Tribal Government Today

Tribal Government Today

Politics on Montana Indian Reservations

James J. Lopach,
Margery Hunter Brown,
and Richmond L. Clow

Westview Press
BOULDER, SAN FRANCISCO, & LONDON

A Westview Special Study

The artwork on the cover is adapted from *Eagle Tipi,* painted by Victor Pepion as part of the Montana Writers Project of the Public Works of Art Project, sponsored by the Museum of the Plains Indian, Browning, Montana, 1940–1943. This image was produced in *Painted Tipis by Contemporary Plains Indian Artists* (Southern Plains Museum and Crafts Center, U.S. Department of the Interior, 1973), p. 61.

This Westview softcover edition is printed on acid-free paper and bound in library-quality, coated covers that carry the highest rating of the National Association of State Textbook Administrators, in consultation with the Association of American Publishers and the Book Manufacturers' Institute.

Published in 1990 in the United States of America by Westview Press, Inc., 5500 Central Avenue, Boulder, Colorado 80301, and in the United Kingdom by Westview Press, Inc., 13 Brunswick Centre, London WC1N 1AF, England

Library of Congress Cataloging-in-Publication Data
Lopach, James J.
  Tribal government today : politics on Montana Indian reservations
/ James J. Lopach, Margery Hunter Brown, and Richmond L. Clow.
    p. cm.
  Includes bibliographical references.
  ISBN 0-8133-7868-0
  1. Indians of North America—Montana—Politics and government.
2. Indians of North America—Montana—Reservations. I. Brown,
Margery Hunter. II. Clow, Richmond L. III. Title.
E78.M9L67 1990
323.1'1970786—dc20   89-29015
                                                                               CIP

Printed and bound in the United States of America

The paper used in this publication meets the requirements of the American National Standard for Permanence of Paper for Printed Library Materials Z39.48-1984.

10   9   8   7   6   5   4   3   2   1

Contents

Preface and Acknowledgments

There has been surprisingly little writing about the condition of contemporary tribal government. Library shelves are filled with works on other American and foreign governments, but an inquirer must learn about tribal government incidentally and in piecemeal fashion. This state of scholarship is regrettable because of the importance of the modern Indian self-determination movement. Reservation politics certainly affect the quality of life in Indian communities, and the outlook for Indian self-determination cannot be assessed without an understanding of tribal government.

It is difficult for reservation outsiders to provide this missing analysis of reservation politics. Living daily with the consequences of American Indian policy, reservation Indians have an abiding distrust of whites. Also, reservation Indians have been the subject of endless study by social scientists and often are irritated by yet another intrusion into their privacy. The resulting introversion is a barrier to research, and this withdrawal is more pronounced when the interviewee is not part of the reservation's leadership.

Fully aware of this methodological obstacle, the authors chose extended conversations with selected political leaders on the reservation as the best way of learning about tribal government. This set of interviews did not constitute a scientific sample, nor was it as large as a generous research budget would have permitted. But in most instances, the interviewees were among the political elite of the reservation. They had thought-through positions and strong feelings about tribal government. Often they had not had the opportunity to express themselves, or they did not realize that outsiders viewed tribal affairs as significant and of interest. It is common practice to publish interviews with at-large political personages or observers of politics for the sake of the insight provided because of the interviewee's rank, long tenure, or reflective qualities. For example, the remarks of a reform-minded governor, a federal budget officer, or a presidential adviser are widely deemed worthy of notice. The interviews in this study are in most instances of individuals who have comparable credentials but concerning reservation politics.

In these conversations, the authors did not use a strictly structured interview technique because of the presumptuousness that would have been implied in a rigorously ordered schedule of questions. The appearance, based upon fact, had to be maintained that the authors were the students and the reservation politicians were the experts. For the authors to have presented in the rhetoric of their questions a fixed hypothesis of reservation politics would have branded them as prejudiced and arrogant. The interviews, therefore, were "nonscheduled," but not wholly without structure. Prior to the interviews the authors reviewed the tribal constitutions and read available materials concerning the tribes' history, culture, government, and economy. From this reading and from one author's teaching of Indian law and experience as director of an Indian law clinic, interview topics were selected that seemed to be at the heart of reservation politics and would be provocative of free and frank conversation. Respondents were selected because of their reputation of being politically knowledgeable and key participants in reservation politics. The interviewers used their remarks to stimulate reflection on personal experiences.

Not all interviews were a success. There were desired sources who failed to keep appointments, some quite obviously avoiding contact with the researchers. Some respondents were ill at ease during interview sessions, probably fearful of censure or of jeopardizing their people's welfare. Some putative spokespersons were inarticulate or not discerning. And even the highest tribal officials could, on occasion, deal solely with the trite and the pedestrian. These were the exceptions, however. The rule was long conversations with well-placed political figures who, because of frustration or outside ignorance or delight in conveying an insight, wanted to talk. Here was a chairman who, because of longevity and centrality, was synonymous with tribal government; a judge who was so disturbed by governmental irregularities that the whistle could not be blown loud and long enough; a councilman who spent a winter evening giving his analysis of tribal government despite an impending return trip to the reservation on dangerous roads.

The resulting study is a discussion of the organization, legal principles, and practical politics of contemporary tribal government. Unlike many studies of the past, it is not an analysis of American Indian policy through the years or an explication of jurisdictional conflicts between tribes and other governments. One contribution of this study could be to make Indian reservations a more common subject of political scholarship. Certainly the observations and conclusions of the present authors about the nature of tribal government can be challenged and built upon by insiders and better-placed outsiders.

The authors thank Dr. Raymond C. Murray, associate vice president for research at the University of Montana, for grant assistance to conduct field research and especially thank members of the Montana Indian tribes who shared their insights during interviews.

James J. Lopach
Margery Hunter Brown
Richmond L. Clow

LINCOLN

GLACIER

Blackfeet

TOOLE

HILL

LIBERTY

FLATHEAD

PONDERA

CHOTEAU

SANDERS

LAKE

Flathead

TETON

MINERAL

CASCADE

MISSOULA

LEWIS & CLARK

JUDITH
BASIN

POWELL

MEAGHER

GRANITE

BROADWATER

RAVALLI

DEER
LODGE

JEFFERSON

SILVER
BOW

GALLATIN

PARK

Paul B. Wilson, Cartographer
Department of Geography
University of Montana

BEAVERHEAD

MADISON

SCALE OF MILES

50   0   50   100

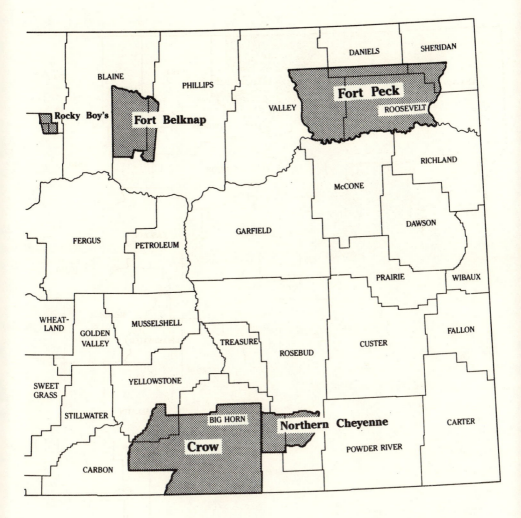

MONTANA INDIAN RESERVATIONS

1

The Contours of Reservation Politics

A century and a half ago the area which is now Montana was part of the homeland of the great Indian tribes of the northern plains. From the Rocky Mountains to the confluence of the Yellowstone and Missouri and from Canada to the Little Bighorn, Native American peoples carried out the independent and ordered lives of sovereign nations. Today, following military conquest and colonial rule, these tribes are striving to reestablish self-government and to regain economic self-sufficiency on the fragments of land they have preserved from deception and betrayal. This study deals with these two central themes of contemporary tribal politics. Its focus is the workings and results of tribal government on Montana's seven dissimilar Indian reservations.

Ten tribes live on Montana's reservations. Their pasts differ in many ways. Native territories included the Great Lakes and Pacific Northwest as well as the upper Midwest. Not all were initially hunters. Some fished, some were agriculturalists, and some trapped for furs. The tribes reacted to whites in different ways. Some were hostile, while others earned a reputation of hospitality. In their intertribal relationships, the Montana Indians showed a similar variety of behavior. Some tribes were allies but most engaged in warfare, even against those with whom they would be induced to share a reservation years later. Different views of life included a respect for nature and a disposition to exploit for immediate gain, an openness to new ways and refuge in the past fueled by suspicion of the present. Brief sketches of the ten tribes—and chapter-length treatment below—will highlight some of these differences.

The Indians of the Flathead reservation are principally the Salish and the Kootenai. They were Plateau Indians, living in the Pacific Northwest between the Cascades and the eastern slopes of the Rocky Mountains. The Salish (or Flatheads) were exceptionally sociable and borrowed heavily from the culture of the Plains Indians. They inhabited the buffalo range of the Upper Missouri until Blackfeet warriors and smallpox in the late eighteenth century drove them across the mountains into the Bitterroot Valley. The Kootenai, from the upper Columbia drainage, were not as friendly to outsiders and receptive to new ways as the Salish and came to represent a conservative influence on the Flathead reservation. Their shared reservation home would ultimately be located in the Jocko and Mission Valleys, about seventy-five miles from the Bitterroot Valley.

The Blackfeet nation was a proud, independent, and aggressive people who dominated a territory which extended from the Judith Basin north into Canada and from the Musselshell River west to the Rocky Mountains. Their life was centered on the buffalo hunt, and they fiercely protected this resource from intruders. Eventually the Blackfeet reservation occupied only the northwestern corner of the tribe's vast homeland.

The tribal territory of the Crow Indians was the country of the Upper Missouri, the Yellowstone, and the Bighorn. The Crow were hunters and perpetual enemies of the Blackfeet, Cheyenne, and Sioux. Toward whites, however, they generally were friendly, and they had the almost unique reputation of being humanitarian in their conduct of war with other tribes. The Crow reservation today lies at the center of the tribe's former homeland.

The Cheyenne originated in the Great Lakes region of northern Minnesota and supported themselves by planting and fishing, becoming hunters only after they were driven westward by the Cree, Assiniboine, and Sioux. In the 1830s the Cheyenne split into southern and northern bands. The Northern Cheyenne in 1884 came to the Tongue River in Montana after an arduous 1,500 mile journey out of a southern exile. This hill country was declared the Northern Cheyennes' reservation in the late nineteenth century.

The Assiniboines' history is linked closely with the Sioux. The two tribes separated in Minnesota in the seventeenth century and became distinct peoples. In the early nineteenth century the Assiniboine moved into the country of the Upper Missouri and for a time dominated that region as hunters and warriors. Weakened by smallpox fifty years later, the Assiniboine were able to preserve only a small hunting ground from the onslaughts of the Blackfeet, Crow, and Sioux. The Assiniboines' two reservations in Montana are shared with the Sioux and the Gros Ventres.

The early homeland of the Sioux was extremely large, including parts of Minnesota, the Dakotas, Wyoming, Nebraska, and eastern Montana. The Sioux were numerous and had the reputation of being uncompromising in battle. In their government the Sioux were tightly organized and severely regulated. These qualities caused them to be both feared and respected. The Fort Peck reservation of the Montana Sioux, which is shared by the Assiniboine, occupies the northeastern corner of the state and traces its lineage to survivors of Custer's Last Stand.

Studies of the Gros Ventre Indians trace their roots variously to the Crow and Arapaho tribes. The Gros Ventre also had a long association with the Blackfeet, dwelling with them and adopting their language for some purposes. The westward movement of the Gros Ventre first stopped at the Milk River and later ended further south near the Missouri. Frequent fighting with the Assiniboine and Crow was necessary to protect their hunting territory. The reservation home of the Gros Ventre at Fort Belknap is along the Milk River and is shared with the Assiniboine.

The Chippewa and Cree were Great Lakes tribes and of common ancestry. The Cree were Canadian Indians who in their trek westward evolved from woodlands trappers to buffalo hunters. The Chippewas' home was south of Lake Superior where they supported themselves by fishing and planting. Some of the Chippewa who migrated westward linked up with bands of Cree. Both tribes were excluded from the reservation movement of the late nineteenth century, and in the early 1900s in Montana they lived in poverty on the outskirts of white communities. Establishment of the Rocky Boy's reservation in 1916 was more to ease the state's conscience than to create a homeland capable of subsistence.

The seven Indian reservations in Montana are not any more identical than are the ten tribes that dwell there. Together these reservations occupy 8.3 million acres, which is 9 percent of Montana's land area. The reservation Indian population of just over 28,000 is under 5 percent of the state's residents. The significance of reservation features, however, lies far more in intertribal comparisons than in collective proportionality to the State of Montana. Table 1.1 supports several judgments about some critical differences between the reservations.

The Montana reservations vary considerably in geographical size, Indian population, tribal land holdings, white presence, natural resource wealth, and unemployment. The acreage of the Crow reservation, for example, is larger than Rocky Boy's by a factor of twenty, and the Blackfeet Indian population is more than three times that of Fort Belknap. On the Northern Cheyenne reservation only 3 percent of the acreage is owned by non-Indians, while whites hold title to 32 percent of the land within the adjacent Crow reservation. The Flathead reservation has great income potential from timber, water resources, and recreation; the Crow and Northern Cheyenne reservations have coal deposits of worldwide significance; and the Blackfeet, Crow, and Fort Peck reservations already have realized considerable revenue from oil

TABLE 1.1 Montana Reservations Compared

Features	TRIBES						
	Flathead	Blackfeet	Crow	N. Cheyenne	Ft. Peck	Ft. Belknap	Rocky Boy
Number enrolled	6,150	12,498	6,927	5,185	8,151	4,425	2,800
Indians on Reservation	4,277	6,716	5,165	3,657	4,415	2,025	1,857
Reservation acreage*	1,242,696	1,525,712	2,282,764	444,885	2,093,123	651,118	108,015
Tribal acreage	570,747 45.9%	240,206 15.7%	400,251 17.5%	302,030 67.9%	390,108 18.6%	180,291 27.6%	108,015 100%
Individual Indian acreage	47,511 3.8%	702,759 46.0%	1,139,691 49.9%	130,760 29.4%	525,887 25.1%	408,464 62.7%	None 0%
Non-Indian acreage	623,421 50.1%	582,610 38.1%	741,422 32.4%	12,095 2.7%	1,177,128 56.2%	62,363 9.5%	None 0%
Tribal forest acreage	449,000	119,248	164,591	148,836	Insignif.	29,309	15,862
Tribal oil and gas leases	None	280 leases 130,000 A production	400 leases 135,000 A production	exploration contracts	35 leases 90,000 A production	6 leases 2,200 A dry wells	30 leases 11,000 A dry wells
Tribal coal reserves	Insig.	Insig.	17 bil. T	8 bil. T	Insig.	None	Insig.
Unemployment	48%	53%	48%	44%	33%	70%	65%

Source: U.S. Bureau of Indian Affairs; Billings, Montana Area Office; November 1983.

*Note: In some instances, the reservation acreage figures include more land than the total of the three subcategories. The discrepancy can be attributed to such uses as reserved federal government land, reserved state school land, railroad right of way, and other takings and acquisitions.

wells (an average of $400 per member in 1980).[1] At the other extreme, the Fort Belknap and Rocky Boy's reservations are natural resource poor and have the highest unemployment rates.

The differences in these figures are not politically neutral. While conflict is present in any community, the task of governing amidst divisiveness will vary from reservation to reservation depending upon economic opportunities and expectations. What principally differentiates these struggles over public matters is the range and complexity of the issues, the variety and skill of the participants, and the effectiveness of governmental machinery. So numerous are the various combinations that an Area Director of the Bureau of Indian Affairs said that "in Montana every possible BIA and tribal situation exists."[2] Such classifications of Montana reservations can cut several ways: those with a potentially strong economic base and those almost totally dependent on federal assistance; those who are innovative and aggressive and those who merely adopt the forms of bureaucracy; those with a good chance for self-government and those who must rely upon their federal managers.

The aim of this study is not only to scrutinize the workings of Montana's seven reservation governments but also to identify what is representative of tribal politics throughout the West. Contemporary discussions of Indian governments suggest some categories for analysis. Such analytical departure points include the reservation setting and economy, the historical evolution of reservation government, the distinctive brand of politics found on a reservation today, and characteristics of contemporary governmental structure. These four perspectives will be maintained throughout this study and will be discussed briefly below.

The setting of Indian reservations has greatly influenced their fate. They generally are rural settlements in sparsely populated and poorly developed parts of the United States. Marginal land divided into small tracts is capable of providing a living for only a few as farmers and stockmen. Given the limited agricultural capacity of the land, most reservations are overpopulated. The Montana reservations are homelands for some of the nation's largest Indian groups.[3] In relatively few cases, the presence of marketable energy resources compensates somewhat for a reservation's social and economic isolation. Four of the seven Montana reservations are among the 15 percent of the country's approximately 300 tribes which have the potential to develop in this way.[4] Such economic opportunity, though, increases even more the likelihood of white interference and manipulation and of state governmental challenges to tribal authority.

The setting of Montana's seven Indian reservations has a governmental aspect that is as significant as their geography. Probably the clearest statement of this context is that reservations do not exist in a governmental vacuum. Tribal governments have constant contacts with officials of local, state, and national governments, and these external relationships affect tribal operations just as do internal political relationships.

The boundaries of a reservation can include parts of several counties. Such overlapping jurisdiction can create intergovernmental conflicts. The reservation's presence can affect demand in a county for public services and legal process, while a reservation can experience regulatory problems because its jurisdiction extends to several counties and both Indian and non-Indian owned land. Certain legal and political realities can make the situation extremely difficult: Indians are citizens of the state in which they reside and therefore eligible to participate in the health, welfare, and educational programs of the state; the presence of a reservation within a county can withdraw a significant portion of the county's area from the base of its property tax; and Indian tribes may exercise some forms of civil jurisdiction over non-Indians whose activities have a direct effect on the tribe's political integrity, economic security, or health or welfare. At times intergovernmental understandings have been used to resolve jurisdictional problems. Tribal governments and county sheriff departments have, for example, cross-deputized officers to achieve more effective law enforcement.

State officials provide no less a governmental presence on Indian reservations. In Montana, the Department of Fish, Wildlife and Parks has sought to regulate Indians' off-reservation hunting; the Department of Health has the authority to administer various regulatory schemes on the reservation to achieve effective statewide programs; the Department of Social and Rehabilitation Services contracts with the tribes for the provision of aging services; and the Department of Natural Resources and Conservation seeks to answer the question whether the state has any jurisdiction over reservation water. As a result of these relationships and pressures, it is impossible for tribal officials to concentrate only on local matters.

The tribal-federal point of contact is the most common and most difficult intergovernmental relationship. The federal government's principal representative to the tribe is the Bureau of Indian Affairs. The Bureau's continuous and immediate contact with tribal governments affects their law enforcement, economic development, financial administration, land management, and even constitutional reform. In carrying out its essential governmental functions, a tribe cannot avoid the regulatory presence of the Bureau. The tribes also have frequent contact with other federal agencies. Tribal housing authorities receive grants from the Department of Housing and Urban Development. The American Native Programs of the Department of Health and Human Services provide for certain needs of reservation residents throughout their life. The Department of Labor oversees many federal job training programs on the reservation, and the Forest Service and the Bureau of Land Management monitor or jointly administer with the tribe many kinds of land use ventures. One Montana reservation deals constantly with the Federal Energy Regulatory Commission concerning ownership and operation of a hydroelectric dam. No tribal intergovernmental relationship is as critical as the one with the Bureau of Indian Affairs, but tribal politics is influenced by a wide range of federal mandates and pressures.

The features of a tribe's pre-Indian Reorganization Act government provide another perspective for viewing contemporary tribal government. Prior to 1934, reservation governments evolved, changing to accommodate new situations and struggling to preserve cultural values. Traditional forms were dropped or modified and new forms were incorporated into reservation structures as conditions dictated. For example, United States Indian agents instituted administrative bodies when they sought tribal help to run the reservation. High-level federal officials added to reservation governance in other ways. Commissioner of Indian Affairs Ezra H. Hayt ordered Indian agents in 1878 to create reservation police forces to maintain law and order, and in 1883 Secretary of the Interior Henry M. Teller added American trial and punishment procedures in his directive authorizing the creation of Courts of Indian Offenses,[5] later known as "25 CFR" courts. Tribal governing bodies during these years presided over land sales and land leases and eventually assumed greater responsibility for general reservation welfare. On the northern plains, tribal decision-making bodies varied from a general council operating with an unwritten constitution to a small business committee made legitimate by a written document. The Indian Reorganization Act of 1934 and the ensuing tribal constitutions minimized differences between tribal governments and addressed the continuing issue: how to reconcile traditional practice with contemporary pressures.

Politics in any setting has to do with conflict over issues of public policy and the resolution of that conflict. Reservation politics—a third vantage point on contemporary tribal government—always tend to be lively, but the factionalism that gives rise to the conflict can have various sources. It can stem from several tribes being confederated on one reservation. It can be based upon differences among clans, religions, places of residency, blood quantum, and the patronage practices of tribal administrations. It can be the result of different views of past events, such as treaties or the Indian Reorganization Act. The rate and mode of political participation on reservations can also vary. Differences can be found in election turnout and in the use of other participation mechanisms such as special committees, council hearings, and general meetings. On a specific reservation, political participation may be heightened because of a strong tradition of involvement or an abiding distrust of tribal politicians. The politics of a reservation can be distinctive because of the dominant values used to resolve conflicts. One reservation, for example, could promote natural resource conservation, while another could emphasize development and equal sharing of the proceeds. In varying degrees, therefore, the politics of a reservation can be characterized by factional loyalties, watchful participation, and the application of traditional values. As in other political forums, astute leadership is needed on a reservation to manage affairs amidst intense conflict in order to improve the general welfare. This skill also can be present in varying degrees.

The fourth analytical perspective which is applicable to Indian reservations generally is the strength and vulnerability of their contemporary governmental structure. After Congress enacted the Indian Reorganization Act in 1934, 181 tribes voted to accept the law while 77 tribes rejected it.[6] Five reservations in Montana were among those which chose to adopt a constitution under the law; the Crow and Fort Peck reservations continued with their general council forms of government outside of the Indian Reorganization Act. Since that time reservation governments (both IRA and non-IRA) have evolved variously, but most still possess common strengths and weaknesses. On the positive side, reservation governments, uniquely among American governments, have the explicit responsibility of developing and managing the tribe's resources for the benefit of the membership. Partially as a result of this duty, they command the close attention of tribal members and rarely fail to address immediate problems. Reservation governments, therefore, are frequently the centers of community life. They are also the principal employer of tribal members and the primary provider of skills training and political experience. On the negative side, reservation governments are characterized by too little continuity, accountability, and professionalism. With few exceptions, the council tends to smother executive power and to subjugate the tribal judiciary to its will. Tribal bureaucracy is at times more of a badge than a governing process. And the local representatives of the Bureau of Indian Affairs have rarely struggled against that agency's traditional paternalism. Additionally, the duty of managing the tribe's economic resources for the collective good frequently comes into conflict with the Indian traditions of informal involvement and generosity. Most reservation governments, therefore, could benefit from structural reform.

The representativeness of Montana's reservations can also be seen in a long line of cases decided by the United States Supreme Court. Litigation arising out of Montana's Indian politics (just as in Arizona, New Mexico, or Washington) contained issues which the Supreme Court scheduled for argument and decision because they were sufficiently important and interesting. The Court, for example, held that the Northern Cheyenne tribe, and not the Montana district court, had jurisdiction over adoption proceedings involving tribal members living on the reservation;[7] adjudicated the extent of the Crow tribe's inherent power to exercise civil authority (here, hunting and fishing regulations) over the conduct of non-Indians on non-Indian land within the reservation;[8] ruled that the State of Montana could not impose its cigarette tax on sales by Indians to Indians on the Flathead reservation, but could require the tax on reservation sales by Indians to non-Indians;[9] and held that a state court had jurisdiction under federal law to adjudicate the water rights of the Northern Cheyenne tribe.[10] By refusing to schedule another case for review, the Supreme Court upheld the Flathead tribes' right to regulate non-Indian owned docks and breakwaters on the south half of Flathead Lake within their reservation (two Justices would have granted certiorari to overturn the lower courts' ruling in favor of the tribes).[11] The Crow hunting and fishing regulation case was especially important; although limiting Crow regulatory authority, it provided an expanded statement of tribal civil authority and spawned a series of related cases from other reservations.

There are few systematic treatments of the politics and government of contemporary Indian reservations. A 1975 monograph, *Indian Tribes as Governments,* was based upon reports of law students involved in both internships and field research on reservations throughout the country. The editor prefaced this work by noting the "complete absence of available research data dealing with the subject matter of tribal government."[12] Prior to and since that time there have been many articles and several books concerning the nature of tribal criminal and civil jurisdiction and the extent of its conflict with state and federal authority. Tribal government was at times indirectly or secondarily dealt with in these works, as it has been in other writings on Indian policy and tribal economies. There also have been several studies focusing on the organization and proceedings of tribal courts, one being *American Indians, American Justice* (1983). This work, while laying a solid foundation for future in-depth study of reservation politics, warned that "[a]ny attempt to analyze contemporary tribal governments must of necessity be flawed."[13] The understandable reason was that many such studies would be undertaken by non-Indian scholars who could easily fall prey to the "uncritical acceptance of cultural evolution as the definitive experience of our species."[14]

This present study, possibly with unhappy results, took up that challenge. The authors are reservation outsiders by race and residence. They are mindful, however, of America's sorry history of Indian-white relations, and they are in full agreement that Indian self-government means essentially that. Their aim is to use their professional talents as political scientist, historian, and lawyer to comment upon Native American self-determination. The authors do not claim to be first in line with fresh insights or reform suggestions. National commissions, congressional committees, associations of tribal officials, and constitutional review committees have previously studied the reservation situation and called for various changes. The contribution of this study is assessment of frequent reform suggestions—such as stronger leadership, an independent judiciary, and increased procedural rigor—from the perspective of the political realities of seven reservations. The resulting account of tribal government is but one cautious voice in a very important contemporary discussion.

Subsequent chapters, then, are principally concerned with the question of whether the Montana tribes in particular and all Indian reservations in general can achieve self-government. The following chapter presents the legal history and legal foundations of contemporary tribal government. The idea is that the understanding and practice of reservation politics are well served by appreciation of the complexity of this area of law and by identification of persisting patterns and developing principles. This historical and legal analysis provides the context for the next seven chapters—separate sketches of how the Montana reservations actually function. These case studies focus on the dominant characteristics of each reservation's political economy, and in so doing they demonstrate the differences in the capabilities of tribal governments. These essays are the basis for more generalized reflection in the final chapter. Here, reservation governments are discussed in terms of common strengths, weaknesses, and opportunities. Reform considerations are suggested with the variety of reservation situations in mind. The unfortunate conclusion is that self-government, in its ordinary meaning, is not a realistic goal for all reservations.

Notes

1. Jim Richardson and John A. Farrell, "The New Indian Wars," *The Denver Post*, November 20, 1983, to November 27, 1983 (eight-part series), p. 16 of reprint.

2. Interview with Richard Whitesell, Director of the Billings Area of the Bureau of Indian Affairs, August 22, 1983.

3. Theodore W. Taylor, *American Indian Policy* (Mount Airy, MD: Lomond Publications, 1983), p. 163.

4. Richardson and Farrell, "The New Indian Wars," p. 16.

5. William T. Hagen, *Indian Police and Judges: Experiments in Acculturation and Control* (Lincoln: University of Nebraska Press, 1980, Bison Edition), pp. 104–105.

6. Theodore H. Haas, *Ten Years of Tribal Government Under IRA,* Tribal Relations Pamphlet No. 1 (Washington, DC: U.S. Indian Service, 1947), p. 3.

7. *Fisher v. District Court of Sixteenth Judicial Dist. of Montana, In and For Rosebud County,* 424 U.S. 382 (1976).

8. *Montana v. United States,* 450 U.S. 544 (1981).

9. *Moe v. Confederated Salish and Kootenai Tribes of Flathead Indian Reservation,* 425 U.S. 463 (1976).

10. *Arizona v. San Carlos Apache Tribe,* 463 U.S. 545 (1983).

11. *Confederated Salish and Kootenai Tribes v. Namen,* 665 F. 2d 951 (9th Cir. 1982), cert denied, 459 U.S. 977 (1982).

12. Alan Parker, *Indian Tribes as Governments* (New York: John Hay Whitney Foundation, 1975), p. 8.

13. Vine Deloria, Jr., and Clifford M. Lytle, *American Indians, American Justice* (Austin: University of Texas Press, 1982), p. 108.

14. Ibid., p. 1.

2

Indian Law and Tribal Government

The extent of the sovereignty or self-governing powers of Indian tribes is not generally understood, in the way that Americans understand the powers of their nation, states, counties, and municipalities. Montanans are no exception. Despite the presence of seven Indian reservations within the state's boundaries, the governments of tribal communities have not been adequately addressed in the past in the standard works on the history and politics of the state and region. More often than not, the Indian frontier was treated as one of several frontier eras that marked Montana's progression to the present. Textbooks chronicled the Indian presence in Montana before the coming of white explorers and fur traders. They treated the interaction of fur traders and Indians, missionaries and Indians, and then, the military and Indians, after the influx of miners and settlers radically altered the homeland that Montana had been for many tribes. The dominant themes of Montana's history that then unfolded—copper and timber kingdoms in the western mountains and valleys, and stockgrazing, homesteading, and large-scale ranching on the eastern plains—eclipsed Indian themes.

What was regarded as the problem of the Indian barrier to successive white frontiers appeared to be solved by treaties and agreements that diminished Indian country in Montana to ever-narrowing reservations. Scholarship scarcely addressed Indian self-government within the reservations.

Inadequate attention among whites to tribal governing powers also stems from the complexity of those powers. They are defined by a mosaic of federal law—constitutional, statutory, and administrative—and in great measure by judicial decisions of the United States Supreme Court. These decisions proclaim and define the trust relationship between the federal government and the tribes, the scope of tribal self-governing powers, and the relationship between the tribes and the states.

The process of judicial interpretation commenced in the decades of the 1820s and 1830s with Chief Justice John Marshall's enduring opinions for the nation's highest court. Not surprisingly, the cases arose from situations on the frontier: the attempted transfer of tribal lands to individual purchasers in Illinois, and Georgia's determination to extend state law into Cherokee country and obliterate tribal governing powers within state borders.

To reach his decisions, Marshall interwove concepts of international law with the practical experience of European nations generally, Great Britain specifically, and the United States as a new nation. In 1823 in *Johnson v. McIntosh,*[1] Marshall set forth the discovery doctrine and its implications for rights of title and possession of Indian lands and the sovereignty of Indian tribes. Discovery of land in the New World, stated Marshall for the Court, gave the discovering European sovereign title good against all other nations and the sole right of acquiring the soil from the natives and establishing settlements upon it. The Indians retained the right of possession, and they were recognized as rightful occupants of the land. Their rights could only be extinguished through purchase or conquest by the sovereign who held ultimate dominion over the land. After the Revolutionary War, the United States succeeded to Britain's position in relation to Indian tribes within the nation's borders. The *Johnson v. McIntosh* opinion helps explain why, after acquiring western lands by warfare and peacemaking or by purchase from European powers, the United States still had to negotiate a long series of treaties and agreements to secure tribal rights to land as white settlements advanced on the western frontier.

The right to dispose freely of land, except to the United States, became the first sovereign power removed from Indian tribes by judicial opinion. Soon afterward, in the Cherokee decisions,[2] Marshall declared further federal common law about Indian tribes, and the substance of his opinions remains at the center of Indian law today. Because of the discovery doctrine and the protective terms of treaties, the Cherokees were held to be not a foreign nation but a domestic dependent nation, with a relationship to the United States resembling that of a ward to a guardian. In the Cherokee opinions, Marshall identified a second power lost to Indian tribes within the United States as a result of their status: they could not enter direct commercial or governmental relations with other nations of the world.

Despite this additional reduction of tribal sovereign power in external relationships, the Cherokee opinions provided firm assurance about the persistence of tribal self-governing powers. European discovery had not annulled the preexisting rights of Indians to govern themselves. Before the age of discovery, they were "a distinct people, divided into separate nations, independent of each other and of the rest of the world," with institutions and laws of their own for governing themselves. While first Great Britain and then the United States held the exclusive right of purchasing lands that the Indian nations were willing to sell, neither country had attempted to interfere with the internal affairs of the Indians. By statute and treaty, the United States recognized that Indian nations were distinct political communities with territorial boundaries within which their authority was exclusive. Moreover, the United States had assumed the duty to protect these Indian rights.

Marshall stated that the settled doctrine of the law of nations was that a weaker power did not surrender its independence or right to self-government by association with a stronger power. A weak state could "place itself under the protection of one more powerful without stripping itself of the right of government and ceasing to be a state."

Marshall's historical and constitutional analysis placed the nation's relationship with Indian tribes exclusively within the scope of federal power. As a consequence, the treaties and laws of the United States "contemplate[d] the Indian territory as completely separated from that of the states." At the heart of the Chief Justice's analysis were provisions of the United States Constitution which conferred on Congress the powers of war and peace, of making treaties, and of regulating commerce with the Indian tribes. Because the whole intercourse between the Cherokees and the United States was vested in the national government, Georgia's intrusion into Indian country was held to be prohibited by the constitution, laws, and treaties of the United States. The Court's admonition to Georgia was blunt: within Cherokee country the laws of Georgia had no force, and the citizens of Georgia had no right to enter Cherokee lands without the assent of the Indians or by conforming to treaties and acts of Congress.

The Cherokee judicial victory afforded little protection from the policy of Congress and the executive in the 1830s to remove Indian tribes in the eastern United States to a vast Indian country west of the Mississippi River, which the United States promised to secure and guarantee forever. Far to the west, white settlement commenced in the future Territory and State of Montana with the coming of Catholic missionaries to the Bitterroot valley a decade after the Marshall Court's decisions. In the fifty years that followed, events in Montana reflected national Indian policy, which often overshadowed but did not erase judicial decisions related to Indian tribes.

By the time the United States entered into treaties with the Montana tribes in the 1850s, the policy of removal to an expansive Indian country was giving way to the creation of specific and ever narrowing reservations for Indian tribes. Initially the United States negotiated with several western Indian nations at Fort Laramie in 1851. The treaty acknowledged large tracts of country as the territories of the respective tribes and gained for the United States the right to establish roads and military and other posts within Indian lands.[3]

Montana tribes were also included in the negotiations conducted in the mid-1850s by Washington territorial governor Isaac I. Stevens to gain land cessions for the United States in the Pacific Northwest and Northern Rocky Mountain region. The Flathead Treaty of 1855 with the Kootenai, Pend Oreille and Salish Indians opened a large area west of the Continental Divide to white settlement. The Flathead reservation was established in the Jocko and Mission valleys south of Flathead Lake, and Stevens left for future determination the question of whether the Salish in the Bitterroot would be required to move north to that reservation or be permitted to remain in their valley.[4] Assurances of peace among the Montana tribes and agreement on a common Indian hunting ground were the primary goals of Stevens' subsequent negotiations with the Blackfeet, Flathead, and other tribes. The 1855 Blackfeet Treaty included these provisions and marked out expansive Blackfeet territorial boundaries. The treaty also incorporated the Indians' acknowledgment that United States citizens could live in and travel through their lands, and that within those lands the United States could build roads, telegraphs lines, and military posts.[5]

Montana was organized as a territorial government in 1864, and four years later the Crow Tribe and the United States agreed on a treaty establishing a reservation for the Crows in southern Montana, greatly reduced from the Crow territory marked out by the earlier Fort Laramie Treaty.[6] Within the twenty-five-year territorial period, executive orders and successive United States–Indian treaties and agreements constricted Blackfeet, Gros Ventre, and Crow lands. The Northern Cheyenne reservation, just east of the Crow lands, was initially established by executive order in 1884. Without the benefit of a long-promised presidential survey, the Salish were instructed to leave the Bitterroot valley and join the Kootenai and Pend Oreille on the Flathead reservation. Shortly before Montana achieved statehood in 1889, the United States negotiated a vast reduction of Indian lands in northern Montana. The Blackfeet reservation was again decreased in size, and separate reservations were established at Fort Belknap for the Gros Ventre and Assiniboine and at Fort Peck for the Assiniboine and Sioux.[7] Additional land cessions were obtained from the Blackfeet and Crow in 1896 and 1904, and in 1916 Congress created the Rocky Boy's reservation for the Chippewa and Cree from lands within the former Fort Assiniboine Military Reservation.

The treaties, agreements, and executive orders customarily provided that reservation lands would be set apart as permanent homes for the tribes. The money paid to the tribes for their land cessions was made available in annual installments and expended for implements, livestock, food, medical supplies, clothing, training in agriculture and mechanical arts, and schooling for Indian children. The treaties foreshadowed the presence of whites who were employed or authorized by the federal government as agents, traders, and teachers. The treaties also served notice that Indian lands would be included in the grid of railroads and telegraph lines crossing the country as there were provisions for rights-of-way and assurances of compensation to the tribes for the rights-of-way.

The insulation of tribal lands from the authority of both the Territory and State of Montana was specifically addressed in the territorial organic act, the enabling act opening the way for statehood, and in Ordinance No. 1, appended to Montana's Constitution of 1889. Each document contained a disclaimer of right and title to Indian lands and acknowledgment that until title might be extinguished by the United States all Indian lands would remain under the absolute jurisdiction and control of the United States Congress.[8]

In Montana, as elsewhere on the Northern Plains and in the Pacific Northwest, alteration of the communal character of the Indian land base opened the door to significant white settlement within Indian reservations. It was the first event in a chain of events that created new questions for courts to answer about the breadth of tribal governing powers and the permissible extension of state authority within reservation boundaries.

The conversion of Indians from the life of hunters and gatherers to cultivators and home-dwellers had been discussed and urged since the early days of the American republic. Individual rather than communal or tribal rights in property became an article of faith for successive Commissioners of Indian Affairs. They equated private land ownership with enterprise and achievement, and regarded it as an essential replacement for the Indian perspective that regarded great expanses of land as home and seasonal movement on the land as necessary and desirable.

Treaties with Montana tribes generally encouraged individual tribal members to enclose and improve their own plots of land. In addition, the 1855 Flathead Treaty indirectly referred to potential allotment of the Flathead reservation, and plans for allotment were specifically included in the 1868 Crow Treaty and the 1882 Crow Act.[9] These manifestations of federal policy predated the General Allotment, or Dawes Act, enacted by Congress in 1887.[10] That measure gave broad authorization to the President to have any reservation with good agricultural or grazing lands surveyed in whole or in part and allotted to individual Indians. Initially, family status was to determine allotment size, with 160 acres assigned to heads of families. As amended, the act provided for 80 acres for each individual Indian on allotted reservations, and the acreage was to be doubled if lands were chiefly valuable for grazing instead of farming. Early in the life of the Dawes Act, amendments authorized the leasing of tribally held lands and of individually allotted lands, if allottees were regarded by the Bureau of Indian Affairs as unable to farm their land.

At first, the allotted lands were to be held in trust by the United States for 25 years; later amendments made it permissible either to lengthen or shorten the protective trust period, depending on the Bureau's determination of the competency of the allottees. United States citizenship was conferred on Indians receiving allotments under the Dawes Act, and at the end of the trust period allottees were to have the benefit of and be subject to territorial or state laws.

The Dawes Act also provided for the acquisition of reservation land by whites. If the President determined that it was in the best interests of a tribe, the Secretary of the Interior was to negotiate for tribal consent to the purchase or release of unallotted lands. Agricultural lands sold or released were to be held by the federal government for actual settlers who could obtain homesteads on the reservations in tracts not exceeding 160 acres.

Support for the Dawes Act and its implementation came from those who believed the legislation would serve Indian interests and from those who saw a welcome opportunity for homesteaders and stockraisers to acquire land that otherwise would be inaccessible to them. Indian sympathizers hoped that the presence of white homesteaders would be beneficial, believing that white farmers would be good teachers. They also were convinced that the allotment program would guarantee Indian rights in allotted lands. More wary observers forecast the overall loss of Indian land that later occurred. The act's sponsor viewed the legislation as a solution to the entire Indian problem: with land ownership and citizenship for the Indians, reservations would vanish, and so, too, would the federal bureaucracy serving Indians.[11]

Nationally and in Montana, the result of the allotment of tribal lands was disastrous for Indian communities and the Indian land base. Between 1887 and 1934, Indian lands nationwide were reduced from 138 million acres to 48 million acres. Much of the most valuable farm land passed out of Indian hands through the opening of the "surplus" land, sales to whites, or forfeiture for nonpayment of state taxes at the end of the trust period.

The loss of Indian lands and the deteriorating state of tribal communities—in health, educational progress, and economic and political well-being—spurred reform efforts and official inquiry in the 1920s. These concerns led in 1928 to the influential Meriam report, *The Problem of Indian Administration.*[12] It was a precursor to further congressional investigation and to the Indian legislation achieved as part of the Roosevelt New Deal in the 1930s.

Montana Senator Burton K. Wheeler, chairman of the United States Senate Committee on Indian Affairs, joined Nebraska Congressman Edgar Howard to introduce the 1934 Wheeler-Howard, or Indian Reorganization, Act.[13] The bill's actual architects included John Collier, reform-minded Commissioner of Indian Affairs; Department of the Interior Solicitor Nathan R. Margold; and Felix S. Cohen, then an attorney in the Solicitor's Office. Their legislative blueprint for new directions in United States Indian policy was altered as it moved through Congress, but fundamental provisions survived.

At the outset of the process set in motion by the IRA, Indian tribes were to determine through elections whether they wished the act to apply to their reservations. For Indian lands, the IRA halted further allotment, extended the trust period indefinitely, and provided that unsold "surplus" lands could be returned to tribal ownership. The principle of sustained yield was henceforth to guide the management of Indian forests, and restriction of livestock grazing and other measures were to protect Indian rangelands from deterioration. The act also authorized the expenditure of $2 million annually to help restore the Indian land base. A revolving loan fund was authorized to spur tribal economic development, and educational loan funds were also authorized to assist individual Indians. Tribes could elect to receive federal charters of incorporation in order to organize for economic progress.

The right of Indian tribes to organize for their common welfare was expressly stated in the IRA. Tribes could adopt constitutions and bylaws which would be effective when ratified by a majority of adult Indians voting in a special election called by the Secretary of the Interior. There was an enumeration of specific powers of tribal governments organized under the IRA, and the act expressly provided that a tribe or tribal council would also possess all powers vested in an Indian tribe or tribal council by existing law. In order that this provision be understood, Solicitor Margold was asked to prepare a formal opinion on the extent and kinds of powers vested in an Indian tribe prior to the passage of the IRA. His opinion, "Powers of Indian Tribes,"[14] first cautioned that the question could not be answered in detail for each Indian tribe without reference to hundreds of special treaties and acts of Congress. Margold did, however, draw from judicial decisions this fundamental principle: "those powers which are lawfully vested in an Indian tribe are not, in general, delegated powers granted by express acts of Congress, but rather, inherent powers of a limited sovereignty which has never been extinguished."

Margold's 1934 opinion recognized that American Indian tribes had lost external powers of sovereignty and that the tribes had been brought under the control of Congress. Internal powers of sovereignty had remained intact unless expressly restricted or limited by treaty or statute. The Solicitor also noted the judicial rule that acts of Congress affecting the powers of an Indian tribe were to be construed liberally, with doubtful expressions resolved in favor of the Indians. The Margold opinion summarized statutes, case law, and administrative rulings in describing inherent powers of the tribes over their governments, members, territory, and over nonmembers accepting privileges of trade or residence within reservation boundaries.

More than two-thirds of the 258 tribes voting on the issue accepted the IRA, agreeing on constitutions and electing new tribal councils. There were significant rejections, including the Navajo in the Southwest and the Crow tribe and the Assiniboine-Sioux of the Fort Peck reservation in Montana. The Confederated Salish and Kootenai Tribes of the Flathead reservation were first in the nation to accept the IRA, and they were later joined by the Blackfeet, the Northern Cheyenne, the Chippewa-Cree at Rocky Boy's reservation, and the Fort Belknap Indian Community. The Secretary of the Interior halted allotment on both IRA and non-IRA reservations, and there were few long-range distinctions in BIA treatment of IRA and non-IRA tribes. The Crow tribe adopted its modern-day constitution in 1948, and the Assiniboine-Sioux Tribes at Fort Peck took that step in 1960.

The IRA was designed as a congressional revitalization of tribal economies and tribal governing structures and powers, reversing many aspects of federal Indian policy of the preceding years. Those years had been distinguished by laws and practices that minimized the role of tribes as self-governing entities. Congress had declared in 1871 that tribes were no longer to be regarded as nations to be negotiated with by treaty, although existing treaty rights were to be respected, and agreements ratified by both houses of Congress came to replace the formalities of treaty-making. The Major Crimes Act of 1885 had subjected Indians to federal jurisdiction for serious offenses. Allotment of Indian lands was designed to break up tribal cohesiveness. United States citizenship was bestowed by Congress in 1924 on all Indians who had not acquired citizenship through treaties, special acts, or the allotment process. As a consequence, all Indians were also citizens of the states encompassing their reservations. In the entire period, the paternalistic attitudes and procedures of the Bureau of Indian Affairs left little room for tribes to function as governments.

The restored self-government of the IRA tribes was not full-blown. Restraints of time and funds resulted in the expedient adoption of tribal constitutions patterned closely on a model document prepared by the Bureau of Indian Affairs. The IRA stipulated that the Secretary of the Interior was to approve both the constitutions and their subsequent amendments. Similarity, rather than distinctiveness, also characterized the new law and order codes adopted by the tribal councils. The presence of the Bureau within the compass of tribal government continued in force. The typical IRA tribal constitution included requirements for the Secretary of the Interior to approve or review tribal council action on such matters as levying assessments on non-members trading or residing on reservations, regulating the inheritance of real or personal property other than allotments, providing for the appointment of guardians for minors, and excluding from Indian lands individuals without a legal right to reside upon them,

Despite later shifts in federal Indian policy, the IRA's vitality continues to the present day. It details basic procedures for tribal governments accepting its provisions, and the Bureau's relationship to all tribal governments has been shaped in great measure by the IRA. Certain of the provisions urged, but not enacted in 1934, have been implemented by later legislation.

Also a byproduct of the Indian New Deal was the preparation of the first comprehensive treatment of federal Indian law. Under the principal authorship of Felix S. Cohen, *The Handbook of Federal Indian Law* was first published by the Department of the Interior in 1942. It later appeared in a revised version, and then in a facsimile reprint of the 1942 edition. The immense growth of Indian law made substantial rewriting imperative, and a new *Felix S. Cohen's Handbook of Federal Indian Law* was published in 1982. It was commissioned by the Department of the Interior and prepared by a board of authors, editors, and several contributing writers, all teachers or practitioners of Indian law.[15]

There has been no straight line in the development of federal Indian policy in the more than half-century life of the IRA. While Montana Senator Wheeler continued to support the provisions of the law that protected the tribal land base and encouraged economic development, he became disenchanted with Collier's implementation of the IRA and moved unsuccessfully in 1937 for repeal of the act. Both Collier and the Bureau remained under critical congressional scrutiny until Collier's resignation in 1945. Meantime, the nation's attention was diverted away from Indian issues during World War II, and the war drained away

Indian leadership from the reservations. The postwar mood was not supportive of tribal self-determination or of the continued role of the federal government in tribal affairs. Both the Bureau and the tribes became targets of attacks on federal bureaucracies and federal expenditures. Indians returning to their reservations after military service or wartime employment encountered another innovation in national Indian policy: assistance in relocating to urban areas away from reservation homelands. Inroads on the IRA's protection of Indian lands came with legislation placing new discretion with the Bureau to end the trust status and approve conveyances of individually-held Indian lands.[16]

There had long been voices in Congress which urged that Indians should be subject to state laws and that the states should bear the primary responsibility for their Indian citizens. Serious attention was given in the late 1940s to terminating the special status of the tribes, and applying the termination policy to selected tribes became the express goal of Congress in 1953.[17] Although the Confederated Salish and Kootenai Tribes were initially designated as a tribal government and people that should be freed from federal supervision and control, specific termination legislation did not extend to the Indians of the Flathead reservation or to any other Montana tribes. Instead, the threat of termination kindled concerted reaction among the tribes, and by the 1960s national policy again moved toward a position of encouragement for tribal self-determination, protection of tribal resources, and continued federal support.

By the Indian Civil Rights Act of 1968, Congress imposed many of the same obligations on tribal governments that the Bill of Rights and the fourteenth amendment to the United States Constitution imposed on federal and state governments. Some of the protections were already included in tribal constitutions, but the Indian Civil Rights Act made guarantees of equal protection, due process, most first amendment rights, and many criminal procedure safeguards a mandatory part of the law of all Indian tribes in the United States.[18]

The presence on reservations of federal agencies in addition to the Bureau and the Indian Health Service was also a mark of the 1960s and 1970s. The development assured additional assistance in housing, job training, economic planning, legal services, and community development, and tribal governments and people became active participants in and administrators of the programs. Education policy also shifted to give tribes greater control over federally funded public school programs and increased resources to establish tribal community colleges. A hallmark of the period was the Indian Self-Determination and Education Assistance Act of 1975. It gave life to a measure first urged by the drafters of the IRA in 1934 by establishing that tribes could contract to perform services being provided by the Departments of the Interior and Health and Human Services.[19]

Economic growth and tribal initiatives were addressed by such measures as the Indian Financing Act of 1974, providing capital on a reimbursable basis for the development of tribal resources; the Indian Mineral Development Act of 1982, expanding alternatives for tribal mineral resources management; and the Indian Tribal Governmental Tax Status Act of 1982, providing for Indians tribes a tax status similar to that of state and local governments. The congressionally-created American Indian Policy Review Commission concluded a two-year study in 1977. Its majority report recommended strengthening tribal sovereignty and the trust relationship and providing increased assistance for the economic development of tribes.[20] Commencing in the 1960s, presidential policy statements proclaimed support for tribal self-determination and recognition of the nation's responsibilities in Indian affairs, none more forcefully than President Nixon's message to Congress in 1970. More recently, the Reagan Administration stressed a government-to-government relationship between the United States and the tribes. Emphasis was directed to economic self-sufficiency, and the way marked out by the Reagan Administration was for tribes to encourage a larger role for private capital in the development of reservation resources and enterprises.[21]

Executive and congressional support for tribal self-sufficiency has coincided with reservation developments to produce more vigorous tribal governments. Increasingly, young and well-educated tribal members are returning to their reservations to join tribal elders in leadership positions—to serve on tribal councils and as staff members of newly created tribal administrative departments. Essential to their work is modernization and expansion of the brief law and order codes borne of the IRA. Tribal leaders today recognize that if self-sufficiency is to be attained, tribes must be able to tax to secure income from resource development or commercial activities. If land, water, and other resources are to be protected and carefully developed, regulatory ordinances must be enacted. If tribal courts are to discharge the responsibilities defined for them by federal and tribal law, court procedures must be reformed and court resources increased.

Few of these recent steps toward self-determination have gone unchallenged, and challenges have led inevitably to litigation and an ever-enlarging role of the judiciary in defining the interrelationships of federal, tribal, and state law within reservation boundaries. Even at the time when Chief Justice Marshall characterized Indian nations as distinct political communities possessing exclusive authority within their territorial boundaries, inroads had been made on that concept.

For instance, Congress had already extended the reach of federal law to offenses committed in Indian country, except for crimes by Indians against Indians and when treaties placed exclusive jurisdiction with the tribes. Later, an additional exception was made for Indians who had been punished by the local law of tribes. As noted above, Congress brought serious Indian offenses, regardless of the race of victims, within the sphere of federal jurisdiction in 1885.[22] The United States Supreme Court upheld this intrusion into tribal internal affairs by linking the Major Crimes Act to the nation's duty to protect Indians.[23] Congressional power to abrogate treaties and to diminish tribal territory has also been sustained by the United States Supreme Court, although recent decisions make clear that Indians must receive full value for lands taken by Congressional action.[24]

Litigation also presented the argument that Congress decreased tribal territory or terminated reservation status by opening "surplus" lands to white settlement. In ruling on these questions, the United States Supreme Court has attempted to ascertain congressional intent by analyzing the language of the opening acts, their legislative history, and surrounding circumstances. No Montana reservation has been held to have been diminished as a result of allotment and the sale of lands to whites.

Federal law governing reservation crime was codified in 1948, and the codification included a definition of Indian country, later construed as applying in both criminal and civil matters. The definition addresses legal uncertainties common to reservations checkerboarded by Indian and non-Indian land ownership patterns. For jurisdictional purposes, Indian country includes all land within the limits of any reservation, including rights-of-way, regardless of land ownership.[25]

Just as assertions of national power can impinge on the sphere of tribal governing power within Indian country, so, too, can state authority be extended to reservations and challenge tribal self-government. The courts have declared that congressional authorization is essential for state law to affect Indians and Indian interests, and the judiciary is often involved in testing the legality of state authority within reservation boundaries. The practice commenced in the late 1800s in the context of criminal law, when the United States Supreme Court upheld state jurisdiction over reservation crimes between non-Indians and created an exception to the federal statutory scheme for reservation criminal jurisdiction.[26] More recently, judicial rulings relating to the exercise of state authority on reservations have been concerned with civil, as well as criminal, jurisdiction, and these decisions are summarized below.

The sovereign power of an Indian tribe to define and punish offenses by tribal members has been recognized consistently by federal courts. As part of the 1968 Indian Civil Rights Act, Congress restricted tribal court penalties to six months' imprisonment or a $500 fine, or both, but did not limit the offenses that tribes could make punishable under their laws. In 1986 maximum penalities were increased to a fine of $5,000, and imprisonment for no more than one year. As noted, the Indian Civil Rights Act guaranteed most Bill of Rights protections to anyone affected by tribal governments and tribal courts. In criminal procedure, ICRA provisions differ from Bill of Rights guarantees in excluding the right to free, court-appointed counsel for indigents and the right to indictment by a grand jury. Defendants accused of a crime punishable by a jail term are assured the right of a trial by jury of at least six members.[27] As a matter of tribal law, service on tribal court juries is customarily restricted to tribal members.

In a landmark decision in 1978, the United States Supreme Court held that tribal courts do not have criminal jurisdiction over non-Indians. The *Oliphant v. Suquamish Indian Tribe*[28] opinion addressed the assertion of jurisdiction by the Suquamish tribal court over two non-Indians. Tribal charges against them included assaulting a tribal officer, driving at high speed on reservation highways, and damaging a tribal police vehicle. The tribe's jurisdiction was upheld in federal district court and in the Ninth Circuit Court of Appeals. The analysis of the Ninth Circuit Court followed the approach outlined by Margold's 1934 Interior Department opinion. The court proceeded from the premise that the power to preserve order on a reservation and to punish those who violate tribal law was part of the sovereignty originally possessed by the Suquamish. The court then looked to treaties with the Suquamish and to federal statutes to find if the tribe's inherent powers of criminal jurisdiction had been expressly limited. Finding no limitations in treaties or statutes, the court posed a final question, which it also answered negatively: in the circumstances, tribal criminal jurisdiction did not interfere with or frustrate the policies of the United States.[29]

In reversing the decision of the Ninth Circuit Court of Appeals, the United States Supreme Court articulated a different analytical framework for determining whether tribes retain inherent sovereign powers. Writing for the Court, Justice William H. Rehnquist stated that Indian tribes are proscribed from exercising both those powers of autonomous states that are expressly terminated by Congress and those powers inconsistent with their status. He also declined to restrict the "intrinsic limitations" on Indian tribal authority to the powers removed from the tribes by Chief Justice Marshall's decisions.

Failing to find express limitations of criminal jurisdiction over non-Indians either in statutes or treaties, Justice Rehnquist reviewed nineteenth century developments and accorded considerable weight from that review to what he characterized as "the commonly shared presumption of Congress, the Executive Branch, and lower federal courts that tribal courts do not have the power to try non-Indians." In *Oliphant,* the Court asserted that both treaties and statutes "must be read in light of the common notions of the day and the assumption of those who drafted them." The *Oliphant* opinion ultimately was based on the interests of the United States as overriding sovereign. By submitting to the sovereignty of the United States, Indian tribes, according to the Court, had given up the "power to try non-Indian citizens of the United States except in a manner acceptable to Congress."

Although the Court acknowledged the prevalence of non-Indian crime within reservations, the increasing sophistication of tribal courts, and the protections afforded by the Indian Civil Rights Act, these developments were described as irrelevant to the issue of whether tribes retain inherent jurisdiction to try and punish non-Indians. They were merely "considerations for Congress to weigh in deciding whether Indian tribes should finally be authorized to try non-Indians."

In the years since the *Oliphant* decision, Congress has not acted to authorize tribal criminal jurisdiction over non-Indians. It has deliberated inconclusively on establishing a magistrate system to increase federal law enforcement on reservations. Meantime, non-Indian crime continues to pose a serious problem for tribal governments and reservation residents. One response of the tribes has been to substitute civil penalties for criminal sanctions in order to be able to impose tribal regulations on motor vehicle operation, fishing and hunting, and other activities on Indian lands.

The United States Supreme Court has not utilized a single set of guidelines in deciding questions of tribal civil jurisdiction in the years since *Oliphant.* In a 1980 decision, *Washington v. Confederated Tribes of the Colville Indian Reservation,*[30] the Court applied the reasoning of *Oliphant* to uphold the retention of tribal sovereign powers to tax cigarette sales to nonmember purchasers. Writing for the Court, Justice Byron R. White pointed to the common recognition of executive branch officials, the courts, and Congress in the nineteenth century that federal law had not brought about a divestiture of Indian taxing power. The viewpoint of the executive branch was found in an 1881 Attorney General's Opinion and in Margold's 1934 Solicitor's Opinion. Justice White cited decisions by federal courts dating to the early 1900s that acknowledged tribal power to tax non-Indians engaging in economic activity on reservations. Congressional recognition of tribal authority to tax was traced to the tribal powers under "existing law" confirmed by the Indian Reorganization Act.

The Court's *Colville* opinion linked implicit divestiture of tribal powers to the overriding interests of the national government, not to the tribes' dependent status. The tribal taxes were upheld on two grounds: there was a widely held understanding within the federal government that tribes still possessed the power to tax, and no overriding federal interest was frustrated by the tribes' taxation of cigarette sales.

Within a year after the *Colville* decision, the Supreme Court ruled in *Montana v. United States*[31] that the Crow Tribe could not regulate nonmember hunting and fishing on reservation lands no longer owned by the tribe or individual Indians. Justice Potter Stewart's opinion for the Court first recognized that *Oliphant* had restricted inherent tribal authority in criminal matters, but then drew support from *Oliphant's* underlying principles for the "general proposition that the inherent sovereign powers of an Indian tribe do not extend to the activities of nonmembers." Having narrowly defined the range of tribal self-government, the *Montana v. United States* opinion then set forth broad grounds for exceptions; as a consequence, the opinion is most frequently cited in support of tribal governing authority over non-Indians. Often quoted from *Montana v. United States* is this passage, drawn from earlier case law:

> . . . To be sure, Indian tribes retain inherent sovereign power to exercise some forms of civil jurisdiction over non-Indians on their reservations, even on non-Indian fee lands. A tribe may regulate, through taxation, licensing, or other means, the activities of nonmembers who enter consensual relationships with the tribe or its members, through commercial dealing, contracts, leases, or other arrangements. . . . A tribe may also retain inherent power to exercise civil authority over the conduct of non-Indians on fee lands within its reservation when that conduct threatens or has some direct effect on the political integrity, the economic security, or the health or welfare of the tribe. . . .[32]

There have been unsuccessful challenges in the 1980s to a tribal oil and gas severance tax and to other tribal taxes, including a leasehold interest tax and a tax on receipts from the sale of services and the sale of property produced or extracted from reservation lands. In a 1982 decision, *Merrion v. Jicarilla Apache Tribe,*[33] the United States Supreme Court characterized the tribe's authority to tax non-Indians who conduct business on the reservation as "an inherent power necessary to tribal self-government and territorial management." Justice

Thurgood Marshall's majority opinion quoted the Court's observation in *Colville* that a tribe's interest "is strongest when the revenues are derived from value generated on the reservation by activities involving the Tribes and when the taxpayer is the recipient of tribal services."

Organized under the IRA, the Jicarilla Apache Tribe had adopted a constitution that required the approval of the Secretary of the Interior for any tax levied against nonmembers. The Supreme Court found assurance that a tribal tax would be consistent with national policies because of the requirement for federal approval and the existence of federal power to take away the tribe's taxing authority.

The effect of the Indian Reorganization Act was also discussed in the Supreme Court's 1985 decision, *Kerr-McGee Corporation v. Navajo Tribe of Indians.*[34] The Navajo Tribal Council's possessory interest tax and business activity tax were challenged after the Bureau of Indian Affairs informed the Navajo, who had not organized under the IRA, that no federal statute or regulation required that the Secretary of the Interior review the taxes. The Supreme Court agreed and found no Congressional or tribal requirement for federal review of Navajo tax laws. Again the Court referred to Margold's 1934 opinion in concluding that Congress had not limited the established, pre-existing power of the Navajo to levy taxes by enacting the IRA. The Court emphasized that the federal government is firmly committed to the goal of promoting tribal self-government. Essential to self-government, stated the Court, is "[t]he power to tax members and non-Indians alike." Further, the Navajos could "gain independence from the Federal Government only by financing their own police force, schools, and social programs."

Territorial management for Indian tribes increasingly has included the enactment of regulations requiring land-use planning and zoning and imposing building, health, safety, and environmental regulations on individuals and enterprises within reservation boundaries. Federal district and appeals courts have upheld these forms of tribal regulatory authority, and until 1988, the United States Supreme Court declined to review their decisions. The Ninth Circuit Court of Appeals applied rules from both *Colville* and *Montana v. United States* in upholding the right of the Confederated Salish and Kootenai Tribes to enact a shoreline protection ordinance regulating docks and breakwaters on the south half of Flathead Lake. The Court found no impediment to the tribe's regulations in the *Colville* rule (divestiture of only those powers inconsistent with overriding national interests) and it placed the tribal ordinance squarely within the exception recognized in *Montana v. United States* (the retention of inherent power over the conduct of non-Indians on fee lands when their conduct has a direct effect on the political integrity, economic security, or health or welfare of the tribe).[35]

Applying the second *Montana* exception, the "tribal-interest" test, the Ninth Circuit Court in 1987 concluded that the Yakima Nation in the state of Washington has the authority to zone non-Indian fee land within reservation boundaries. The underlying litigation concerned conflicting tribal and Yakima County zoning ordinances as applied to fee lands in an "open" checkerboarded area of the reservation in which nearly half of the land is in private ownership, and as applied to fee lands in a "closed" area, long protected for its economic and cultural resources, in which only a small percentage of land is privately held. In June 1989, the United States Supreme Court reversed in part the Ninth Circuit Court's decision. As a result of the combined opinions of the justices, county and not tribal zoning ordinances may be applied to fee land owned by nonmembers of the Yakima Nation in the "open" area, and tribal zoning ordinances may be applied to fee lands in the "closed" area. Under two differently reasoned opinions and over the strong dissent of three justices, zoning of fee lands of nonmembers in the "open" area was not brought within the scope of tribal authority under either treaty rights or the second *Montana* exception. Instead, as explained in Justice White's opinion, the Yakima Nation has a protectable interest under federal law which must be recognized and respected by Yakima County zoning authorities. If the impact of a land use on fee land within the reservation is "demonstrably serious and . . . imperil[s] the political integrity, economic security, or the health or welfare of the tribe," the tribe can seek relief in federal court.[36]

Tribal rights of self-government and federal protection of these rights have been at the core of United States Supreme Court decisions upholding the adjudicatory authority of tribal courts in civil matters. The Court's 1959 opinion in *Williams v. Lee*[37] recognized the exclusive jurisdiction of the Navajo court over an action by a non-Indian to collect a debt resulting from goods sold on credit on the reservation to a Navajo Indian and his wife. The Court stated that to permit state court jurisdiction instead of tribal court jurisdiction in the circumstances "would undermine the authority of the tribal courts over Reservation affairs and . . . infringe on the right of the Indians to govern themselves."

The Supreme Court further underscored tribal rights and responsibilities in 1978 by holding in *Santa Clara Pueblo v. Martinez*[38] that tribal forums, not federal district courts, have jurisdiction over claims brought under the Indian Civil Rights Act. Justice Thurgood Marshall's opinion for the Court declared that the Indian Civil Rights Act did not waive a tribe's sovereign immunity from suit, and that federal jurisdiction to enforce the act was restricted to habeas corpus actions. Earlier Supreme Court decisions were cited for the proposition that tribal courts are the "appropriate forums for the exclusive adjudication of disputes affecting important personal and property interests of both Indians and non-Indians."

In the wake of these decisions, many tribes amended their constitutions and codes to remove restrictions on tribal court jurisdiction over nonmembers. White plaintiffs readily utilized tribal courts to collect debts and settle disputes, but there was often resistance to the exercise of tribal court jurisdiction over non-Indian defendants in civil matters. A challenge to a Crow tribal court default judgment in a tort action against a Montana school district within the Crow reservation reached the United States Supreme Court in the 1984 term. In its decision in *National Farmers Union Ins. Cos. v. Crow Tribe of Indians,*[39] the Supreme Court indicated only tentative views on tribal court civil jurisdiction over non-Indian defendants, but firmly upheld the right of federal courts to review the jurisdictional question.

The lawsuit arose from schoolyard injuries sustained by a young boy, a member of the Crow Tribe. His guardian filed suit in Crow Tribal Court against the school district. The complaint was served on the chairman of the school board, but no answer to the complaint was filed in the tribal court. In accord with its rules of procedure, the Crow Tribal Court issued findings of fact, conclusions of law, and a default judgment against the school district. Soon afterward, the school district and its insurer bypassed the tribal court and obtained an injunction against any execution of the tribal court judgment from a federal district court in Montana. The injunction was issued because the federal district court could find no basis for the Crow Tribal Court's jurisdiction in statutes or treaties or by applying the general rule and exceptions of *Montana v. United States.*[40] That ruling was appealed to the Ninth Circuit Court of Appeals.

The Ninth Circuit Court of Appeals reversed the decision of the federal district court on jurisdictional grounds. The lower court had based its own jurisdiction on the section of the United States Code giving federal district courts jurisdiction over civil actions arising under the Constitution, laws, or treaties of the United States. The Supreme Court had already held that federal question jurisdiction under the statute can be based on federal common law.

Other federal district courts and the Ninth Circuit Court had found similar jurisdictional grounds when tribal powers had been challenged in other contexts, but the Ninth Circuit Court refused to subject tribal adjudicatory jurisdiction to the same kind of review. Relying on *Santa Clara Pueblo v. Martinez,* the Ninth Circuit Court interpreted Congressional purpose in enacting the Indian Civil Rights Act as limiting federal court interference with tribal court proceedings. The Court did not recognize a federal common law cause of action in addition to the habeas corpus remedy specified in the Indian Civil Rights Act.[41] The litigants were advised to seek a jurisdictional determination in tribal court, and the Ninth Circuit ruling was in turn appealed to the United States Supreme Court.

The United States Supreme Court did not agree with the Ninth Circuit Court's insulation of tribal court jurisdiction from federal court review. Without differentiating between jurisdiction to review regulatory and adjudicatory powers, the Supreme Court held that the question of "whether an Indian Tribe retains the power to compel a non-Indian property owner to submit to the civil jurisdiction of a tribal court" must be answered by reference to federal law and may be determined by a federal court. The Supreme Court, however, declined to extend the rule of *Oliphant* to tribal court civil jurisdiction over non-Indians, primarily because of the manner in which Congress and executive officials had historically differentiated between the criminal and civil jurisdiction of Indian tribes.

Having removed any automatic bar to tribal court jurisdiction, the Supreme Court ruled that a tribal court must have the opportunity to examine and rule on its own jurisdiction before any jurisdictional review can occur in federal court. The Court justified the requirement on several grounds. Giving a tribal court whose jurisdiction is challenged the first opportunity to evaluate the challenge is in keeping with the congressional "policy of supporting tribal self-government and self-determination." The orderly administration of justice also will be served. Tribal courts will be encouraged to explain the precise basis for accepting jurisdiction, and if further judicial review occurs, other courts will benefit from the expertise of tribal courts in these matters. The Supreme Court also set out guidelines for tribal courts to follow in answering the question of whether they have the power to exercise civil jurisdiction over non-Indians in such suits as the Crow case. In doing so, the Court restated the analytical framework it had utilized in the 1970s and 1980s in its own review of tribal jurisdiction:

> . . . the existence and extent of a tribal court's jurisdiction will require a careful examination of tribal sovereignty, the extent to which that sovereignty has been altered, divested, or diminished, as well as a detailed study of relevant statutes, Executive branch policy as embodied in treaties and elsewhere, and administrative or judicial decisions.[42]

The United States Supreme Court again addressed tribal court civil jurisdiction over non-Indian defendants in 1987 in a case arising on the Blackfeet reservation in Montana.[43] After a tribal member sued a

ranch and its insurer over injuries sustained in the course of employment, the insurance company sued in federal district court, alleging
diversity of citizenship as the basis for federal court jurisdiction. The
Supreme Court held that the exhaustion requirement of *National Farmers Union* should apply in federal diversity cases as well as in federal
question cases. The Court reasoned that in both situations, "uncon-
ditional access to the federal forum would place it in direct competition
with the tribal courts, thereby impairing [their] authority over reservation affairs."

In the *Iowa Mutual Insurance Company v. LaPlante* decision, the
Supreme Court noted the "[t]ribal courts play a vital role in tribal self
government, . . . and the Federal Government has consistently encouraged their development." Although recognizing *Oliphant's* holding that
the criminal jurisdiction of tribal courts was subject to substantial
federal limitation, the Court stated that "their civil jurisdiction is not
similarly restricted." The Court appeared to move a step beyond its
National Farmers Union opinion by stating:

> Tribal authority over the activities of non-Indians on reservation lands
> is an important part of tribal sovereignty. . . . Civil jurisdiction over
> such activities presumptively lies in the tribal courts unless affirmatively
> limited by a specific treaty provision or federal statute. "Because the
> Tribe retains all inherent attributes of sovereignty that have not been
> divested by the Federal Government, the proper inference from silence
> . . . is that the sovereign power . . . remains intact."

In the same period in which it has reviewed tribal self-governing
powers, the United States Supreme Court has also had to decide
questions concerned with the assertion of state authority within reservation boundaries. Frequently, the two issues are involved in a single
case. In the *Colville* decision in 1980, a tribal tax on cigarette purchases
by non-members was upheld, and so, too, were Washington state taxes
on the same cigarette sales. A related ruling in 1976 required that
Indian smokeshops collect for the state a Montana tax on cigarette
purchases by non-Indians.[44]

The Supreme Court historically has approached questions of the
extent of state governing power within reservations by proceeding from
the premise that Indian activity on reservations is immune from state
law unless Congress has authorized the exercise of state authority. More
typically, questions before the Court have been concerned with state
attempts to exercise authority over the conduct of non-Indian activity
on reservations through regulation, taxation, or the assertion of adjudicatory jurisdiction. It was in this context that the Supreme Court

framed its *Williams v. Lee* analysis in 1959 as an inquiry into whether state action infringes "on the right of reservation Indians to make their own laws and be ruled by them."[45]

For several years after 1959, although continuing to recognize interference with tribal self-governing rights as an independent barrier to the exercise of state authority, the Supreme Court increasingly turned to a special federal preemption analysis in assessing the legality of the extension of state law to both Indian and non-Indian activity within reservations. The emphasis on preemption treated tribal sovereignty as a backdrop for applicable treaties and federal statutes.[46] Under the analysis, protective federal law and policy can merge with tribal self-governing powers to create a bar to state jurisdiction. In the 1980s, the Court has detailed a framework for analyzing the legality of state law in Indian country which requires a "particularized inquiry" into the federal, tribal, and state interests involved.

In *Colville* in 1980, the Court stated that "[t]he principle of tribal self-government, grounded in notions of inherent sovereignty and in congressional policies, seeks an accommodation between the interests of the Tribes and the Federal Government, on the one hand, and those of the State, on the other."[47] In *White Mountain Apache Tribe v. Bracker,*[48] also a 1980 decision, the Court explained that an inquiry into the nature of state, federal, and tribal interests was "designed to determine whether, in the specific context, the exercise of state authority would violate federal law."

Today, the approaches and results of the Supreme Court's answers to questions related to tribal self-governing powers and the application of state law in Indian country are far from clear. After balancing federal, tribal, and state interests, the Court has both upheld and prohibited the exercise of state jurisdiction in cases it has decided in the 1980s. In the Southwest, the Court has disallowed state taxes on a logging company's activities under a contract with a tribe, on sales of farm machinery to a tribe, and on a contractor's income from school construction for a tribe.[49] The Court also analyzed federal, tribal, and state interests before upholding the tribe's exclusive right to regulate all hunting and fishing on reservation lands in its 1983 decision in *New Mexico v. Mescalero Apache Tribe.*[50] Judicial balancing of federal, tribal, and state interests and a finding of interference with tribal self-government determined that Montana could not impose its large severance and gross proceeds taxes on mineral production by non-Indian developers of Crow coal-resources.[51] Not long after that decision, however, the United States Supreme Court held that New Mexico had the authority to collect a much smaller severance tax and a school emergency tax from a non-Indian company producing oil and gas from

leases on tribal trust land on the Jicarilla reservation despite the fact
that the Jicarilla Apache Tribe was also imposing tribal taxes on the
leases.[52]

What is clear from the recent United States Supreme Court treatment
of Indian law cases is that the judiciary's role has been enlarged and
that the interests which dictated Chief Justice Marshall's decisions a
century and a half ago have changed. The Court has moved from
holding that Congress alone has plenary power in Indian affairs to
declaring that the power of the entire federal government, including
the judiciary, is plenary over the Indian tribes. The federal law that
must be consulted to determine federal interests in protecting the
individual, territorial, and political rights of Indian tribes is "implemented by statute, by treaty, by administrative regulations, and by
judicial decisions."[53] State interests, too, are to be weighed in the
judiciary's decisions which will shape in a fundamental way the future
course of tribal self-government.

The application of state law to Indian activities within reservations
has also resulted from congressional and tribal authorizations. In the
General Allotment Act, for example, Congress provided that state heir-
ship laws may apply to the descent of land of allottees. Federal law
also provides that state criminal laws are to be applied by United
States courts in the prosecution of reservation crime for which there
is no specific federal criminal statute. Tribal councils also frequently
incorporate state law into tribal codes to give either a mandatory or
permissive choice of law in civil matters if tribal or federal law provides
no rule of decision for a case before a tribal court.

Prior to 1953 Congress had authorized the extension of state jurisdiction to Indian reservations in statutes pertaining to a single state
or to designated reservations within a state. In 1953 Congress enacted
Public Law No. 280, which broadly authorized the extension of state
criminal and civil jurisdiction to reservations. The jurisdictional arrangement was mandatory for six states. Other states, including Montana, with Indian reservations within their borders, were given the
option of assuming jurisdiction as provided in the act.[54] Between 1953
and 1968 the second group of states could have moved unilaterally to
extend state jurisdiction to Indian reservations. During the period
Montana limited its utilization of Public Law 280 to a jurisdictional
agreement with the Confederated Salish and Kootenai Tribes of the
Flathead reservation. The arrangement provides for concurrent state-
tribal jurisdiction over criminal offenses and over eight subject areas
in civil litigation.[55]

Commencing in 1968, Congress required that tribal consent precede
any further extension of state jurisdiction under Public Law 280. The

United States Supreme Court ruled in 1971 in a case arising on the Blackfeet reservation that under the statute tribal consent had to be expressed by a majority vote of the enrolled members of the affected tribe, and that there could be no extension of state jurisdiction to reservations unless all of the provisions of Public Law 280 were strictly followed.[56]

Montanans had the opportunity to re-examine the relationship between the state and Indian tribes in writing and adopting a new constitution in 1972. Article I states that all provisions of the 1889 enabling act and Ordinance No. 1 of the 1889 constitution will continue in full force and effect until revoked by the consent of the United States and the people of Montana. Expressly carried forward from the 1889 provisions is a reaffirmation that "all lands owned or held by any Indian or Indian tribes shall remain under the absolute jurisdiction and control of the Congress of the United States." Recognition of the distinct and unique cultural heritage of American Indians is reflected in the Article X statement that Montana is committed in its educational goals to the preservation of Indian cultural integrity.[57]

The period since 1972 has been marked by increased attention to Indian affairs by Montana courts, the executive branch, and the legislature. Montana Supreme Court decisions reflect a gradual recognition of modern developments within the tribal judicial system. Initially, the Court noted the apparent deference of tribal codes in Montana to state law and jurisdiction in the field of domestic relations and observed the failure of tribal courts to exercise the jurisdiction that the United States Supreme Court held to be exclusively theirs. The reaction of the Montana Supreme Court was to uphold state jurisdiction over domestic relations cases involving Indians within reservations and to design a jurisdictional test. The Court ruled that before a state district court could assume jurisdiction, it had to find: whether applicable federal treaties or statutes preempted state jurisdiction, whether the exercise of state jurisdiction would interfere with reservation self-government, and whether the specific tribal court was currently exercising jurisdiction in such a manner as to preempt state jurisdiction.[58]

The Montana Supreme Court's subsequent decisions reflect faithful application of the analysis it devised. The Court took note of tribal code amendments removing jurisdictional barriers and ambiguities and of the actual practice of tribal courts in exercising jurisdiction over domestic relations suits and other civil litigation. When the Montana Supreme Court was convinced that Indian parties had adequate tribal remedies, it refused to uphold competing state jurisdiction and expressly overruled an earlier opinion sustaining state jurisdiction in an Indian divorce action.[59]

In 1982 the Montana Supreme Court ruled that a valid tribal court judgment can be enforced through a special proceeding in a state district court. The Supreme Court stated that "tribal court judgments are treated with the same deference shown decisions of foreign nations as a matter of comity." Once a special proceeding is instituted to enforce a tribal judgment, state law creates a presumption that the judgment is evidence of rights between parties. Defenses are limited to evidence of a lack of jurisdiction or notice or of collusion, fraud, or clear mistake of law or fact.[60]

The office of the Coordinator of Indian Affairs is part of the executive branch of Montana state government. The statutory duties of the Indian Affairs Coordinator are to understand the problems of the Indians of Montana and to provide information and recommendations to the legislature, the executive branch, and the Montana congressional delegation. The Indian Affairs Coordinator is to act as spokesman for Indian organizations and groups on their request. Also housed within the executive branch is an Indian legal jurisdiction project, established in 1977 to conduct research and handle litigation. The activities have received substantial funding from the legislature, and attorneys associated with the project have vigorously represented the state in court contests against Montana tribes over jurisdiction, water rights, mineral taxation, and other matters.

Since 1979 five interim committees of the Montana Legislature have been created to gather information about Indian affairs and to provide a forum for state and tribal representatives to discuss mutual concerns. Initially, the interim committees on Indian affairs were reluctant to venture into sharply contested areas, but the reluctance soon gave way to a willingness to consider major problems in state-tribal relations. The committees have determined their agendas after soliciting ideas for study topics from state agencies, tribes, tribal organizations, and interested individuals, and their hearings and deliberations have been productive. In addition, most legislative recommendations of the select committees have been successful. The committees have provided a forum in which problems related to the interaction of tribal, state, and local governments can be addressed, and enactment of the Montana State-Tribal Cooperative Agreements Act in 1981 was a direct result of the recommendations of the 1979–1980 select committee on Indian affairs. The measure authorizes state agencies and local governments to enter into agreements with Montana tribal governments to perform any functions that the parties to the agreement can lawfully perform.[61] Keeping informed about the progress of cooperative agreements and encouraging their implementation have been important activities for subsequent Indian affairs committees.

The 1983–1984 Indian affairs committee recommended procedural changes to facilitate state-tribal agreements, and the 1985 legislature enacted the changes. Another recommendation resulted in legislation permitting the exchange or sale of state lands within reservations through agreements with tribal governments. Other subjects for the committee's deliberations in 1983–1984 were: delivery of social services including the provision of mental health care; excise taxes on alcohol, gasoline, and cigarettes; natural resource taxation and tax credits; education issues; fish and game matters; and water rights. The committee also recommended the creation of a more permanent and better funded Indian affairs committee. That recommendation was not successful. The 1985–1986 Indian affairs committee had four legislator-members instead of the usual eight, and the life of the committee was again limited to two years. Although several topics were addressed, the committee concentrated on Indian child welfare matters and alcoholism programs. Committee recommendations resulted in legislation in 1987 establishing the position of Indian child welfare specialist in the Montana Department of Social and Rehabilitation Services and requiring the participation of a person knowledgeable about Indian cultural and family matters when foster care review boards deliberate on the care of Indian children. In 1987–1988, a four-member committee on Indian Affairs studied cross-deputization and extradition agreements, Indian students in postsecondary education, and Indian health care, and reviewed the subject of a state-tribal cooperative agreement for the assessment and collection of taxes, licenses, and permits. The 1989 legislature reestablished the four-member committee on Indian Affairs as a statutory rather than interim committee.

Agreements between the tribes and state and local governments place Montana within the national movement for increased cooperative activities between non-Indian and Indian governments. For example, Montana has been a leader among the states in pursuing negotiation as a substitute for litigation to determine federal and Indian reserved water rights. Negotiation of tribal-state compacts is the primary mission of the Reserved Water Rights Compact Commission, created in 1979.[62] Because of the complexity and time-consuming nature of the negotiations, budget and staff have increased, and the successful Fort Peck–Montana Compact of 1985 has engendered strong hopes for other agreements worked out through the negotiation process. By 1988, departments of Montana state government had entered into more than forty agreements involving all of the tribal governments in the state and dealing with many areas of social services in addition to resource issues.

Encouragement of such endeavors has been the principal aim of the Commission on State-Tribal Relations formed in 1978 under the sponsorship of the National Conference on State Legislatures, the National Congress of American Indians, and the National Tribal Chairmen's Association. The rationale for mutual undertakings is simple: tribes, local governments, and states have many shared interests and common problems. Coordinated work in such fields as law enforcement, wildlife management, environmental protection, and land use planning and zoning is essential if common problems and common needs are to be effectively addressed.

Montana's success in state-tribal relations, though, is partial. The state has not developed a consistent or uniform policy in Indian affairs. Instead, Indian policy often appears diffused, and contradictory expressions of Montana's position in state-tribal relations are common. Litigation resolves one conflict at a time and seldom erases the friction or practical problems that lead to law suits. Progress toward reaching common ground by the tribes and the state and local governments in Montana is slowed and often blocked by misunderstanding, skepticism, and deep-seated hostility. No ready answer can be given to the question of whether historic antagonisms and mistrust will prevail or whether Montana and the tribes will turn increasingly to mutual approaches to shared problems.

Notes

1. *Johnson v. McIntosh,* 21 U.S. (8 Wheat.) 543 (1823).
2. *Cherokee Nation v. Georgia,* 30 U.S. (5 Pet.) 1 (1831); *Worcester v. Georgia,* 31 U.S. (6 Pet.) 515 (1832).
3. Treaty of Fort Laramie with Sioux, Etc., 1851, 11 Stat. 749.
4. Treaty with the Flatheads, &c., July 16, 1855, 12 Stat. 975.
5. Treaty with the Blackfoot Indians, Oct. 17, 1855, 11 Stat. 657.
6. Treaty with the Crow Indians, May 7, 1868, 15 Stat. 649.
7. Act of May 1, 1888, 25 Stat. 113.
8. Organic Act of the Territory of Montana, Act of May 26, 1864, 13 Stat. 85; Enabling Act for North Dakota, South Dakota, Montana and Washington, Act of February 22, 1889, 25 Stat. 676; Ordinance I, appended to Montana Constitution of 1889.
9. Treaty with the Crow Indians, May 7, 1868, 15 Stat. 649; Act of April 11, 1882, 22 Stat. 42.
10. Act of February 8, 1887, 24 Stat. 388; 25 U.S.C. Sec. 311 et seq.
11. Lake Mohonk Conference Proceedings, 1887, p. 9, cited in D.S. Otis, *The Dawes Act and the Allotment of Indian Lands* (Francis Paul Prucha ed.) (Norman: University of Oklahoma Press, 1973), p. 58.

12. Institute for Government Research, *The Problem of Indian Administration* (L. Meriam ed.) (Baltimore: The Johns Hopkins Press, 1928).

13. Act of June 18, 1934, 48 Stat. 984; 25 U.S.C. Sec. 461 et seq.

14. 55 I.D. 14 (1934).

15. F. Cohen, *Handbook of Federal Indian Law* (1942); F. Cohen, *Handbook of Federal Indian Law* (2 ed. 1958); F. Cohen, *Handbook of Federal Indian Law* (U.N.M. ed. 1971); F. Cohen, *Handbook of Federal Indian Law* (1982 ed.).

16. Act of May 14, 1948, 62 Stat. 236; 25 U.S.C. Sec. 483.

17. H.R. Con. Res. 108, 83d Cong., 1st Sess. 67 Stat. B132 (1953).

18. Pub. L. No. 90-284, 82 Stat. 77; 25 U.S.C. Sec. 1301 et seq.

19. Pub. L. No. 93-638, 88 Stat. 2203; 25 U.S.C. Sec. 450 et seq.

20. American Indian Policy Review Comm'n, 95th Cong., 1st Sess., *Final Report* (Comm. Print 1977).

21. President's Statement on Indian Policy, 19 Weekly Comp. Pres. Doc. 98 (Jan. 24, 1983).

22. The principal federal statutes governing reservation crime are the General Crimes Act or Enclaves Crimes Act, 18 U.S.C. Sec. 1152, and the Major Crimes Act, 18 U.S.C. Sec. 1153.

23. *United States v. Kagama,* 118 U.S. 375, 384 (1886).

24. *Lone Wolf v. Hitchcock,* 187 U.S. 553 (1903); *United States v. Sioux Nation of Indians,* 448 U.S. 371 (1980).

25. 18 U.S.C. Sec. 1151.

26. *United States v. McBratney,* 104 U.S. 621 (1881).

27. Pub. L. No. 90-284, 82 Stat. 77; 25 U.S.C. Sec. 1301 et seq.

28. *Oliphant v. Suquamish Indian Tribe,* 435 U.S. 191 (1978).

29. *Oliphant v. Schlie,* 544 F.2d 1007 (9th Cir. 1976).

30. *Washington v. Confederated Tribes of the Colville Indian Reservation,* 447 U.S. 134 (1980).

31. *Montana v. United States,* 450 U.S. 544 (1981).

32. *Montana v. United States,* 450 U.S. 544, 565–66 (1981).

33. *Merrion v. Jicarilla Apache Tribe,* 455 U.S. 130 (1982).

34. *Kerr-McGee Corporation v. Navajo Tribe of Indians,* 471 U.S. 195 (1985).

35. *Confederated Salish and Kootenai Tribes v. Namen,* 665 F.2d 951, 963–964 (9th Cir. 1982), cert. denied, 459 U.S. 977 (1982).

36. The Yakima zoning controversy resulted in two cases brought by the Confederated Tribes and Bands of the Yakima Indian Nation in federal district court, separate appeals to the Ninth Circuit Court, and three petitions to the United States Supreme Court for writs of certiorari. The federal district court opinions are at 617 F. Supp. 735 and 617 F. Supp. 750 (1985); the opinion of the Ninth Circuit Court of Appeals is at 828 F.2d 529 (1987), and the opinion of the United States Supreme Court is at 109 S.Ct. 2994 (1989).

37. *Williams v. Lee,* 358 U.S. 217 (1959).

38. *Santa Clara Pueblo v. Martinez,* 436 U.S. 49 (1978).

39. *National Farmers Union Insurance Companies v. Crow Tribe of Indians,* 471 U.S. 845 (1985).

40. *National Farmers Union Insurance Companies v. Crow Tribe of Indians of Montana,* 560 F. Supp. 213 (1983).

41. *National Farmers Union Insurance Companies v. Crow Tribe of Indians,* 736 F.2d 1320 (1984).

42. *National Farmers Union Insurance Companies v. Crow Tribe of Indians,* 471 U.S. 845, 855 (1985).

43. *Iowa Mutual Insurance Company v. LaPlante,* 480 U.S. 9, 107 S.Ct. 971 (1987).

44. *Moe v. Confederated Salish and Kootenai Tribes of Flathead Indian Reservation,* 425 U.S. 463 (1976).

45. *Williams v. Lee,* 358 U.S. 217, 220 (1959).

46. *McClanahan v. Arizona State Tax Comm'n,* 411 U.S. 164 (1973).

47. *Washington v. Confederated Tribes of the Colville Indian Reservation,* 447 U.S. 134, 156 (1980).

48. *White Mountain Apache Tribe v. Bracker,* 448 U.S. 136 (1980).

49. *White Mountain Apache Tribe v. Bracker,* 448 U.S. 136 (1980); *Central Machinery Co. v. Arizona State Tax Commission,* 448 U.S. 160 (1980); *Ramah Navajo School Board v. Bureau of Revenue,* 458 U.S. 832 (1982).

50. *New Mexico v. Mescalero Apache Tribe,* 462 U.S. 324 (1983).

51. *Crow Tribe v. Montana,* 819 F.2d 895 (9th Cir. 1987), aff'd mem., 484 U.S. 997 (1988).

52. *Cotton Petroleum Corporation v. New Mexico,* 109 S.Ct. 1698 (1989).

53. *National Farmers Union Insurance Companies v. Crow Tribe of Indians,* 471 U.S. 845, 851 (1985).

54. Act of Aug. 15, 1953, 67 Stat. 588; 25 U.S.C. Sec. 1321 et seq., 18 U.S.C. Sec. 1162, 25 U.S.C. Sec. 1321–1326, 28 U.S.C. Sec. 1360.

55. Montana Code Annotated, Sec. 2-1-301 et seq.; The Law and Order Code of the Confederated Salish and Kootenai Tribes of the Flathead Reservation, Montana, Ch. 1, Sec. 2 (3) (4).

56. *Kennerly v. District Court of Montana,* 400 U.S. 423 (1971).

57. *Montana Constitution of 1972,* Article I and Article X, Sec. 1 (2).

58. *Iron Bear v. District Court,* 162 Mont. 335, 512 P.2d 1292 (1973).

59. *In re Limpy,* 195 Mont. 314, 636 P.2d 266 (1981).

60. *Wippert v. Blackfeet Tribe,* 201 Mont. 299, 654 P.2d 512 (1982).

61. Montana Code Annotated, Sec. 18-11-101 et seq.

62. Montana Code Annotated, Sec. 2-15-212.

3

The Blackfeet:
Their Own Government
to Help Them

The Blackfeet are among the oldest residents of the Northern Plains.[1] They also were the most powerful Indian people north of the Missouri River. The nation consisted of three tribes, the Blood and Blackfeet who lived far to the north and the Piegan who lived south of the present forty-ninth parallel. Early accounts described them as an independent people, renowned both for their happiness and for their hostility when challenged. Early traders said that the Blackfeet were high-spirited and easygoing, but they also knew that the Blackfeet's fearless brand of warfare had effectively prevented white expansion to the north. The Blackfeet dominance was appreciated by other tribes as well as by pioneering whites. The Blackfeet lived with a proprietary sense on the plains as buffalo hunters and fur traders, the buffalo both charting the territory of the Blackfeet and influencing their political organization.

Today's Blackfeet reservation is a true homeland, although it consists of only a small portion of the territory once claimed by the three tribes. In the early nineteenth century, the Blackfeet would hunt from southern Canada to the Missouri River and from the Judith Basin west to the Rocky Mountains. The basic topography and climate of their lands are unchanged. Rolling plains, crossed by rivers and creeks, rise gradually to the hills and then to the peaks of the Rockies. The continental climate of hot and dry summers and long and cold winters has consistently made the point that this is grazing and not crop land.

The social forms that bound the Blackfeet together evolved from their life as hunters. As long as the buffalo was the basis of the Blackfeet economy, small groups were the basis of their political organization. Hunting bands were a fluid social form, as families were free to change their membership based on the success and generosity of the band leaders. The band's flexibility also extended to the selection of chiefs and their relationship to members. Consensus would form as to who possessed leadership qualities, such as war and hunting skills and a caring nature. Also, matters of importance to the band were resolved only after the band leader presented these issues to the council of male members for discussion and decision. The Blackfeet traditionally, then, prized the traits of self-reliance, independence, and involvement.

After 1888 the Blackfeet Indians were confined to reservation life, their freedom and individualism giving way to subjugation to an overseeing power. For years a series of Indian agents took steps to destroy reliance on the tribe's political structure and to make the Blackfeet dependent on the federal government's system of reservation governance. Not until 1935 were the Blackfeet able to regain some influence in designing a political system of their own. In the constitution[2] adopted in that year and in subsequently proposed and sometimes ratified amendments can be seen elements of the Blackfeet's traditional political culture. Values of structural fragmentation and broad participation, especially, have been adhered to most strongly. The principal question of this chapter is whether continued adherence to such forms is conducive to economic and political self-determination.

Blackfeet Indian Agent John Wood initiated governmental change in 1875, encouraging the tribesmen to elect reservation representatives to leadership positions. Typical of nineteenth century reservation governments, the Blackfeet general council responded by electing tribal leaders to serve as reservation administrators. Until 1911, the general council elected an eighteen-member administrative body. These were "reliable" men with "good judgment" who exerted beneficial influence upon the rest of the community by maintaining discipline.

Agent Wood also pushed the Blackfeet to adopt a code of laws and to create a tribal tribunal, composed of the agent and three principal leaders, to administer justice.[3] Involving tribesmen in their own affairs improved reservation conditions.[4]

The Blackfeet Court of Indian Offenses, organized in the nineteenth century by the federal government, but run by the tribesmen, functioned very well. For example, in 1928 the tribal court was "very efficient" and able men presided. "Their procedure is simple, they get the plain facts of the case, summon witnesses and examine them. . . . This is all done in the presence of the defendant and he is allowed to make statements and other defenses as he cares to make." After the court's decision, defendants did not question the verdict. The punishment was not a fine but usually "an industrial sentence which many times starts some of the younger people along the lines of industry."[5]

The court's self-rule was not emulated in the tribal governing body's experience because of increased federal interference. Superintendent Arthur McFatridge pushed for the replacement of the general council with a smaller five-member business committee in 1912. This went against the tribe's participatory politics, and the council was increased gradually. The membership was twelve by 1917, and increased to fifteen by 1920. Because of the outside interference, the tribe's early twentieth century politics was steeped in conflict. The tribal leaders' opposition to federal directions caused the superintendent to label the council a body of troublemakers with nothing better to do. The early twentieth century business council established a confrontational political style which carried into the Indian Reorganization Act debates and beyond.[6]

The Blackfeet government today under the 1935 tribal constitution is dominated by the nine-member Business Council. The nine positions are allocated among four geographic districts, but district boundaries are for filing purposes only. The entire reservation electorate votes in each primary and general election, choosing council members for two-year concurrent terms. From its membership the Council chooses a chairman and a vice chairman, while a secretary and sergeant-at-arms can come from either within or outside the Council. The constitution seems to anticipate that these officers will be subordinated to the Council, as it has both lawmaking and executive authority. Characteristic of Indian Reorganization Act governments, it also has economic as well as political duties. The Council, accordingly, is empowered to "promulgate ordinances," "manage all economic affairs and enterprises of the Blackfeet Reservation," and "manage tribal affairs in an acceptable and business-like manner and in accordance with the administrative plan."[7] The By-laws of the Blackfeet tribe, published along with the constitution, lists presiding at council meetings as the only duty of the chairman.

The Council has followed two administrative plans, one adopted by resolution in 1966 and a more detailed plan drafted in the early 1980s. In both versions of the "Plan of Operation," the Council spelled out the governing roles and responsibilities of tribal entities. For several years the tribal government followed the most recent administrative plan even though the Council had never formally adopted it by resolution. A Bureau of Indian Affairs official on the Blackfeet reservation believed that such usage "probably would not withstand a challenge."[8] Because of this legal vulnerability, the Council in 1984 returned to the 1966 administrative plan as its source of guidance.[9] The later plan is important, however, because it gives some indication of what contemporary tribal leaders believe is the proper political relationship between the legislative and executive branches. While the plan treats the administrative roles of the Council and chairman in a hazy manner, the dominant impression is that the Council would be made the paramount force.

The ambiguity of the more recent plan stems from the tribe's unwillingness to identify and assign administrative responsibilities clearly. Instead, great value is placed on shared authority, broad involvement, and an informal mode of proceeding. Initially the Council is given the responsibility "to become involved in the vast number of Tribal and Tribally-sponsored Programs to develop and maintain a centralized organization of administration."[10] Then an executive committee, made up of the chairman, vice chairman, secretary and treasurer, is created to receive the administrative responsibility and functions of the Council. Yet, other provisions of the plan both vest "management of Tribal business"[11] in the Council and charge the chairman, as "Chief Executive Officer,"[12] with "general supervisory authority over Tribal employees, Tribal property and Tribal projects."[13] On top of this administrative triangle of Council, chairman, and executive committee, the plan of operation authorizes the Council to establish the following: advisory committees of tribal members, Council members, and program directors for the purpose of program oversight and development; tribal task forces which are temporary committees for accomplishment of a definite objective; and administrative boards and committees "to properly administer certain Tribal functions,"[14] comprised solely of Council members. These several authorizations raise conflicting expectations and could create an administrative atmosphere of confusion and competition.

The fragmented nature of Blackfeet government has been further enhanced by the activism of the agency superintendent, the Interior Department's representative on the reservation. In the early 1980s the federal government's policy of Indian self-determination should have tempered somewhat the longstanding paternalism of the Bureau of Indian Affairs. Thus the superintendent should have been facilitating tribal takeover of reservation government rather than continuing to provide an institutional check on the tribe. But the Bureau on the Blackfeet reservation during these years interpreted its role more in line with direct participation than with the option of withdrawal. The superintendent, for example, emphasized reviewing constitutional amendments, ordinances, budgets, resolutions, and codes; checking for compliance with contracts under which the tribe had assumed program operation from the Bureau of Indian Affairs; providing technical assistance and approving contracts and leases dealing with such tribal natural resources as oil, gas, and grazing land; and initiating tribal council action and even recruiting and supporting candidates for Council positions.[15] The Bureau of Indian Affairs agency on the Blackfeet reservation was a force in tribal government, at times a controlling influence, because of its unusual involvement in tribal affairs.

This fragmented system of administration presides over a government of not insignificant size and stakes. In 1983 the Blackfeet reservation had a tribal enrollment of 12,498, out of which 6,716 members lived on the reservation. Total acreage within reservation boundaries is 1,525,712 acres. Of this total, the tribe owns 240,206 acres; individual Indians own 702,759 acres; and non-Indians own 582,610 acres, which amounts to 38 percent of the total. The major concern of government is economic development, as unemployment among the work force has in recent years been above 50 percent. The most likely areas for economic development have been stock raising, oil and gas production, tourism, and small businesses. For example, the maximum grazing limit on tribal trust and allotted land is 55,000 cattle.[16] Presently, this potential is being realized, but by 24,000 Indian-owned cattle and 31,000 head owned by whites grazing under contract with Indians. Oil and gas development is the most hopeful area of economic development. In 1983, 280 exploration leases covered 130,000 acres. Oil and gas royalities in 1981 amounted to $3,021,772, when the tribe's total income was $4,573,807.[17] The 1983 tribal budget was approximately $7.9 million, and mineral revenue contributed $6.2 million of that amount.[18] The Blackfeet tribe has had many failures in small business development. Its sole success, the Blackfeet Writing Company, manufactures pencils, pens, and calendars and has 125 employees. The major employer, though, is the tribal government itself with nearly 400 full-time positions on its payroll.[19]

An analysis of the tribe's operating budget demonstrates the scope of tribal government and how it is similar to and different from other governments. Programmed expenditures for fiscal year 1981–1982 were $4,898,700.[20] Major outlays were for the principal departments and services of the tribe's government, whose functions and responsibilities are similar to those of a county or municipal government. Some examples follow:

tribal council salaries	$ 122,419
council staff salaries	15,824
finance department	96,424
head start program	270,305
job training center	90,016
nursing home	230,535
community health program	140,055
economic development	195,060

| tribal court | 117,847 |
| debt service | 228,925 |

The Blackfeet tribe, however, has assumed responsibilities that distinguish it from other governments. The poverty of the reservation has placed pressure on the tribal government for special kinds of responses. For example, in 1981 the Council set aside $851,822 for "per capita payments,"[21] each member of the tribe receiving $50.00. This direct payment represents a policy of sharing whereby the Council says, "the tribe's natural resources are being managed successfully and all partake in this good fortune." Another budget item necessitated by reservation conditions is a program of individual grants costing over $194,000.[22] These are extraordinary welfare payments for medical and educational emergencies, natural disasters, burial, and other hardships. In this instance, the tribe is providing its members with help when all other sources have failed. The detoxification program is another outlay that is not unique to Indian governments but of special concern given the determination to reduce the high rate of alcoholism that has prevailed in the past. In 1981–1982, the Medicine Pine Lodge received $82,175.[23]

Although it has attempted to respond to community needs, there are indications that the Blackfeet government, as presently conceived and operating, is not providing effective management of tribal affairs. Any reservation government is confronted with major problems. These include cultural isolation, poverty, an untrained work force, severely restricted revenue sources, limited potential for economic development, and relative inexperience with governing under a bureaucratic system. The design of government alone cannot remedy these weaknesses, but structural values and features can have an effect on the tribe's ability to identify, discuss, and respond to problems. The Blackfeet government's characteristics of informality, administrative fragmentation, and Council domination seem to be holding back the progress of the tribe.

According to a former Blackfeet tribal councilman who is also an attorney, the special character of Blackfeet government—and of most reservation governments—is that it is an integral part of a closed community.[24] The Blackfeet reservation is a homeland for approximately 7,000 members whose attention is directed principally inwards—toward family, relatives, neighbors, reservation events, and the activities of those who have the temerity to seek prominence. The center of life is the governmental "complex," a collection of cinder block structures and converted frame houses in Browning. Most families on the reservation have daily dealings with tribal and agency officials housed in these buildings. Here family members work, come with problems and to conduct business, or sit to watch the activity and idle away the hours.

This proximity is the glue of the closed community. Because of inside information and shared gossip, most members believe that they know what is happening on the reservation. This opportunity to observe and relate is fueled by an ethic of equal station and jealousy: Blackfeet generally do not take pleasure in seeing other tribal members get ahead financially. The political consequence of the closed community is a disposition of tribal members to suspect and second-guess the decisions of governmental officials and to involve themselves in tribal matters.

The Council functions as a highly visible and elite group amidst this social network.[25] Council members have good salaries (over $27,000 in 1982) and benefits (a $64,499 off-reservation travel budget in 1982),[26] and Council membership is important because of authorizations in the constitution and plan of operations. These powers and perquisites of office have an inevitable influence on the councilmen, and tribal members seek favors in proportion to the officials' display of power and importance. The Council members' difficulty in saying "no" to constituents is enhanced by their election schedule. Every two years each member of the Council faces the prospect of re-election or defeat. The result of frequent contact with the Blackfeet voters is the candidates' reinforcement of the impression that Council members can solve problems. Easy access to tribal officials, however, does not result in true governmental responsiveness because a single Council member's signature will not secure a job or a loan and a Council member acting alone cannot make or alter policy.

The essential weakness of the Blackfeet government stems from the Council's formal status and its mode of operation. Power is so centralized in the Council that there is a broad expectation that the Council will manage the business of the tribe. This means, for the most part, attending to the details of government. In 1983, for example, the Tribal Council passed 548 resolutions dealing with housekeeping matters (such as approving a particular site for a lease) and enacted only six ordinances of general application.[27] The politics that accompanied these routine administrative tasks pitted the Council members against each other and the Council itself against any competitor for power. The Council collectively takes the position that it must be in charge, while members individually maneuver for individual advantage.

An example of the dysfunction of this "Council mystique"[28] is the tribe's economic development effort. Because the Council has insisted on being the director of the tribal economy, many business failures have resulted, such as a campground and a racetrack. The Council's assertiveness has a basis in law. The tribe's corporate charter issued by the federal government authorizes the Council to "exercise all of the corporate powers hereinafter enumerated."[29] These authorizations include the power to "engage in any business that will further the economic well-being of the members of the Tribe. . . ."[30] The business failures result because the Council is unwilling to delegate to others. In the past the Council has refused to hire a tribal manager and business managers who would earn salaries higher than those of Council members. Economic development projects then became subject to the political ambitions and jealousies of Council members. Only the writing company succeeded, and this was because the investors insisted on retaining management control separate from the Council.

The deficiency of the Blackfeet Council goes deeper. Its failure to install a centralized administrative office has lead to internal management problems.[31] In 1983 the tribal government spent $400,000 beyond its budget, primarily because of Council indiscretions. For example, a five-day business trip to Houston cost $9,000 and another trip to Washington, D.C., cost $35,000. Tribal member and attorney Joe McKay remembers how, in the past, persons resigned from the Council and denounced such practices. The Council system, they alleged, took money from the people and spent it on a few—for example, high fees for consultants, unnecessary travel and overhead, and wining and dining for officials. They argued that the Council taught the young exactly the wrong lessons—do little, provide no supervision, travel all of the time, and exploit the tribe for private gain.

Some resistance to the Council's inadequacies does exist, but it is principally due to an incumbent's force rather than official roles, to outrage rather than routine procedures. The appointed tribal treasurer, somewhat like a clerk and recorder in a rural county, to a degree can hold the government together because of longevity in office and location at the hub of operations.

The treasurer, absent a true chief executive, is the only employee who knows everything that is occurring. The treasurer can remain free of the Council's political squabbles and, therefore, has the neutrality to bring the Council financially into line. This check, though, is more accidental than systematic. Institutional restraint could have been expected from a tribal chairman who served on the Council for thirty years and as chairman for twenty-four years. The chairman, though, was only nominally a chief executive, defining his role instead in terms of a leader in the national Indian movement, a member of the Council, and a listener to the complaints and problems of tribal members. As a member of the moderate faction on the Council, the chairman vacillated without taking a stand; by gaining national recognition, the chairman traded time in Washington for time on the job; and as an ear for the tribal members, he became a broker instead of a leader.

The other form of resistance to Council failures is political retribution that can occur when the electorate detects conspicuous consumption or abuse of office. A member of a leading Blackfeet political family notes that the surest way to ruin a political career on the reservation is to buy a pickup truck soon after election to the council.[32] The ethic at work, he says, is "don't get too far ahead too quickly." Similarly but more seriously, a charge of nepotism can be the undoing of a tribal official. Word quickly gets around the reservation that someone "is finished," and resident voter turnout can be as high as 44 percent.

Electoral accountability is also furthered by the existence of factionalism on the reservation. Policy positions are important, and Council members have tended to group along pro-development, traditionalist, and do-nothing lines.

Generally, no faction has sufficient votes to control, so the Council is reduced to wrangling and reacting to crises. The well publicized disputes and Council salaries, though, help to attract a full field of candidates. Incumbents have felt the hot breath of competition when as many as sixty-four persons have contested nine Council positions. Blood quantum and family ties also figure into campaigning and political rhetoric, but charges of "He's a goddamn Cree" or "He's only a half-breed" are generally covers for policy differences.[33] Taken together, jealousy, suspicions of nepotism, ideological differences, and bloc voting by families can defeat an incumbent at election time.

This discussion of tribal politics should not be taken to mean that the Blackfeet are more tolerant of malfeasance than other communities. Investigations have been conducted routinely, and on occasion members have been willing to address reform. An audit of tribal compliance with twenty agreements under which the tribe had assumed $1.5 million of federal responsibilities found only one disputed contract.[34] Periodically the Blackfeet have constituted a special body to consider governmental revision, and proposals for change have been adopted. The process to amend the tribal constitution and by-laws is set out in the constitution.[35] A proposed amendment can be put on the ballot by a two-thirds vote of the Council or by a petition signed by one-third of the tribe's qualified voters. Adoption of an amendment is dependent upon approval by a majority of those voting in a special election and a turnout of at least 30 percent of the electorate.

The last amendment to the tribal constitution was the 1978 addition of a primary election. Under the present scheme, Council candidates file by district and run in an at-large primary election. The top two candidates for each position then can advance to the general election by a very small plurality vote.

In 1983 a referendum committee appointed by the Council was at work. Tribal elders made up this committee, reflecting the Blackfeet's deference to experience and age. The committee had a full agenda of possible constitutional reforms, and its first priority was strengthening the position of chairman. The committee ultimately made three recommendations for amending the constitution: popular election of the chairman on an at-large basis, changing council terms from a concurrent to a staggered system, and lengthening council terms from two to four years. The Blackfeet chairman gave these proposals little chance of passage.[36] It was thought that the Council would deny the chief executive measure the necessary two-thirds Council support because councilmen did not want an administrative challenger. Also, tribal members seemed apathetic to governmental reform issues, appearing to be more interested in the cost of the committee and the family ties of committee members.

The effective opponent of the reforms, however, turned out to be the Bureau of Indian Affairs. The superintendent killed the proposals even though the constitutional review committee was properly established and it had been procedurally correct in conducting its work. The superintendent explained his action by saying that the committee had been created by one Council, and in the interim a new Council had been elected. Another interpretation of the Bureau's opposition was that the superintendent disliked the philosophy of government behind the reform proposals—a stronger and more accountable executive and a council characterized by more experience and stability.[37]

In the summer of 1984, the new Council revived and slightly revised the recommendation of the referendum committee. The four-year term and staggered election proposals were combined into one ballot item. The tribal electorate, in late 1984, defeated the amendment by a two-to-one margin. While the rejection can be attributed in part to members' lack of understanding and the Council's failure to communicate sufficient information, the major reason for the voters' opposition was probably the Council's contemporaneous refusal to convert a $1 million energy company bonus into per capita payments.[38] The Council had turned back, for both technical and policy reasons, a petition calling for such a distribution. The petition contained an insufficient number of signatures, and the Council had already decided to commit the money to establishing a bank in the reservation town of Browning. One councilman concluded that the referendum outcome was more a result of political retaliation than a judgment on the merits of the proposed amendment.[39]

Not all attempts at constitutional reform on the Blackfeet reservation have been piecemeal. In 1974 a Blackfeet constitutional convention proposed a new tribal constitution.[40] This document, though never adopted, can serve as an example of contemporary Native American philosophy of government. Constitutions adopted in the 1930s after passage of the Indian Reorganization Act, on the other hand, have been derided by Indians as representative of the ideas of white lawyers and anthropologists hired by the federal government.

The themes of the 1974 constitution stress the Blackfeet's past, present, and future. The experience of the past is reflected in the framers' desperation and their conclusion that this is the last chance for the Blackfeet to succeed. The future, though, seems promising; the framers believe that the economic and political means of success are presently in place. This optimism and sense of mission are captured in the "Declaration" and "Preamble":

. . . we arise, refreshed with due strength, declaring to all men that we shall form a new government, a new way of life, recapturing our pride and our dignity and fostering our culture and our heritage.

. . . we wish to make sure that our people will continue to live here, that they will have their own government to help them and that they will be a good people.

. . . we have been pushed back to this land, the last of our home country.

The proposed 1974 constitution has interesting features throughout its articles. It is a blend of innovative and borrowed provisions, bold statements of power, and tangled administrative arrangements. The borrowed characteristics are among the traditional strengths of American governments; the innovations and aggressive stance include honest admissions of weakness and assertions of political presence and jurisdiction; and the structural features reflect the Blackfeet's traditional unwillingness to isolate power in a centralized position of authority. A brief overview of the articles will identify these characteristics of the draft constitution.

Article I claims for the tribe "exclusive jurisdiction of the territory within the exterior boundaries of the Blackfeet Reservation. . . ." Tribal power extends to "[a]ll persons and property" within these borders.

Article II resolves the dispute of who shares in the tribe's resources by creating two classes of membership: (1) those with one-fourth and more of Blackfeet blood would enjoy all rights, including per capita distribution of tribal monies; and (2) those with less than one-fourth Blackfeet blood would have all rights except for sharing in per capita payments.

Article III, "Government," creates a complex system with the following parts: a Big Council, a Little Council, an administrator, and two chairmen. The aim seems to be generous distribution of governing power, adequate checks, and public involvement. The Big Council is the principal governing body and has twenty-two members—two representatives serving two-year terms from each of eleven sub-communities. It meets once a year for no more than forty-five days. The Big Council's powers parallel those of the present Council and include such authorizations as management of all tribal economic affairs, licensing of businesses, levying of taxes, regulation of land use, regulation of personnel and administrative practices and procedures, review of all administrative operations, budget approval, and delegation of powers. The Big Council selects five of its members to form the Little Council. Its main powers are to exercise authority delegated by the Big Council, hire an administrator with the Big Council's approval, oversee the management of tribal affairs, act as the official representative of the tribe, and oversee implementation of the Big Council's rules and resolutions. Each Council selects its own chairman from its own membership.

Article IV creates a tribal court of three judges elected to six-year staggered terms. The article attempts to gain for the judges a measure of independence by asserting that they "shall have the respect of the tribe," by prohibiting the Big Council from reducing their salaries while in office, and by proclaiming that the court "shall be recognized as an independent branch of government which shall not be subject to the control of any governing body or official of the Blackfeet Tribe."[41] The constitution further enhances the stature of the court by vesting it with the American institution of judicial review (". . . to declare tribal laws void if such laws either are not in agreement with this Constitution or imperil the existence of the Blackfeet Tribe") and creating a special action whereby any tribal member has standing to accuse a tribal official or employee of misuse of tribal money or property.

Article V establishes an election board to adjudicate election disputes and provides for an appeal to tribal court. Additionally, the article calls for a secret ballot, absentee voting, eighteen-year-old voting age, and nomination by filing (thus, no primary election).

Article VI provides for removal from office either by a Big Council two-thirds vote of expulsion for cause or by a recall election pursuant to a petition signed by one-fourth of the voters in the particular sub-community.

Article VII is a detailed compilation of land-use provisions. It contains a prohibition on the transfer of any land by a tribal member "into the possession of any person not of Blackfeet Indian descent" and requires the tribe to set aside 25 percent of its annual income for the purchase of land, timber, and mineral and water rights.

Article VIII deals with "Water Rights" and consists of a strong assertion of the tribe's absolute ownership of all reservation waters and authorization of tribal regulation of this resource.

Article IX borrows from the Montana Constitution's assertion of an environmental duty:[42] "The Blackfeet Tribe and each person, shall maintain and improve upon a Clean and Healthful Environment for the enjoyment, health and protection of the Tribal members and others." Broad authorizations for the tribal government follow regarding environmental quality, reclamation, recreation, and Indian heritage lands.

Article X deals with education and mandates an elected board of education to administer a tribal educational system, the earmarking of 10 percent of annual tribal income for educational purposes, and a system of education "founded in principles of humanity according to the Good Spirit."

Article XI proposes liberalization of the tribe's direct legislation processes. Initiative and referendum would be allowed by a petition of one-sixth of the Blackfeet electorate and effected by majority vote. In the present constitution there is no initiative feature and the referendum requires a petition of at least one-third of the qualified voters.

Article XII proposes an amendment process that could be more restrictive than the method in place. An amendment would be initiated by a petition of one-sixth of the electorate or on motion of the Council (compare the present one-third petition and two-thirds Council requirements), but a turnout of a majority of the qualified electorate would be required (now a 30 percent turnout is needed).

Article XIII is a bill of rights and has guarantees similar to those of the present constitution, with the following exceptions. In accordance with the 1974 constitution's assertion of broad jurisdiction, the article extends the protection of basic civil liberties and rights of criminal defendants not only to members of the tribe but also to reservation residents and visitors. These rights include, among others, privacy, to be tried in the Blackfeet language, and "due process of Blackfeet law." A separate section on rights of members includes preferential tribal hiring for tribal members.

There are many provisions in the 1974 draft constitution which would represent a strengthening of the present tribal government. These include the strong judiciary, land, water, environmental, and rights articles and elimination of the Secretary of the Interior's authority to review Blackfeet ordinances. The heart of the document, however, possibly would represent a step backwards rather than forwards because the disintegration of the present tribal government would be continued.

While the "Government" article, to its credit, would perpetuate the traditional Blackfeet ethic of broad-based involvement and shared responsibility, its provisions for a Big Council, Little Council, two chairmen, and administrator would at the same time preclude the strong leadership and administrative accountability that the present government lacks.

One longtime and perceptive observer of Blackfeet government, tribal member and attorney Joe McKay, has said that, ultimately, the legitimacy of tribal government will be determined by outsiders and not by members. His observation rests on his assessment that the critical operations of tribal government involve external as well as internal relationships. He also believes that a continuing "mystique of tribalism" has little basis in reality and is damaging, whereas attention to the administrative needs of tribal government is compelling. Thus, if tribal constitutions and governments are to survive, then "tribes must begin to act like governments," he says. This means that "tribal governments must come to fit outsiders' views of proper government, or they will be terminated."[43]

Accordingly good tribal government would include such features as a governing body that is essentially in a policy making role, a full-time chief executive who is a strong and competent administrator, a judiciary that is independent and respected, adequate checks and balances inside the governmental system that do not include the oversight of the agency superintendent, formalized procedures of governing to offset divisiveness, the clear location of official responsibility so that accountability to the electorate and policy leadership can emerge, and a mode of operation that demonstrates that the tribe can be responsible and fair. "The tribes," Joe McKay concludes, "must act how we expect to be treated."

Such a government would not be blind submission to the dominant white culture of American society. It would be recognition of the fact that economic development and self-governance must be based on experience and professional and accountable administration, not on romanticization of the past. Frequently it is emphasized that the Blackfeet are a self-reliant people. Today realization of this goal depends upon a carefully designed government that looks outward and ahead and not only inward and to the past. Such a government can help achieve the hope expressed in the preamble of the proposed 1974 constitution:

> . . . we wish to make sure that our people will continue to live here, that they will have their own government to help them and that they will be a good people.

Notes

1. The historical overview of the Blackfeet is derived from Thomas P. Wessel, *Historical Report on the Blackfeet Reservation in Northern Montana,* Docket No. 279-D (Washington: U.S. Indian Claims Commission, 1975) and William Brandon, *Indians* (New York: The American Heritage Library, 1985).

2. *Constitution and Bylaws of the Blackfeet Tribe of the Blackfeet Indian Reservation, Montana,* 1935.

3. John C. Ewers, *The Blackfeet: Raiders on the Northwestern Plains* (Norman: University of Oklahoma Press, 1958), p. 273.

4. Superintendents' Annual Narrative and Statistical Reports from Field Jurisdictions of the Bureau of Indian Affairs, 1907–1938, Blackfeet, 1911: Microcopy 1011, Frame 69. Hereafter cited as Superintendents' Annual Report with agency name and year.

5. Superintendents' Annual Narrative and Statistical Report, Blackfeet, 1928, Frame 807.

6. Superintendents' Annual Narrative and Statistical Report, Blackfeet, 1917, Frame 252; 1920, Frame 354; 1923, Frame 645.

7. *Constitution,* "Article VI—Powers of the Council."

8. Interview with Edie Adams, Tribal Operations Officer of the Blackfeet Agency, August 1, 1983.

9. Interview with Joe McKay, tribal member, attorney, and former Blackfeet councilman, February 26, 1986.

10. *Blackfeet Plan of Operation,* "Final Draft—Pending Approval by Tribal Council," Ch. II, sec. 1.

11. Ibid., Ch. II, sec. 8.

12. Ibid., Ch. III, sec. 1.

13. Ibid.

14. Ibid., Ch. II, sec. 13.

15. Interview with Joe McKay, tribal member, attorney, and Blackfeet councilman, July 7, 1983.

16. Interview with Ted Hall, Natural Resource Officer of the Blackfeet Agency, July 8, 1983.

17. Blackfeet Tribe, *Fiscal Year 1981–82 Operating Budget,* September 7, 1981, p. 4.

18. Interview with Michael A. Fairbanks, Superintendent of the Blackfeet Agency, July 6, 1983.

19. Blackfeet Tribe, *Fiscal Year 1981–82 Operating Budget, passim.*

20. Ibid., p. 4.

21. Ibid., p. 83.

22. Ibid., p. 82.

23. Ibid., p. 54.

24. The reflections on the Blackfeet reservation as a "closed community" come from the 1983 interview with Joe McKay.

25. Interview with Joe McKay, 1983.

26. Blackfeet Tribe, *Fiscal Year 1981–82 Operating Budget.*

27. Interview with Edie Adams.

28. The analysis of the Blackfeet economic development effort is based upon the 1983 interview with Joe McKay.

29. *Corporate Charter of the Blackfeet Tribe of the Blackfeet Indian Reservation,* A Federal Corporation Chartered Under the Act of June 18, 1934, p. 2.

30. Ibid., p. 3.

31. Interviews with Joe McKay (1983) and Edie Adams.

32. Interview with Joe McKay, 1983.

33. Ibid.

34. Interview with Michael A. Fairbanks.

35. *Constitution of the Blackfeet Tribe,* Art. X.

36. Interview with Earl Old Person, Blackfeet Tribal Chairman, July 6, 1983.

37. Interview with Joe McKay, 1986.

38. Ibid.

39. Ibid.

40. *Blackfeet Constitution of the Blackfeet Nation,* Proposed by Members of the Blackfeet Constitutional Convention, 1974.

41. One particularly harsh critic of the Blackfeet tribal court is Samuel J. Brakel, *American Indian Tribal Courts: The Costs of Separate Justice* (Chicago: American Bar Foundation, 1978). He charges that the court has been characterized by incompetence, political interference, favoritism, and a law and order mentality.

42. The *Constitution of the State of Montana* (ratified June 6, 1972) lists as an "inalienable right" in Article II, "the right to a clean and healthful environment." Then Article IX of the Montana Constitution reads: "The state and each person shall maintain and improve a clean and healthful environment in Montana for present and future generations."

43. Interview with Joe McKay, 1983.

4

The Crow: A Politics of Risk

On the Crow reservation, the words of Plenty Coups, an esteemed former leader, are often heard: "This place is located in the right place."[1] Ample evidence does exist of bountiful natural resources and of their potential to sustain a good quality of life for the Crow Indians. Coal, for example, is as abundant as anywhere in the nation, and the natural grasses provide unmatched grazing. The means of putting these resources to work for the Crow people, however, have been lacking. A deeply ingrained patronage system has frequently prevented the Crows from taking a farsighted view of tribal affairs. This chapter will analyze how this traditional practice has jeopardized the welfare of the Crow people and ask why this politics of risk has characterized the Crow government.

The Crow reservation covers more than 2.2 million acres, the largest of Montana's seven Indian reservations. It is located in southeastern Montana, east of Billings and north of the Wyoming border. The Crow tribe itself owns 18 percent of the reservation acreage, while members of the tribe hold 50 percent of acreage through individual allotments. Non-Indians own 32 percent of the land within the reservation boundaries. The trend in holdings has been a decrease in allotted acreage and an increase in both tribal and non-Indian owned land.

The non-Indian presence on the Crow reservation extends beyond white land ownership. Approximately three-fourths of the land owned by individual tribal members is leased to non-Indian agricultural operators, primarily ranchers. About 77 percent of reservation land is devoted presently to grazing, the land's best use, while dryland farming occupies about 13 percent of the acreage. Increasingly, though, range land is being broken out for dryland wheat farming. Individual Indians have been attracted by the $12.00 per acre dryland farming fee they can get for their lands, compared to $1.50 per acre for grazing.[2] An example of white use of Indian land on the Crow reservation is the Antler Ranch, a cattle operation of more than 100,000 acres of which

65,000 acres are leased from individual Indians and the tribe. Non-Indians, therefore, derive significant economic benefit from the "finest grasslands on the continent."[3] The economic future of the Crow tribe, however, rests with coal and not grass. The mineral wealth of the reservation is undetermined because it is so vast. Estimates of the tribe's coal run as high as 19 billion tons, which would be the largest reserves in the United States.[4] Major energy companies have demonstrated substantial interest in the coal, proposing both strip mining and power plant projects. One proposal for mining and generating electricity on the reservation has an estimated cost of $1.4 billion.[5]

The economic interests of the tribe extend to more than the coal seams under reservation land. In 1983 the Crow presented to the federal government a formal proposal to reclaim 36,164 acres of tribal lands which had been excluded from the reservation in 1891 because of a surveying error. Counsel for the Crow assigned 1982 values of $6.7 million to the surface land and $97 million to the coal reserves.[6] In a 1984 legal action concerning a strip of land north of the reservation ceded to the State of Montana in 1904, the tribe asked for a determination that it had retained mineral rights and that Montana's coal severance tax did not apply to the coal held by the United States in trust for the Crow tribe. The tribe also sought return of as much as $93 million in coal taxes paid to the state. After losing in federal district court in Montana, the Crow tribe ultimately prevailed in the Ninth Circuit Court of Appeals. The Ninth Circuit Court invalidated Montana's severance tax on both the ceded strip and reservation lands. That decision was affirmed by the United States Supreme Court.[7]

Economic self-determination seems to be within the Crow tribe's grasp. One coal consultant estimated that if a third of the tribe's coal is developed "each person in the tribe will be worth $1 million."[8] A state witness in the 1984 ceded strip trial testified that even moderate coal development and a tribal severance tax and royalties would result in an average annual income of $32,000 for every family on the reservation by the year 2010.[9] Although the true dollar dimension of the coal is not clear, there is no doubt that the Crow economic opportunity is as great as any other reservation in Montana. The ability of the tribe to realize this potential, though, is in doubt because the Crow do not have an effective system of managing their public affairs. The tradition of political patronage and an ethic of individual gain have in the past endangered general economic well being.

The Crow tribe had its birth in factionalism, and divisiveness has marked its social organization ever since.[10] In the seventeenth century the Crow resided with the Minnetarees along the Missouri River in what is now the Dakotas. A quarrel between leaders of two major factions resulted in a battle, each chief's relatives taking part, and as a result about one-half of the nation—the Crow—left the Missouri and made their way to the plains at the foot of the Rocky Mountains. Here the Crow have remained, initially as hunters and then as residents of a homeland whose boundaries were first recognized by the 1851 Treaty of Fort Laramie.

Scholars of the Crow people describe some early characteristics which are helpful in explaining tribal politics today.[11] One such trait was a quarrelsome disposition. Differences arose more frequently among the Crow than among other plains Indians. The reason for this contentiousness was another tribal characteristic. While other tribes frequently resorted to bloodshed to settle differences between members, the Crow had the custom of settling disputes by abusing one another or stealing the other's horses. Disagreements among the Crow were common because violence, including murder, was not a likely consequence.

Another traditional characteristic of the Crow was the central role of family and clan. Crow legends contrasted the political opportunities of a youth with parents to the sorry social condition of an orphan. The boy with parents had access to relatives on the side of both his mother and father "to aid and shield him."[12] This network was especially useful on the maternal side as clan organization was matrilineal. These "clansfolk recognized mutual obligations, which characteristically overrode their sense of duty to any larger group."[13] A "large body of kindred," therefore, was a "social factor" of success.[14]

The traditional Crow political system emphasized both social position and individual freedom. The power of formal positions, such as camp chief and police, was very limited, to the degree that "the people hardly felt the weight of authority."[15] Other than on a few special occasions, "everyone was allowed to act much as he pleased."[16] An exception to this autonomy was the significant informal power that could be exercised by a well-born individual—that is, one with wealth, attractive personality, and many relatives. This person was different from a chief because his eminence was not derived from good deeds. Instead, this leader "who had somehow acquired power might selfishly make the most of it."[17] With the aid of his relatives, this exception to the Crow ideal of autonomy could use the absence of formal checks to "easily dominate a band of a few hundred souls."[18]

Another influence on contemporary Crow politics is the tribe's religious tradition. The Crow had "no idea of a Supreme Being, a first cause, or of a future state."[19] Additionally, the Crow did not worship the natural world, a unified life force, or ancestors. The basis of Crow religion, instead, was the "all-sufficiency of personal revelations."[20] Crow religion, as a result, was highly personal and material in its orientation.

In the practice of religion, the individual Crow was an "opportun-
ist."[21] First, he was constantly alert to a chance encounter with some
supernatural power who might afford a special favor. This advantage,
though, was transitory as the mystical forces of life were not constant.
Secondly, if a Crow were lucky enough to experience an "individual
vision,"[22] the supplicant would not ask for moral elevation but "some
material benefit."[23] Crow religion, therefore, was a means of acquiring
power and getting ahead; its essential implications were personal and
not social. This view of life undoubtedly had some carry-over to Crow
politics: in a world of shifting values and individual vulnerability, a
person would not be criticized for watching out primarily for himself.
   The principal arena of Crow politics for centuries has been the
general council. Crow reservation government experienced in 1910 a
temporary transition from the traditional general council to a small
business committee. The new business committee was based on three
representatives elected from each of the six farm districts. A superintendent reported that this tribal government was a hindrance to progress
and that the tribal representatives were "intelligent" but not "reliable."[24]
The business committee was a benefit in that it helped the superintendent to dispose of tribal business quickly as compared to working with
the general council.[25]
   The federal government's subsequent manipulation of the business
committee disturbed the Crow representatives. They refused to permit
tribal government to remain "in an advisory capacity" and demanded
that "the affairs of the Reservation should be as they [the Crow] might
determine." Because of this confrontation, the superintendent circumvented tribal dictate by controlling the committee's call into session
and establishing the agenda. Some full-bloods supported the superintendent's action as a means of gaining lost powers.[26] Generally, though,
the Crow detested outside plotting, and they abolished their business
committee of eighteen and returned to a voluntary general council.
Out of a desire for efficient government some tribal members in 1918
planned another business committee. But fearing outside interference,
the Crow gathered "to talk, talk, talk," and refused to establish another
business committee. The general council continued operation and created
instead "hand-picked" subcouncils to conduct business. The result was
unpredictable politics: "anyone who desires a certain action can go out
and pick a council from different localities and get them to do what
he wants done, and someone else could go out and pick a council that
would do exactly the opposite thing the next day."[27]
   The Indian Service constantly encouraged the tribe to move away
from the general council, and, when they did not, federal officials
established a seven-member Crow business council in 1921. Refusing

to dishonor tradition, committee members deferred questions to a general council and did not exercise their powers. The Crow finally rejected this government, which was not of their selection, by refusing to vote for the representatives. This protest forced the federal government to deal with the general council.[28]

The practice of general council government during the early twentieth century enabled the Crow to maintain cohesiveness, minimize outside interference in tribal affairs, and preserve their sovereignty. Even though the Crow people promised throughout the 1920s to eliminate the general council in favor of a business committee, they failed for an obvious reason—they simply wanted to fail. The tribe's rejection of the Indian Reorganization Act reflected the Crow political climate, and their 1948 tribal constitution preserved the general council.

The Crow today continue to support their general council political system because it allows the perpetuation of custom. Sylvester Knows His Gun, an elderly member of the Crow Tribe with intimate knowledge of Crow politics, said that "the Crow system reflects their outlook on life."[29] On the positive side, this tie to the past is reflected in tribal members' ability to participate directly in general council meetings— to hold forth in their native language for an hour or more and question the policies of their government. But this link between the present political system and the past has a darker side. Sylvester Knows His Gun emphasized that the Crow perspective could also mean a short view of events, a preference to be without laws or regulations, and a disposition "to get as much out of the tribe as possible."[30] The Crow tribe prefers a radically democratic form of government not only for its openness but also because of the personal advantage it permits.

The Crow democratic form of government is unique among Montana tribes. In its basic design, the Crow government is essentially unchanged from the way the tribe managed its affairs in ancient times. It also is representative of how other tribes functioned before the imposition of outside influences. The adaptability of the democratic form to manipulation by powerful individuals also has been long known and practiced. For example, a contemporary tribal leader said that the agency superintendent in 1948 (who was a Crow), when the Crow constitution was adopted, advocated this form "so that he could control tribal government."[31] These entwined features of Crow government—democratic participation and manipulation for personal gain—will be discussed in detail below.

The Crow Council is the heart of the tribe's government. All other features are defined and function in relation to the Council. The Council is not a representative body. Instead, its membership is comprised of all female tribal members of eighteen years and older and all male tribal members of twenty-one years and older. Because the Council is the tribe's governing body, Crow government is based on the principle of direct democracy, similar to the traditional town meeting form of government in New England.

The Council meets regularly four times a year, on the second Saturdays of January, April, July, and October. Special meetings are anticipated by the constitution, although the procedure for calling them is not clear. The applicable constitutional language is, "All meetings shall be called by the Chairman and the Committee" (this is a fourteen-member executive committee, to be discussed below).[32] In practice, special meetings are held infrequently. The method of disposing of tribal matters is determined at each Council meeting by the membership. The constitution mentions voting by "voice, standing, hand-raising or secret ballot."[33] In three different sections, the constitution requires the Council to take formal action by majority rule.

Constitutional officers are chairman, vice-chairman, secretary, and vice-secretary. The chairman is the most powerful officer because of two duties. The constitution makes the chairman the presider at all Council meetings, although his vote is authorized only to break a tie. The chairman, without clear constitutional authorization, also supervises the government during the periods between Council meetings. The vice-chairman's role comes into play in the Chairman's absence or at the Chairman's request. The secretary's constitutional duties extend to the Council minutes, records, correspondence, and agenda. The only significant constitutional power concerns the agenda, as the secretary in providing notice of Council meetings is able to determine the order but not the content of the agenda. The secretary also has the responsibility to call elections and approve their results. The council elects these four constitutional officers to two-year terms. The election is held at a May Council meeting in even-numbered years. Election is by secret vote using a printed ballot.

The Crow constitution also provides for a fourteen-member executive committee, made up of two representatives from off-reservation tribal members and from each of six reservation districts. The constitution mentions two duties of this committee: "work with the officers under the general direction of the Council"[34] and, together with the chairman, determine the items on the Council's agenda.[35] Observers of Crow politics emphasize that the only real power of the committee is its participation in fixing the agenda. Like the constitutional officers, the committee members are elected to two-year terms at a May Council meeting, although this election occurs in odd-numbered years and is conducted on a district basis.

Crow tribal government also includes a court, although its authorization is not in the constitution.[36] The court's role in the Crow political system is influenced by the fact that the Council created the court and could abolish it. The Crow court has three judges, elected by the Council to concurrent four-year terms. Depending upon budgetary constraints, court personnel have included at various times several clerks, a juvenile counselor, a probation officer, a prosecutor, a lay defender, several lay advocates, and an attorney-advisor. The Council's authorizing resolution also provides for the three judges to sit together and serve as an appellate panel, but this process has been little used. The court's funding comes from a contract with the Bureau of Indian Affairs which requires an annual contribution from the tribe. A law and order committee of the tribe oversees the court's operations. The civil work of the court consists largely of contractual and family matters, while the voluminous criminal docket is managed primarily by dismissals and non-jury proceedings. Despite the court's political vulnerability, there are indications that it can make positive contributions to reservation government. Some signs that the court is establishing itself as an arm of tribal government are its use of contempt power, judgments enforcing payment schedules in contract disputes, development of forms to regularize various procedures, and use of judicial review to void an executive committee election and require new balloting. Despite this maturation, the tribal court has not been a significant force in Crow politics.

The law and order committee of the Council is part of a system of "appointed special committees" authorized by the Crow By-laws.[37] These committees are established by Council resolution and there is no consistent method of choosing committee members. For example, the Council has chosen the members of some committees, and other committees have been constituted under the Chairman's direction. Understanding their role and operation is difficult because, according to an attorney for the tribal court, "legal procedures are not followed very closely."[38] At a minimum, the committee system provides a method for direct participation by members in tribal administration. There are six committees: Land and Resources, Credit, Industrial Development, Health, Education, and Law and Order. Each committee has six members, one from each district (Education is an exception with seven members, one being an off-reservation representative). Committee members are not salaried but receive a stipend for each meeting, which sometimes occur weekly. In theory, the committees establish an administrative reporting relationship. Tribal departments report to their overseeing committee, and the committee chairmen work with the tribal chairman to oversee program operations. Committee performance has been weakened by the practice of concurrent terms and by the chairman's neglect.[39]

The Crow government has the responsibility of administering a large budget[40] and activities of considerable variety and importance. Federal and state contracts and grants amounted to $5.8 million in fiscal year 1980 and again in fiscal year 1981. The lease income of the tribe, consisting primarily of coal revenue and grazing fees, was $8.6 million in fiscal year 1980 and $2.3 million in fiscal year 1981. In fiscal year 1982, income to the tribe from coal leases alone was $2.7 million. Coal dollars are the most significant and promising kind of income. The 1980 lease figure included a Shell Oil Company advance payment of $5 million, and the 1981 lease figure included $1.8 million under a Westmoreland Resources coal lease. The Shell Oil coal lease would have been the source of significant future income for the Crow tribe, but it was cancelled by the company in 1986. Under its terms, the tribe was to receive an additional $7 million in several large payments prior to the start of mining. The agreement also called for a minimum royalty payment of $3 million a year.

The variety and size of Crow tribal involvements are also evident in activities previously mentioned. In its lawsuit brought in federal district court against the State of Montana, the tribe challenged the state's application of its coal severance tax to Crow coal and sought return of as much as $93 million. In discussions with coal industry consultants, the tribe was approached with a proposal to construct a $1.4 billion mining and generating project on the reservation. Tribal attorneys also have proposed to the federal government a $104 million settlement in exchange for title to Crow land which had been erroneously excluded in a nineteenth century survey. Thus, Crow government, a form of direct democracy characterized by frequent election, direct participation, and infrequent general councils, has the responsibility of responding to major opportunities and guiding the tribe toward self-government and self-reliance.

The Crow tribe's ability to achieve economic and political self-determination depends as much upon the reservation's style of politics as upon the governmental structure. The distinctive feature of Crow politics is its traditional practice of patronage. This system has markedly mixed results. On the one hand it makes Crow government familiar, accessible, and personally rewarding. On the other hand, Crow government becomes unstable, uncertain, and unprofessional. One result is that outside organizations attempting to establish a business relationship with the Crow tribe often are not confident that agreements will be implemented and maintained. Whereas the tribe is able to act with dispatch and conclusiveness in litigation or negotiation through legal counsel, its own internal business can become mired in the narrow motives of job politics.

The tribe's peculiar brand of politics exists because of Crow culture and the mechanics of the general council meeting. Tribal and Bureau of Indian Affairs officials on the Crow reservation have variously described the dominant Crow philosophy as: ". . . it's OK if you don't get caught";[41] "Crows would do anything for money";[42] and ". . . get as much out of the tribe as possible."[43] If these reservation officials are correct, improvement of one's own financial condition is not an accidental benefit of political involvement; rather, personal economic advancement is a principal aim of Crow politics. The resulting political ethic is a dangerous politics of spoils. The winner understandably uses the system of government to reward supporters in order to secure sufficient support to govern; but considerations of general welfare and long-term benefit are thereby downplayed.

The Crows' conduct of their general council meeting makes it a perfect vehicle for perpetuating a patronage system. This is because that kind of politics needs a reliable method of rewarding friends and punishing enemies. Council meetings are held in the tribal gym amidst an atmosphere of moment and festivity. Seven hundred to one thousand members are in attendance, and the proceedings are conducted generally in the Crow language. A heavy amount of politicking takes place up to the time of the vote on actually reading the minutes of the last meeting, and this ballot is the most significant of the day. The vote on reading of minutes is a test vote to determine the power alignment of the meeting. At every general council, the several factions vie for control of Crow government. A voice vote on the minutes will indicate whether one faction is in control of the meeting or whether the split is close. If it is close, a division of the house will be determined by "walking through lines,"[44] a voting procedure in which each member passes between counters and thereby declares one's preference. Once a locus of power has been determined, the meeting uses voice vote to dispose of the agenda. The critical aspect of this procedure of public voting is that it allows factional leaders to identify their supporters and opponents.

Each Council meeting amounts to a vote of confidence on the incumbent chairman. Before each meeting, the chairman and his lieutenants work vigorously to secure a strong turnout of supporters from among the tribal factions. The opposition does the same. The basis of the factions is not ideological, and the factional composition is not fixed. To some degree the factions are defined by clan allegiances. But even this identification is fluid. Family leaders swing clan support, and "like grass-hoppers clans jump back and forth between factions."[45] An attorney serving as court adviser observed that factionalism in the Crow tribe "is about who controls government and, therefore, who controls jobs and the dispensation of benefits."[46] All factions know about the "joy of spoils"[47]—high salaries, travel, prestige—because they have been in control. The opposition at each Council meeting can defeat the chairman's agenda and overturn past policies, creating a political vacuum until the next election. A chairman who prevails, on the other hand, can enact his policies and ignore the items placed on the agenda by the opposition. A prevailing chairman signifies that a majority of the members at the meeting think that they, individually, can get a better deal from the present administration than from the opposition.

The essential step in building or maintaining a majority faction is to work with the system of clans. This approach works for both tribal politicians and outsiders seeking influence within the tribe. It is also used in campaigning for Council action. For example, a chairman's political success depends upon support from a group of clan elders. The elders' political position, in turn, rests upon the fact that clan members stay close to the elders. Most clan members, according to tribal judge Tommy E. Roundface, are politically interested but "unsophisticated and manipulable."[48] This network serves the purposes of the politically wise and resourceful.

Tribal politicians begin the search for support with their immediate families and then reach out in expanding circles to their extended families, their clan, and the tribe. The approach of "Brother, I need your vote,"[49] invokes certain cultural sanctions. An invitation to eat and smoke with the candidate, along with a request for support, cannot be refused without fear of bad luck. Clan standing and the sacred custom of tobacco, though, are not the only incentives to cooperation. In characteristic Crow fashion, the person being courted expects a *quid pro quo*—something for oneself and something to be offered to other clan members who will be persuaded to support the candidate. For the clan "boss"[50] the candidate brings gifts of value: cigarettes, buckskin, a wool blanket, and money. For the clan members to be recruited by the clan leader there are promises of employment. For the general electorate there are feasts at community centers or the fairgrounds. A successful candidate for vice chairman estimated that she spent $5,000 on these campaign feeds for sides of beef and tribal members' travel.[51] It has been said that an election turns on "how many steaks you can buy."[52]

An important official on the Crow reservation has observed that outsiders attempting to influence tribal politics also have used the opportunity provided by clans.[53] Powerful white interests which stand to gain financially by Council decisions, especially concerning land use, have gained the support of family groups through "pay-offs" and thereby established "puppets" in tribal government. Clumsy attempts to use this method, however, have backfired in the past. One energy company representative proceeded indiscriminately with an open checkbook, buying turkeys and other gifts at Thanksgiving time, but not securing any political support. "The turkey" is still a joke on the Crow reservation. The important lesson is that outsiders have understood and benefited from the Crow political system and, as a result, they have been a "critical factor" in Crow government.

Satisfaction with any political system depends on performance more than on promises. There has been, therefore, pressure on the Crow factions to come up with favors for supporters. While almost any resource of the tribe could enter into the system of *quid pro quo,* this political relationship primarily has been "maintained in terms of jobs."[54] Thus, the general belief on the reservation is that "a changeover in administration means a changeover in positions."[55]

It is not difficult to gather rumors concerning excesses and abuses of the Crow government: how the earnings of the 1980 tribal fair "went South";[56] how during the Great Society era "hundreds were hired without meeting program eligibility"[57] in return for pay-offs to the chairman; how "one former chairman got away with over $2 million and raced horses all over North Dakota."[58] Reliable information is a different matter. However, an audit report of the Inspector General of the U.S. Department of the Interior, covering Crow governmental operations for fiscal years 1980 and 1981, provides insight as to the manipulation actually practiced under the Crow political system.

The Department of the Interior audit found a deplorable financial situation on the Crow reservation and blamed both the competence and the attitude of Crow officials. The federal report said that as of September 30, 1981, the Crow tribe "was in a state of technical insolvency."[59] One reason for this condition was that the tribe's personnel system placed little or no value on performance-related hiring criteria. As a result, the auditors concluded, the tribe's "management of its affairs has been inept."[60] More important, though, was the conclusion that tribal officials lacked motivation to change the situation, and this apathy was due to the role personnel practices played in maintaining political power on the reservation: "We believe that the Tribe's political processes . . . contribute to the problems and attitudes of Tribal officials."[61]

Probably the most fundamental observation about Crow politics that is permitted by the audit is that every available resource had been converted to produce jobs. The final report read: ". . . the Tribe used

whatever cash it had to meet payrolls and other expenses regardless of
the original intent of the funds."[62] Examples of such misuses were
$532,000 owed to the federal and state governments for unpaid income
taxes and $240,000 owed to various suppliers of goods and services.
The tribe's total current liabilities exceeded $1.8 million, its long term
debt amounted to $6 million, and it faced $960,000 in questioned and
disallowed costs uncovered by prior audits of federal contracts and
grants.

The audit report's greatest utility for understanding Crow politics is
its documentation of the workings of the patronage system. In the
course of their investigation, federal auditors heard many charges:

> Numerous allegations have been made regarding personnel placements
> based on intra-Tribal political affiliation and friendship with those in
> positions of authority. Also, allegations were made that votes were pur-
> chased through employment under Federally sponsored programs.[63]

The findings of the study allow the judgment that the allegations are
correct. For example, after the May 1980 changeover in tribal government,

> . . . a selection committee was formed. This committee began placing
> personnel into positions even though the positions were already filled. In
> addition and in contradiction to prescribed policy, the members of the
> committee appointed themselves to positions of employment.[64]

The report cites another method of rewarding followers besides finding
employment when jobs did not exist. Time sheets were falsified to
claim more hours than were actually worked, and some employees
turned in several time sheets for one pay period. "For example, one
employee submitted two time sheets and was paid for 240 hours in
the [two-week] period."[65] Another example of job politics is the tribe's
failure to implement successfully a financial management system designed by the federal government. This system, called the tribe's Office
of Management and Budget, was intended to provide comprehensive
and reliable information concerning the status of each program's assets
and liabilities. This office never succeeded in developing policies and
procedures to guide the tribe's fiscal practices. What it did achieve was
the creation of jobs: "Although $307,563 had been expended for OMB
through September 30, 1981, we were unable to identify any tangible
benefits of OMB other than providing employment for Tribal members."[66]

Some findings of the auditors more directly linked the provision of jobs to votes cast by members. Unusual personnel activity was noticed around the time of General Councils:

> An analysis of employees paid on a sporadic or one time basis showed that personnel were employed just prior to the quarterly council meetings, giving credence to the allegations that employment was used as an inducement for favorable voting.[67]

The tribal administration also used revenue sharing money, in addition to temporary employment, for vote buying:

> Employee time sheets were submitted by 292 Tribal members during the two week period prior to the July 11, 1981 Tribal Council meeting. . . . The time sheets would have resulted in approximately $91,700 being paid in one pay period if all of the time sheets had been paid. However, because of insufficient funds only 96 individuals were paid a total of $31,393. The Tribal Chairman signed 248 of the time sheets as supervisor. . . . There was no indication of the work performed by the 248 individuals for whom time sheets were submitted.[68]

The auditors' review of the tribe's Comprehensive Employment and Training Act program discovered similar allegations and disregard of guidelines, and one confession: ". . . one Tribal member admitted to us that he had been allowed to participate in the program in exchange for his influence and votes."[69]

Another means the tribal administration used to respond to the expectations of patronage politics was conversion of a program's supplies and equipment accounts into personnel dollars. For example, a weatherization grant from the Department of Energy required that only $2,044 could be spent for administration during six months in 1981. The tribe, instead, "spent $15,751 for administrative purposes and nothing for home weatherization."[70] Along the same lines, the Department of Housing and Urban Development suspended a housing improvement program because of "excessive administrative costs."[71] While departmental guidelines specified a maximum of $30,000 for personnel, the tribe "reported $41,692 in administrative expenditures versus $247 for program materials."[72] Similarly, the Indian Action Program spent over $203,000 for improving reservation roads and buildings, but the results were no maintenance and no construction.[73]

The Interior Department audit reveals that the spoils of victory in the Crow political system have included more than jobs. Just as hiring abuses have stemmed from the lack of a formal personnel system, misuse of tribal funds, supplies, and services have resulted from inadequate property management and accounting procedures. For example, during the period covered by the audit, no action was taken by the tribe to recover or settle $170,306 in outstanding salary and travel advances. There was a similar laxity regarding court fines and fees. No controls had been in place for over $25,000 in receipts, allowing such practices as payment of unauthorized Christmas bonuses and personal loans to court employees. The absence of procurement and property management regulations allowed thousands of dollars of building materials to be diverted to the personal use of employees and their relatives. The tenant accounts receivable for the Crow Tribal Housing Authority at the end of 1980 was at $354,745, primarily because "elected Tribal officials, BIA employees and IHS employees do not pay, therefore, others do not feel they have to pay."[74]

The findings of the Department of the Interior auditors repeatedly made the point that the personnel turbulence of the Crow tribe resulted in inept and corrupt governmental management. An assumption ran through the audit report that structural changes, for example, new policies and procedures, would result in improved practices. The investigators failed to emphasize that reform would depend upon a change in attitude and that Crow political leaders and their followers—both the ins and the outs—were committed to the present system because they had prospered under it. The pervasiveness of manipulative politics on the Crow reservation, therefore, must be fully appreciated before the auditors' reform recommendations are considered.

The patronage politics of the Crow tribe is only one example of how various features of the governmental system have been bent to serve a faction's advantage. What these practices point to is a political philosophy which stresses partisan gain to the detriment of governmental stability and continuity. An example of such political expediency is the General Council's censuring of a tribal chairman outside of the boundaries of the constitution. Rather than using the constitutional impeachment process, the General Council simply removed the chairman's authority to deal with administrative matters. The Department of the Interior's Deputy Assistant Secretary for Indian Affairs condemned this as one of several "damaging practices of circumventing and undermining the presently established tribal constitution and bylaws."[75]

Another instance of governmental stability being sacrificed to factional maneuvering was the special General Council meeting of December 17, 1983. On this occasion, the faction opposing the incumbent tribal chairman (which also constituted a majority of the executive board) gained control of the meeting. The new ruling faction then proceeded to undo as much of the chairman's program as possible—for example, voting to cancel all action taken at the October General Council meeting presided over by the chairman, adopting a new tribal budget, and expanding the authority of the executive board. This situation was not unique, as the chairman also had lost control of the July, 1983, meeting when his opponents formed a majority behind the vice-chairman. Each such upheaval sets the stage for renewed tension at the next meeting. Thus, the most controversial issue at the January, 1984, General Council meeting was whether to accept the decisions of the special December 17 meeting.

The opposition faction's reworking of the chairman's budget included a new requirement that 60 percent of all tribal money be distributed to members in per capita payments. With this revision, the chairman's opponents were not only striking at the heart of his fiscal program but also attempting to create the basis of continued majority support. Per capita payments are the Crow government's distribution of its assets among the 7,000 tribal members. Traditionally income from mining, grazing, and timber has been shared three or four times a year with payments of between $25 and $40. In 1981, a Shell Oil Company payment of $5 million for a coal lease was distributed in its entirety as per capita payments. Large per capita payments understandably can create the desire and expectation for their continuance, and they become an almost irresistible basis for political appeals. The opposition, accordingly, argued that they would reinstitute large per capita payments, regardless of the tribe's fiscal condition and competing uses for the money.

There is no doubt that the factionalism and manipulation of the Crow political system have left the tribal government in a weakened state. The representative of the Department of the Interior at the Crow inaugural ceremony in July, 1982, reflecting on the department's audit findings, said:

> I come here today to talk with you about your system of government—the Crow Tribal Government. It has problems; the Crow people are divided among themselves within it. . . . events over the past several years have led to damage and to serious divisions within your community.[76]

The most serious weakness created by the persistent factionalism concerns the executive branch. The weakness of the executive has been evident in the members' turning to the agency superintendent for handling routine grievances and administering special projects. This lack of trust robs the chairman of standing and influence, preventing him from performing well his most basic duties. The chairman, for example, has been unable to provide continuity in dealings with outside organizations and to stop the passage of individual Indian land holdings into fee patents and then, through sale, to white outsiders.

The conclusions of the Department of the Interior audit warranted a declaration of bankruptcy and transfer of tribal administration to a more responsible party. Such a step by the federal government, however, could have been interpreted as loss of faith in its policies of Indian self-determination and self-governance. A less drastic approach was chosen, detailed in a "Memorandum of Agreement" concluded by the Department of the Interior and Crow Tribe on July 2, 1982. The agreement concerned short-term and long-term solutions. To begin immediately, the federal government would provide a tribal manager to introduce sound financial practices and restore solvency. Looking to more permanent reform, the federal government would finance and set into motion a constitutional revision study to correct the flaws in the Crow governmental system.

The short-term solution had short-term results. A Department of the Interior employee received a temporary transfer to serve as tribal manager. The manager's most significant accomplishments were establishing a system of centralized accounting and committing the tribe to a payback schedule to retire its debt. The manager also initiated a property procurement and management system. The greatest obstacles to these reforms were the chairman's reluctance to cooperate because of the General Council's quarterly test votes and the necessity of using less than competent staff because of patronage hiring practices. A July, 1983, report by a Department of the Interior review board found that considerable progress had been made:

> . . . the tribe will have retired approximately $1.5 million in short term debt, and in the process restored its standing with the Internal Revenue Service, Unemployment Compensation, Workmens Compensation, and the federal program agencies. It is clear that the Crow Tribe will enter its fiscal year 1984 budget free of most of the short term debt load which had been built up over years of mismanagement.[77]

Areas which still needed attention were travel policy and the personnel system. Concerning travel, the report said that there was "loss of administrative control over tribal travel activities" which was a "source of frustration and dissension within the tribal structure."[78] The conclusion concerning personnel administration was that the absence of a salary and classification system "has led to morale problems" and prevents the achievement of "an effective tribal personnel management program."[79]

The manager's accomplishments, though notable, could persist only for the short-term. This is because the reforms did little to alter the entrenched political values of tribal members and officials. Evidence for this judgment can be found in events that occurred during a two-week absence of the manager. Tribal officials once again placed political pressure on employees and set aside new fiscal management practices. A payday for a two-week pay period was moved up two weeks, in effect creating a bonus, so that employees would have money for the tribal fair. Also, tribal officials were not committed to continuing the manager position after the agreement with the Department of the Interior expired, and some on the reservation suspected that a successor to the manager would be a political lieutenant of the chairman, were one to be hired.

The Interior Department's primary hope for fundamental change in Crow government was comprehensive constitutional revision. The lesson from this effort is an old one in the annals of governmental reform. If change occurs, it comes through imposition by a higher authority or through a genuine grass roots movement. Absent these factors, a review process will conclude by endorsing the status quo. In the Crow instance the Bureau of Indian Affairs was understandably frustrated with the Crow government and deeply committed to reform, but the Crow community was antagonistic or timid in its support, some embracing the review process only for its monetary rewards. Principally, though, reform was stifled because the Crow had too many reasons to hang onto the past.

The Bureau of Indian Affairs and not the Crow Tribe was enamored with the idea of constitutional revision. This rejection of change has been the tribe's tradition. In 1935, a vote of 689–112 opposed organization under the Indian Reorganization Act. The tribe adopted a constitution in 1948 containing its general council form of government, and all subsequent attempts to amend it have failed. There was widespread belief on the reservation that the most recent effort would fare no better. The reasons most frequently given by Crow officials were that the present government was "their government" and members liked its festive and participatory features. The difficult task of the Bureau of Indian Affairs was to show that new ways of governing would not risk the best of old values.

The Department of the Interior initiated the constitutional review process with a pledge of federal money. The tribe committed $60,000 and established a constitutional commission of fifteen members. Each commissioner received $200 a week, plus travel costs. The Department of the Interior also provided a consultant with long experience in tribal government who guided the commission through three drafts. The strategy of the consultant was to borrow considerable language from the existing constitution so that the proposal would be obviously derivative. This approach, though, was not sufficiently conservative to overcome the innate hostility of the tribe. Some tribal members confused the study commission with a call for a representative tribal council to replace the General Council and opposed the movement from the start. Both the ruling faction and the opposition faction resisted change because they feared that the other would benefit from reform. Many tribal members distrusted any interference in their government because of bad experiences with outsiders in the past. And some constitutional commission members, appointed by the incumbent power structure, viewed the study as another patronage opportunity and prolonged the process to increase their compensation. There was, therefore, little commitment to revision for two reasons: a deep love of old ways and attachment to the political manipulation that had been permitted by the traditional system.

The final draft of the revised constitution never went to vote. The Crow court voided a late 1983 election when a tribal member argued more time was needed to study the document. The re-scheduled referendum was never held. The common position of tribal members had come to be, "too much change in too short of a time."[80] The incumbent chairman stopped advocating reform as the biennial spring elections approached. Important off-reservation Crow political interests opposed the proposed change because it could scramble established avenues of political influence. In the end, even the reservation superintendent conceded that reform had become a "dead issue."[81] This concession by the Bureau of Indian Affairs was significant because Bureau officials believed that the document's only chance depended on high level Department of the Interior pressure and support.

Even though the Interior Department gave strong endorsement to the constitutional review process, federal officials could not have been very happy with the substantive features of the proposal. The Department's second tactic (in addition to its public support) was to borrow heavily from the present constitution. This conservative ploy stood in the way of substantial reform. The final document, for example, contained no provisions for a representative council, a secret ballot, or a strong administrative branch. Even if the proposal had been ratified, Crow politics would have remained essentially unchanged.

The proposed constitution, though, is deserving of discussion because of several interesting features and what it reveals about the Crows' commitment to their political culture. The "Tribal Council," comprised of all members over eighteen years of age (under the present constitution males must be age twenty-one), is the governing body. The council would meet every three months, but a petition of one hundred voters could call a special meeting. Special meetings also could be scheduled at the request of the chairman or a new body called the "Tribal Commission." The tribal secretary would set the council agenda, to be amended only by a unanimous vote of the Council. The voting section retains in explicit language the present method of "through the lines" balloting, and additional language about the integrity of each person's vote could be nothing more than a sop to the Crows' critics:

> All voting in any regular or special meeting of the Tribal Council on major issues shall be by standing vote and voting on matters of procedure or minor issues shall be by voice vote as may be determined by the chairman. Since each member of the Tribal Council has a right to exercise his or her vote without interference or harassment, each member should therefore be allowed to vote their own free will in a manner becoming to the dignity of the Crow Tribal Council.[82]

The executive branch emerges as even more fragmented than the present arrangement. There would be four constitutional officers, the chairman, vice-chairman, secretary, and treasurer (which position is substituted for the present vice-secretary). These positions would have four-year instead of two-year terms of office, and a June primary would precede a general election. The chairman's authority of "chief executive officer"[83] is qualified by other conflicting grants of power. The Council can delegate authority to administer its policies to both the chairman and the "Tribal Commission," which is comprised of the Tribal Council officers and officers of six "District Committees."[84] Further confusion is created by the document's establishment of a "Tribal Program Committee" (the chairmen of the various standing committees of the Council) and provision that the administration of tribal programs is the joint responsibility of the standing committees and of a new position called the "Executive Director of Tribal Programs."[85] There is no sorting out of the administrative responsibilities of these positions and bodies.

The draft constitution contained other interesting features, but none changed the basic design of the present government. A membership requirement of one-quarter Crow blood is given constitutional status. Each of the reservation's six districts is given an elected District Committee with planning, welfare, social, and liaison functions. A tribal senate, called the "Council of Elders," is comprised of district representatives and given advisory duties regarding "tribal traditions and customs" and quasi-judicial responsibilities "for domestic and youth problems."[86] The "Tribal Judiciary" gains constitutional status and judicial review authority over the actions of the Council and all officers. Finally, the present amendment process by majority vote is scrapped in favor of a more difficult two-thirds requirement.

The Crow tribe has as much potential as any tribe in Montana to achieve the goals of economic self-reliance and political self-determination. This is because its mineral reserves are so massive. To develop this resource responsibly—that is, so that members' immediate needs, long-term tribal welfare, and environmental integrity are respected—an effective governmental system is necessary. The qualities that are essential and presently lacking in Crow government are voting integrity in the General Council, stability and continuity in administration, and executive leadership that calls the Crow membership to a politics of both vision and restraint.

The lesson of the Department of the Interior audit is that these reforms must come from the Crow people themselves. The audit failed as an opportunity for reform for two reasons: the Bureau's active role in the constitutional review process and the Crow's adherence to traditional values. For reform to occur, the Crow tribe must replace Bureau activism and paternalism with acceptance of the full responsibility of self-governance. This cannot be done, though, as long as the Crow define the central truth, "this is our government," more in terms of past usage than present needs. Until the Crow make this change, the Bureau will remain entrenched on the reservation.

Crow politics is so interesting because it is a rare example of the workings of pure democracy. Tribal members legitimately defend the General Council on grounds of traditionalism. They enjoy its festivity and know firsthand the importance of direct political involvement. But the General Council also has permitted exploitation of pure democracy. Because of the informality of Crow government, tribal leaders can gain broad manipulative power and perpetuate the instability and short-sightedness of a patronage system. Confronting the Crow tribe is the difficult task of reconciling a proud though ambivalent past with the uncertain promise of the future. Only the Crow tribe can make the necessary decisions, and on the Crow reservation these factors make up a politics of risk.

Notes

1. Interview with Wyman Babby, Superintendent of the Crow Agency, August 23, 1983, quoting Plenty Coups.

2. Interview with Clay Gregory, Natural Resource Officer of the Crow Agency, August 25, 1983.

3. Interview with Wyman Babby.

4. Interview with Clay Gregory, and *The Missoulian* (Missoula, Montana), December 18, 1983.

5. *The Missoulian,* December 18, 1983.

6. "Settlement Proposal of Crow Indian Tribe," Memorandum to Crow Chairman, Donald Stewart from Fredericks and Pelcyger, Attorneys at Law, November 3, 1983.

7. *Crow Tribe of Indians v. State of Montana,* 819 F. 2d 895 (9th Cir. 1987), aff'd mem., 484 U.S. 997 (1988).

8. Ben Lusk of Washington, D.C., quoted in *The Missoulian,* December 18, 1983.

9. Kristi Branch of Billings, Montana, quoted in the *Billings Gazette,* January 21, 1984.

10. Edwin Thompson Denig, *Five Indian Tribes of the Upper Missouri* (Norman: University of Oklahoma Press, 1961), pp. 137–138.

11. See Ibid.; Robert H. Lowie, *The Crow Indians* (New York: Farrar and Rinehart, Inc., 1935); and Fred W. Voget, "Adaptation and Cultural Persistence Among the Crow Indians of Montana," *Political Organization of Native North Americans,* ed. Ernest L. Schusky (Washington, D.C.: University Press of America, Inc., 1980).

12. Lowie, p. 7.

13. Ibid., p. 9.

14. Ibid., p. 7.

15. Ibid., p. 6.

16. Ibid.

17. Ibid.

18. Ibid., p. 7.

19. Denig, p. 189.

20. Lowie, p. 239.

21. Ibid., p. 253.

22. Ibid., p. 255.

23. Ibid., p. 253.

24. Superintendents' Annual Narrative and Statistical Report, Crow, 1910, Frame 50.

25. Superintendents' Annual Narrative and Statistical Report, Crow, 1911, Frame 62.

26. Superintendents' Annual Narrative and Statistical Report, Crow, 1913, Frame 106.

27. Superintendents' Annual Narrative and Statistical Report, Crow, 1919, Frame 400.

28. Superintendents' Annual Narrative and Statistical Report, Crow, 1921, Frame 510; 1926, Frame 899.

29. Interview with Sylvester Knows His Gun, Crow tribal member, August 23, 1983.

30. Ibid.

31. Interview with Danetta Fallsdown, Vice Chairman of the Crow Tribe, August 25, 1983.

32. *Constitution and Bylaws of the Crow Tribal Council,* 1948, Art. VI, sec. 2.

33. Ibid., Art. IV.

34. Ibid., Art. VI, sec. 9.

35. Ibid., Art. VI, sec. 4.

36. The assessment of the Crow Tribal Court comes from an interview with Jim Vogel, attorney for the court, August 23, 1983.

37. *Bylaws,* Art. I, sec. 4.

38. Interview with Jim Vogel.

39. Interview with Danetta Fallsdown.

40. U.S. Department of the Interior Office of Inspector General, *Audit Report: Review of the Financial Status, Financial Management System, and Selected Programs, Contracts, and Grants, Crow Tribe of Indians, Fiscal Years 1980 and 1981,* March 1982, pp. 3–4.

41. Interview with Wyman Babby.

42. Source requested to remain anonymous.

43. Interview with Sylvester Knows His Gun.

44. Interview with Kathleen Fleury, Judicial Services Specialist, Billings Area of the Bureau of Indian Affairs, August 22, 1983.

45. Interview with Sylvester Knows His Gun.

46. Interview with Jim Vogel.

47. Ibid.

48. Interview with Tommy E. Roundface, Crow Tribal Judge, August 24, 1983.

49. Interview with Jim Canan, former Director of the Billings Area of the Bureau of Indian Affairs, August 28, 1983.

50. Interview with Sylvester Knows His Gun.

51. Interview with Danetta Fallsdown.

52. Interview with Alvin Howe, Tribal Court Prosecutor, August 23, 1983.

53. The source of this account requested to remain anonymous.

54. Interview with Alvin Howe.

55. Interview with Jim Vogel.

56. Interview with Wyman Babby.

57. Source requested to remain anonymous.

58. Interview with Sylvester Knows His Gun.

59. Inspector General, p. 10.

60. Ibid., p. 52.

61. Ibid., p. 53.

62. Ibid., p. 6.

63. Ibid., p. 24.

64. Ibid.

65. Ibid., p. 26.

66. Ibid., p. 17.

67. Ibid., p. 25.
68. Ibid., p. 41.
69. Ibid., p. 40.
70. Ibid., p. 47.
71. Ibid., p. 48.
72. Ibid.
73. Ibid., p. 43.
74. Ibid., p. 50.
75. Roy Sampsel, Deputy Assistant Secretary for Indian Affairs, Remarks at the Inauguration Ceremony on the Crow Reservation, July 2, 1982, p. 4.
76. Ibid., p. 2.
77. Crow Management Review Board, Memorandum presenting findings of first quarterly management review of Crow Tribe, July 13, 1983, p. 4.
78. Ibid., p. 5.
79. Ibid., p. 6.
80. Interview with Lorna Thackery, *Billings Gazette* reporter, May 7, 1984.
81. Interview with Wyman Babby, Superintendent of the Crow Agency, May 7, 1984.
82. "Proposed Revision: Constitution and By-Laws of the Crow Tribe," Art. V, sec. 7.
83. Ibid., Art. I (By-Laws).
84. Ibid., Art. VI.
85. Ibid., Art. IX.
86. Ibid., Art. VII.

5

The Northern Cheyenne: A Politics of Values

Among the Plains Indians, the Cheyenne had the distinct reputation of being "very much concerned with living up to an ideal of high-minded and responsible behavior."[1] Conversations with Northern Cheyenne tribal members today, from an elderly president to a Vietnam War veteran, leave the impression that the Northern Cheyenne still care deeply about their land and their future. More than other Montana tribes, the Northern Cheyenne have brought their traditional values to bear on their contemporary public affairs. One reason why Northern Cheyenne politics has been an interplay of old beliefs and new challenges is that tribal government has been sufficiently strong to nourish traditional values. This apparent contradiction in the eyes of many— the coexistence of centralized power, balanced government, and respect for the cherished past—has allowed the tribe to adapt to difficult situations with good faith.

Northern Cheyenne religious and ethical values stem from belief in Maheo, the all wise and beneficent Creator.[2] Divine life is present throughout creation, making living things sacred and deserving of reverence. The proper order among all of nature is harmony. Ideal behavior among the Northern Cheyenne, therefore, is understanding and cooperation with one another and respect and preservation of the land.

Belief in Maheo influenced the tribe's concept of itself as well as its attitudes about nature and human relations. The tribe's cultural hero, Sweet Medicine, taught that the Creator's providence was not to be taken for granted. The Northern Cheyennes' welfare, including survival as a tribe, would depend on tribal integrity and fidelity to Cheyenne beliefs. The tribe's sacred Medicine Arrows, gifts of Sweet Medicine, came to symbolize this precarious wholeness. Sweet Medicine left the Northern Cheyenne with a prophecy about temptations the white men would present—how they would lure the tribe away from their traditions and beliefs:

> The white people will try to change you from your way of living to theirs, and they will keep at what they try to do. They will tear up the earth and at last you will do it with them. When you do this, you will become crazy and will forget all that I have taught you. Then you will disappear.[3]

Northern Cheyenne have sought to preserve their heritage and keep Sweet Medicine's prophecy unfulfilled.

The tribe's attempts to be true to its past and maintain a tribal identity have been closely tied to keeping the reservation intact. The hills, canyons, and plains of the Tongue River area in southeastern Montana were not the Cheyenne's aboriginal home. In their earliest days, the Cheyenne lived in the upper midwestern area of the now United States and sustained themselves by trapping, fishing, and agriculture. They were pushed westward by other tribes, splitting into northern and southern branches in the 1830s and becoming hunters of buffalo. The Northern Cheyenne tribe's favorite area came to be the Tongue River, which they occupied after their 1877 surrender to General Nelson Miles, the avenger of George Custer. This land became their reservation in 1884. The Northern Cheyenne view their 450,000 acres in ways beyond the land's economic potential—that is, not only as a resource for grazing, leasing or mining. The characteristic Northern Cheyenne attitude is that the tribe can stand for something unique and of value only if the reservation is maintained as a homeland. This helps to explain why the Northern Cheyenne reservation today is 98 percent Indian owned and 77 percent tribally owned. In recent years tribal government has spent nearly a million dollars to purchase members' land to keep it out of white hands. A traditional and persisting Northern Cheyenne value is that the tribe and its land are identified with each other.

Acceptance by the Northern Cheyenne of one deity and a dominant prophet did not cause the tribe to submit itself to a form of religious tyranny. Instead, strong strains of autonomy are present within the tribe.[4] Traditionally, this value was seen in the tribe's dispersion into ten hunting bands during most of the year, the centrality of the family in the hunting bands, and the preeminence of family ties and responsibilities above all other social relationships. This family ethic was a manifestation of the self-reliance which the Cheyenne way of life made necessary. A hunting economy placed a premium on individual achievement and on taking care of family needs first. The behavioral consequences were a tendency of tribal members to go it alone and an element of social introversion, probably accentuated by the Northern Cheyenne belief in their own uniqueness.

The Northern Cheyenne political ethic honored authority as well as individual autonomy. At special times of the year, a peace council of forty-four would convene. This governing body of the tribe was made up of four chiefs from each of the tribe's ten bands and four principal chiefs. The Council of Forty-four debated and set policy concerning moves to new hunting territory, building alliances with other tribes, and going to war. The Cheyenne War Council of Twenty-four was composed of four members of the six military societies and conducted all war expeditions.[5] Orders of the councils were seldom disobeyed, one probable reason being the consultation between band leaders and members which preceded final decisions. But because of the importance of the chiefs' orders, warrior societies were given the duty of securing implementation and compliance.

Traditional Northern Cheyenne politics, therefore, was characterized by both individual autonomy and subordination to authority. Neither value was pushed to an extreme and, as a result, the traditional system of organization could adapt to different situations. Most of the time the Northern Cheyenne would live in separate groups, but on occasion the bands would form a large tribal camp and formulate generally applicable rules. Northern Cheyenne government accommodated fragmentation for day-to-day pursuits and combination for strategy setting. It valued broad participation and recognized the importance of obedience. As a result, a central feature of early Northern Cheyenne government was flexibility.

From the beginning of Cheyenne reservation life, the reservation government was marked by a sense of responsibility. This characteristic was not diminished by the tribe's split into northern and southern divisions and confinement on different reservations. The Northern Cheyenne organized a fifteen-member business council in 1911. Representation was based on electing three members from each of the reservation's five districts. A superintendent reported that the members were "reliable and intelligent" and their decisions pertaining to "Law and Order and policy were respectfully considered, for the matters thus far handled by the Business Council appear to have been very wisely acted upon."[6] Another assessment was that the members "make very good use of such funds as are paid to them."[7]

Tribal members "resented injustice" and carried a respect for legitimate authority to both the Indian police and the Court of Indian Offenses. Tribesmen generally accepted court decisions: "practically all of its judgments are acquiesced in and carried out by offenders convicted before it." One drawback was the court's lack of jurisdiction over tribal divorce, creating a reservation social problem which had been formerly under tribal control.[8]

Despite limited tribal resources, the Northern Cheyenne demonstrated "considerable determination and stubbornness in being controlled."[9] This adherence to self-rule created confrontations with the reservation superintendent.[10] The Northern Cheyenne's continuing preference to follow their own government and not imposed rule was reflected in their acceptance of the Indian Reorganization Act and adoption of an IRA constitution. Tribal harmony was disturbed during the 1940s and 1950s as younger residents opposed the cohesive older full-bloods. Another source of later factionalism was the Cheyenne military societies continuing to function as social and political groups.[11]

Reservation life today for the Northern Cheyenne is similar to life on other reservations, despite the tribe's efforts to honor its heritage. An environment of adversity has included high unemployment, poverty, and inadequate medical care. Factionalism has not been absent from tribal politics. Conflicting sentiments for development and conservation have threatened the ideal of harmony. Fears that the good things of the past are gone are expressed as often as pride in the preservation of traditional values. The tribe's goal of making the isolated reservation a real homeland, therefore, is not without major challenges.

Lame Deer is the principal reservation community. It is small and dusty and in appearance not unlike a mountain mining town. Tribal and other governmental offices and services are located in Lame Deer, but it is not the headquarters for thriving local businesses. Major employers of tribal members are the tribe, the Bureau of Indian Affairs, the Indian Health Service, and the Western Energy Company. An agreement between the tribe and Western Energy was the basis for 125 tribal members working in 1983 at the Colstrip, Montana, generating plants. There is not much else in the way of reservation jobs. Past ventures on the reservation in the lumber business and manufacturing plastic novelties failed, and a small sawmill has had financial problems. The tribe's business manager, who is responsible for economic development, has talked about bringing a tool and die company to the reservation from Michigan and of developing Asian contacts for the tribe's natural resources. But as is the case with economic development attempts generally, results are more difficult to produce than plans. The Northern Cheyenne unemployment rate has been lower than the figures of most other Montana reservations. Between 1973 and 1983, it ranged from 25 percent to 44 percent.

Similar to many other tribes, the economic potential of the Northern Cheyenne appears to depend not so much on industrial activity as on natural resources. From Lame Deer westward the pine-covered hills recede into grassy plains cut by gullies, and to the east the hills rise to small mountains before falling again to plains. This geography gives obvious promise of timber harvesting and livestock grazing, but excitement recently has been created by plans for mineral extraction. While tribal forest income has fluctuated wildly ($320,000 in 1980 and $30,000 in 1983) and excellent grassland can provide a good living for a few families and a stable but modest income for the tribe, coal and oil revenue could be so great as to alter significantly tribal members' way of life. The reservation's oil and gas potential is unknown, and one contract for exploration resulted in four dry wells. On the other hand, estimates place the tribe's coal reserves at between five and eight billion tons, most of which is recoverable by strip mining.

The presence of factionalism on the Northern Cheyenne reservation also makes its political life typical of other reservations. Factionalism exists because poverty is widespread and questions about the use of tribal resources are political issues to be resolved by the Council. Factionalism has become intensified on the Northern Cheyenne reservation because of the presence of coal. The tribe's ideal of harmony has not been able to quiet voices raised in debate about coal development and coal dollars.

Today's reservation factions, as described by a former tribal president, the late Allen Rowland, are organized along lines of age, ideology, and political candidacy. For example, candidates for the tribal presidency have their own groups of supporters; a separate radical faction urges coal development, which is countered by the arguments of conservationists; and older people emphasize restraint and ties to the past, while some young people advocate "mother earth stuff."[12] An anthropological study of Northern Cheyenne life in the late 1960s found substantial factionalism based on interests somewhat different than those described by the tribe's president. The principal factions, which tended to form antithetical pairs, were mixed blood and full blood, young and old, and Native American church and Christian church.[13]

Factions do not have a consistent and predictable effect on reservation politics. This is because formal group association, outside of the family structure, is not of critical importance to the Northern Cheyenne. As a result, the membership of any faction is diverse and unstable, and the political allegiances of factions shift over time. The key point about factionalism among the Northern Cheyenne is that it is a constant though varying political expression of the conditions and longings on the reservation.[14]

The Northern Cheyenne tribe's limited and fluctuating revenue is another reason why its situation is typical of other reservation governments.[15] For years the chief sources of tribal income were timber contracts and grazing leases, with revenue rising and falling according to market conditions. Between 1977 and 1980, total income for tribal government ranged between $500,000 and $1,000,000. The advent of energy company exploratory activity on the Northern Cheyenne reservation brought substantial, though temporary, increases in the tribal budget. The budget's income line between 1981 and 1983 varied between $2,000,000 and $7,000,000. The large increases were due to short-term energy company payments to the tribe, which fell off drastically in 1984. A major challenge of tribal leadership has been to curtail the expectations of tribal members as the government moves from impoverishment to energy company bonus payments and then back to the reality of revenue limits.

Per capita payments are common to tribal governments, and coal talk and coal money have immersed the Northern Cheyenne tribe in per capita politics. Between 1980 and 1984, the Northern Cheyenne tribe received $15.8 million for exploratory leases from four energy companies. Of this amount, $9.7 million was distributed to the tribe's 5,200 members in the form of per capita payments. The balance was invested or used to purchase the land of tribal members and to pay for routine governmental operations. Rumors circulated throughout the reservation that the total coal payments during this period amounted to $48 million, and a petition signed by 282 tribal members requested the U.S. Senate Select Committee on Indian Affairs to conduct an investigation into alleged misuse of these funds. A local inquiry by the Bureau of Indian Affairs did little to defuse the clamor about corruption and demands for sharing of the wealth. Tribal politics became dominated by the per capita issue when some tribal officials promoted per capita payments even to the point of deficit financing, and a budget referendum was sought to earmark 50 percent of the tribe's 1984 income for a per capita payment of $400. The Northern Cheyenne tribe, therefore, is not immune to conflict which pits short-term needs against long-term benefits. Northern Cheyenne officials, as leaders on other reservations, cannot ignore chronic poverty when attempting to guide the tribe to self-reliance and self-governance.

A final feature of the Northern Cheyenne homeland, which characterizes reservations in general, is its overwhelming isolation. The Northern Cheyenne reservation is located in the least populated corner of a rural and sparsely populated state. The white presence on the reservation is negligible. Only 2 percent of the acreage within the reservation boundaries is non-Indian owned. Leasing by white ranchers also is insignificant, as only three or four white cattlemen lease grazing acreage from tribal members and no white ranchers run their cattle on tribal grass. In contrast, 32 percent of the adjacent Crow reservation is non-Indian owned. Further, the Northern Cheyenne have enhanced their physical isolation with an element of social introversion. As a tribe, the Northern Cheyenne fought long and hard against massive industrial development at Colstrip, Montana, less than twenty miles from the reservation's northern boundary, because of a perceived threat to the tribe's way of life. The tribe also has rejected coal development within its borders and fought nearby coal development in part because of the social intermingling it would produce. The tribe's isolationism also can be seen in its standoffish attitude concerning Montana politics. In the 1980 gubernatorial election, the turnout figure for the Lame Deer precinct on the reservation was 26 percent. The comparable figures on the other six Montana reservations ranged between 48 percent and 73 percent. The Northern Cheyenne reservation seemingly turns in upon itself. Today, if reservation children grow insubordinate and adults shun work, tribal elders demand that leaders shield members from dangerous white influences. The essential task of Northern Cheyenne leadership, however, has been to provide a core strength so that the tribe can reach both inward and outward for the help it needs to survive and prosper.

It is fortunate for the Northern Cheyenne that their traditional and present forms of government have placed high value on strong leadership. In the Council of Forty-four, leadership qualities such as concern for tribal welfare, goodness, knowledge, and decisiveness were prized more than the traits of a warrior. The words of the four head chiefs accordingly "received greater consideration than those of other speakers."[16] This expectation of wisdom and guidance in a chief has carried over to the role of president today.[17] The Northern Cheyenne, therefore, support strength at the head of their government.

The Northern Cheyenne constitution is written in such a way that a strong president is likely to emerge at the head of the council and tribe. The president's constitutional duties include serving as chief executive officer, first officer and presider of the council, and chief spokesman of the tribe in dealings with federal and state officials. The primacy of the president's position is reinforced by the electoral system. The president is the only tribal officer who is chosen by the whole Northern Cheyenne electorate. District meetings nominate both presidential and council candidates, but council members are elected from five districts which are apportioned on a population basis. The constitutionally provided terms of office also strengthen the president's position of leadership. While council members serve concurrent two-year terms, the president's four-year term without limitation allows for experience, continuity, and establishment of a strong base of power.

The tribal council has its own strength, due in part to its traditions also running back to the Council of Forty-four.[18] The council is a large body, in the past having as many as twenty-four members. Only recently was it reduced to sixteen. The people's concept of council service is derived from the traditional functions of the forty-four chiefs. Council membership is "prestigious"[19] because its responsibilities are making policy for the tribe's welfare and staying in touch with the membership. This expectation of responsiveness and accountability has made recruitment of council candidates difficult, one observation being that council service results in "'trouble because everyone kicks at you.'"[20] Compensation is not an attraction, as the pay is less than $2,000 a year. The electorate votes with caution, basing its choice on evidence of "good sense, education, and political activity that has been effective."[21]

The Northern Cheyenne government's reputation of strength and stability stems more from the executive than from the council. The council has reflected the changing moods of the tribal membership. Biennial elections for all of the council positions tend to produce a council sharply divided between newcomers and holdovers. Recently, for example, a "full blood council" was elected in the wake of fears about reckless coal development, replacing a "breed council" which was primarily income oriented.[22] A council divided between newly elected councilmen (only nine women served on the council between 1935 and 1984) and senior members can accomplish little until the newcomers come to accept the impossibility of instant change. The burden of providing this education to eight councils fell to tribal president Allen Rowland, who was an incumbent for sixteen years. He earned respect and power at the head of the Northern Cheyenne government through his unimpeachable character, force of personality, and sometimes ruthless use of constitutional authority. So fortified, he served as the tribe's executive officer, complaint bureau, chief spokesman, and head negotiator and led the council as presiding officer with an invincible veto power.

President Rowland's council opponents, usually led by the vice chairman, repeatedly tried to strip him of his strong executive power. Allen Rowland, however, thwarted these assaults and once used such a scheme so that it became an improvement in the governmental structure. That occasion was the council's creation by resolution of an executive committee. This group is appointed by the president from among the council membership and with the council's approval. It is chaired by the council's vice chairman. The original purpose of the committee was to investigate program operations and expenditures and report to the whole council with findings and recommendations. This intent was abused when the executive committee began to get involved in tribal administration, placing itself between the directors of tribal programs and President Rowland. Some basis for shared executive duties can be found in the language of the tribe's Plan of Operations. Here the president is given "responsibility" for "all employees in the management of Tribal business," and the council is "vested" with the "management of Tribal operations."[23] Resolution of this statutory ambivalence and of the actual conflict created by the executive committee has been through accommodation. Because President Rowland insisted upon his executive prerogatives, the executive committee was forced to adopt a "chain of command"[24] mode of operation. The executive committee, therefore, began to carry its suggestions first to the president and only later, if the president did not take satisfactory action, to the whole council. As a result, the president preserved his position as a "strong and true executive."[25]

The activities that surrounded and followed upon Allen Rowland's retirement in 1984 raise the question whether the strength of the Northern Cheyenne government was due primarily to his incumbency or a result of the reservation's political culture and structure.[26] The answer appears to be that the Northern Cheyenne idea of government does anticipate and can generate strong leadership, but a politician's personal traits must complement the Northern Cheyenne constitutional design before such a president in fact emerges. Against this backdrop, the first post-Rowland presidency was a disappointment. A drop in revenue from energy companies and increased unemployment, the rapidly spreading discontentment of tribal members, and personal problems of the new president were sufficient political reason for a council minority to seek his removal from office.

Windy Shoulderblade, a well-known reservation politician in his early thirties, was elected president in 1984 by a plurality vote from a field of thirteen candidates. He was known for his friendliness, fairness, high ethical standards, and success as a tribal representative in off-reservation affairs, but his greatest asset was Allen Rowland's public backing. Windy Shoulderblade's rapid political decline, ending in impeachment in late 1985, was occasioned both by events and personal weaknesses which were in direct opposition to Allen Rowland's strengths. He was the former president's protégé, while Allen Rowland was extraordinarily independent. Windy Shoulderblade supported the appointment of his chief political opponent as vice chairman, but he lacked his mentor's political base or toughness to minimize the resulting discord. The new president played to the interests of younger members by emphasizing coal development, thus alienating the more politically influential older electorate; Allen Rowland had assiduously courted the traditional faction. The new president stressed his off-reservation duties and bettering relations with outside groups, while Allen Rowland had taken special care of his on-reservation responsibilities and delegated travel to others. Finally, the pressures of his new position caused Windy Shoulderblade to be indiscreet publicly in his behavior, while Allen Rowland had been prudent and beyond reproach in his personal life. The tribal membership would not tolerate misconduct in their leader, and the members' shame became fodder for Windy Shoulderblade's council opposition, culminating in his removal from office. This action was not only the retaliation of a rival faction and the members' rebuke of government because of their worsening economic situation. Impeachment also was a statement that a Northern Cheyenne leader must be characterized by both respect for traditional values and political strength.

The Northern Cheyenne tribe's political assertiveness and sophistication has confounded the Bureau of Indian Affairs. The Northern Cheyenne reservation was the first community in the nation to receive a pristine air classification from the Environmental Protection Agency. The tribe established the Northern Cheyenne Research Project, put in place a computerized system for environmental monitoring, negotiated an innovative exploration contract with a major energy company, concluded a hiring agreement with the state's largest utility, and sought authority to bring violators of tribal civil regulations to court. Left behind by the tribe, the agency superintendent has defined his role in negative rather than positive terms. Not having to prod tribal officials, the superintendent has assumed the task of restraining the tribe. The superintendent could have assisted the tribe by hiring specialized staff to provide otherwise unavailable technical assistance, but he has preferred to stress to the tribe the necessity of living within the confines of federal regulations and its own constitution. The superintendent's position is that "councilmen must realize the BIA is here."[27]

The special strength of Northern Cheyenne government is also seen in its openness to involvement by tribal members. The concentration of power in the executive and legislative branches is offset not only by checks and balances between them (for example, the council vice chairman has almost always been a political opponent of the president) but also by direct participation. The total electorate chooses the president, rather than allowing the council to fill the position from among its membership. A premium is placed on community representation by using the districts of Ashland, Birney, Busby, Muddy, and Lame Deer for both council elections and nominating meetings. The districts also schedule periodic community meetings to debate issues and hear from and question council members. The size of the tribal council also encourages citizen involvement in government through greater ease of candidacy. Additionally, the Northern Cheyenne constitution promotes direct democracy through referendum. This provision allows an election on any proposed or enacted council measure if initiated by 10 percent of each district's electorate. This device was used in 1976 to approve the tribe's application for Class I air status and in 1983 to question the tribal budget. The strength of Northern Cheyenne government, therefore, is in its balance. It incorporates neither extreme centralization nor participation, but uses the merits of each and thereby promotes a healthy flexibility.

There are a large number of actions by the Northern Cheyenne which show that the strength of the tribe's government is in deeds as well as on paper. To be strong, tribal government must be structured to serve each of several purposes. It must be open to the members' involvement, representative of various tribal interests, accountable to the judgment of the electors, responsive to the needs and values of the tribe, and capable of mounting competent and effective leadership in times of crisis and when the interests of the future are jeopardized. The Northern Cheyenne government is designed in such a way that all of these goals can be realized.

The tribal government's handling of financial matters, for example, indicates that it is much more than an arena for the play of reservation politics. In a setting which is fairly typical of many other tribes, the Northern Cheyenne government has made a difference in the lives of the Northern Cheyenne people. Tribal government has been strong enough to practice fiscal restraint. After the tribe began to receive large though temporary payments from energy companies in 1981, the council had the prudence and resolve to invest approximately $3.5 million over a three-year period. When the tribe began to experience a decrease in revenue in 1983, the council initiated "cutback" government. The council's executive committee announced a 19 percent reduction in all program budgets, met individually with program directors to assess the effect of the proposed cuts, and then made final budget adjustments based upon special conditions. The tribal leadership has conducted the entire budgetary process—formulation, adoption, and post review—in accordance with their statement of tribal priorities. The Northern Cheyenne government, therefore, has a sufficiently strong sense of identity and autonomy that it can act responsibly. As a result, its actions have been related to its view of the tribe's welfare.

The tribal government's strength was also revealed in its reaction to the call for congressional investigation of its financial affairs. In 1982, 282 tribal members complained of official corruption and widespread poverty on the reservation and asked, regarding millions of dollars in energy company payments, "Where is the money?"[28] The tribal government had been audited in the past by the Department of the Interior. Because these audits did not criticize the tribe's fiscal practices, the council felt free to hire an accounting firm to conduct a study of the tribe's accounts for three years. The president said there was "nothing to hide,"[29] and the chairman of the executive committee was quoted as saying he found the members' petition to be reasonable:

> A lot of money really comes to the tribe, and the people really don't see much of it. It goes to salaries and programs. One reason we called for the investigation was to let the people see how money is spent on the reservation.[30]

The significance of the council's action is not only that the independent audit reported a clean situation. It also is that the tribal government was open to criticism and responded in a respectful and responsible manner.

The tribe's handling of organizational matters, similar to its fiscal politics, demonstrates governmental maturity. Officials have been willing to identify problems facing the community and make adjustments in the status quo to serve the tribal welfare. An example of such political realism was President Rowland's success on three occasions in securing the removal of the agency superintendent. The president brought pressure on the Bureau of Indian Affairs because the superintendents stood in the way of realizing reasonable tribal goals. The Bureau responded positively and without condescension. The respect shown by the Bureau to the Northern Cheyenne was due to the tribe's ability to speak convincingly with one voice.[31]

Another example of decisive action to correct an organizational defect was President Rowland's removal of tribal judges. The Northern Cheyenne court does not have the prestige or power of the president or council. The council, especially, has been unwilling to afford the court the independence it needs to establish itself as a co-equal branch of government. Council members, wanting to keep the judges "under their thumb,"[32] have put pressure on the court by criticizing its decisions publicly. The court has on occasion bowed to the council's wishes by denying parties a hearing or otherwise ignoring proper procedures. Believing that he was protecting the court as an institution, President Rowland fired two tribal judges seven different times. Although the council reinstated them each time, the inter-branch tension produced beneficial change. The position of court administrator was established to shield the judges from political interference. The result, a more effective tribal court, was due to the president's determination.

The council, as well as the president, is capable of responding to tough problems with firmness. On all reservations, welfare assistance places a great strain on tribal revenues. This was especially so during the Reagan administration when the federal government made substantial cuts in human service programs. Faced with increased pressure for tribal benefits, the Northern Cheyenne council set a "fair share for all"[33] as the tribe's goal. Administrative guidelines were drawn up to avoid such abuses as favorable treatment for well-placed families and playing one official against another. At the risk of angering the politically influential, the council rejected patronage and stressed objective standards and fair procedures in a critical tribal program.

Probably the best evidence of the strength of Northern Cheyenne government is its undertaking of major restructuring. Change of this type is always very threatening to employees, officials, and the community. Successful reorganization, therefore, is an indication of a government's acceptance and self-confidence. The Northern Cheyenne tribe's reform of its committee system under the council in the early 1980s was in two phases. Each stage represented an adjustment to a serious problem facing the tribe.

The stated reason for undertaking reorganization was President Allen Rowland's poor health. Because the president had been absent from the reservation for medical treatment two afternoons every week, concern on the council grew that administrative supervision of tribal programs would suffer. The council's response was termination of all council standing committees and establishment of a four-person council executive committee. The intent was to provide assistance to the president and not to erode his executive position. Despite attempts to use the new arrangement to remove the president from administrative reporting and supervision, the reform succeeded in preserving the president as a true day-to-day executive and maintaining a significant degree of administrative centralization.

President Rowland's illness had raised the possibility that tribal administration would come to be fragmented among the standing committees of the council. To prevent such decentralization, the executive committee was authorized to conduct the budget process and oversee the operation of all tribal programs. Each member of the executive committee was responsible for approximately six tribal programs. President Rowland's constitutional position was respected in that he appointed the executive committee from the council membership, he was the first official to receive the committee's findings and recommendations, and he reserved to himself final approval of administrative policy.

This restructuring amounted to a major change for several reasons. It threatened the political standing of President Rowland, probably the best known and most respected member of the tribe. Secondly, it transferred oversight responsibility from the members of the standing committees to the four members of the new executive committee. Finally, it established an economically favored group. Previously, council members received stipends for both council and committee service; but under the new system four members receive full salaries (of $20,000 in fiscal year 1983, compared to the president's salary of $32,000) for serving on the executive committee. Despite these major obstacles, the reorganization plan went into effect and resulted in preservation of centralized executive control.

The second phase of governmental restructuring concerned the size of the executive committee. Originally there were four members, then the membership was eight, then seven, and in 1984 it was reduced to five. The reason for the progressive reduction in size was to save money. Faced with declining energy company payments, President Allen Rowland and the Northern Cheyenne council mustered courage to cut some of the few high-salaried and high-status positions on the reservation. This was an action of political realism and maturity. When the alternatives have been providing work or cutting budgets, other reservation politicians frequently have found it difficult to say "no" to employment.

The strength of the Northern Cheyenne government, characterized by centralization of power and openness to reform, can be viewed as a threat to the tribe's heritage. The Northern Cheyenne government, however, not only has coexisted with traditional values but also has served as the vehicle of their expression. For example, the council removed President Windy Shoulderblade from office for not exemplifying the members' sense of proper conduct. The tribe's fiscal controls allowed it to purchase members' acreage and to preserve the reservation as a tribal homeland. For similar reasons, the tribe secured Class I air status from the federal government and fought the construction of large thermal generating plants near its borders. The fact that the Northern Cheyenne eventually struck a bargain with the energy company points to strength and not weakness. The agreement resulted in installation at the plants of the "best available pollution control technology,"[34] location on the reservation of air quality checking stations staffed by tribal members trained by the company, and employment of tribal members at the coal mines and in the generating plants with opportunity for advancement to technical and administrative positions. The tribe through its efforts protected the reservation's natural environment, but in addition it gained control of air quality policing and significant employment opportunities.

How the strength of Northern Cheyenne government has been used in the service of tribal values is best illustrated by contemporary dealings with coal and oil companies. A series of three episodes shows a marked development in the tribe's attitude and posture. Initially, the Northern Cheyenne deferred to the Bureau of Indian Affairs in working out agreements with the energy companies. Next the tribal government became involved in negotiations, eventually rejecting an offer which was financially attractive though threatening to the tribe's values. Finally, the Northern Cheyenne bypassed the Bureau of Indian Affairs and demonstrated that tribal self-reliance could result in an agreement which was in the tribe's economic interest and in line with its cultural heritage.

Even though the "pull of the land is powerful and runs deep in Cheyenne blood,"[35] in the 1960s and early 1970s the tribe found itself going along with several Bureau of Indian Affairs-approved contracts with energy companies.[36] These agreements allowed Peabody Coal Company, AMAX Coal Company, Consolidation Coal Company, and Chevron Oil Company to explore thousands of acres of the reservation. The companies gained leasing rights to mine the coal discovered, and the tribe's guaranteed compensation was a bonus of from 12 cents to $9.00 for each acre put into production and royalties ranging from 15 cents to 17.5 cents for each ton of coal mined. The tribe later had doubts about the contracts, and the council petitioned first the Secretary of the Interior and then the United States Congress to cancel them. Reasons the tribe gave for its initial assent to exploration and mining were the poverty of the reservation, blind trust in the advice of the Bureau of Indian Affairs, and belief that mining would not be very extensive or destructive. Because of the tribe's lack of vigilance, however, the council had to seek extraordinary means of redress.

Opposition to the coal lease agreements became especially strong during new negotiations with Consolidation Coal Company in 1972. Consolidation sought an expansion of its existing contract, specifically an addition of 55,000 acres for exploration and mining, the right to mine up to one billion tons of coal, and the right to construct four coal gasification plants on the reservation and to use tribal water in this process. The tribe would receive a bonus of $35.00 for each acre mined (compared to the $9.00 in the Bureau's contract), and a royalty of 25 cents per ton for all coal mined (compared to 17.5 cents in the Bureau-negotiated contract). The tribe thus came to realize that past reliance on the Bureau of Indian Affairs had worked to its disadvantage. Tribal president Allen Rowland alleged that Bureau officials "'had been inept, uninformed, and sadly overmatched.'"[37] The response of the council was to hire expert assistance for securing the federal government's termination of the early coal contracts.

The fight for cancellation was long and ultimately successful. In 1973 the Secretary of the Interior refused to set aside the contracts, but he conditioned any mining under the agreements on his finding that the reservation's environment would not be damaged and on the tribe's approval. Congress in 1980 provided a more comprehensive and satisfactory solution. Concluding that the Bureau of Indian Affairs had acted contrary to federal regulations and in violation of the trust responsibility it owed to the Northern Cheyenne, the Congress cancelled the leases and provided consideration for the companies and the tribe. The coal companies received a promise of preferential treatment for future leasing of federal lands and the tribe received $9.8 million from the coal companies (Peabody—$3.0 million, Chevron—$3.5 million, AMAX—$3.3 million) as damage payments for removing the acreage from any leasing activity for sixteen years. The measure had the support of the tribe and the companies, but it was opposed by the Bureau of Indian Affairs.

The contract cancellation episode reinforced the Northern Cheyenne attitudes of self-reliance and caution. The tribe became part of the Consolidation Coal Company negotiations, and the council gave full consideration to the positive and negative implications of the proposal. The benefits included an estimated total royalty of $250 million, jobs and secondary economic opportunities, and a company donation of $1.5 million for a reservation health center. Arguments against the agreement emphasized destruction of the homeland and the end of the tribe. Tribal member Ted Risingsun said: "'I would rather be poor in my own country, with my own people, with our own way of life than be rich in a torn-up land where I am outnumbered ten to one by strangers.'"[38] The council ultimately rejected the offer, and to this day there has been no coal mining on the Northern Cheyenne reservation.

The third episode in the tribe's recent dealings with the energy companies demonstrates how well the lesson of self-reliance was learned. Oil and gas negotiations with ARCO were conducted by the tribe without the active involvement of the Bureau of Indian Affairs. The Bureau's approval was essential because of the federal trust responsibility, and it came reluctantly. The tribe's new position was that economic self-sufficiency and respect for traditional tribal interests would be realized during development only if the tribe remained in control of negotiations. As a result, the tribe countered the company's first offer with strong demands. The ultimate agreement included protection of the natural environment and cultural areas, employment and training guarantees for tribal members, a 25 percent tribal share of gross production, a $6 million bonus for the opportunity of exploring on the reservation, and an annual acreage rental payment of $1.3 million. The 1980 contract's joint venture feature was pioneering and came to be the basis of a congressional proposal to authorize other tribes to do the same.

The ARCO agreement indicates that the Northern Cheyenne government has become strong enough to watch out for the tribe's interests. The tribe's values and way of life can be protected because its government is able to take control of its affairs, confidently and decisively. In the future, the argument might be made that tribal coal reserves must be mined to guarantee the tribe's continued existence as a separate people. But that decision, in the words of the Northern Cheyenne oil and gas officer, will be for the tribe itself to make: "'We may develop our coal someday, but if we do, it will be in a way and at a pace that suits us.'"[39]

This chapter has made the point that Northern Cheyenne government is strong and that this strength has been developed in a modern reservation setting and with adherence to old values. The judgment of governmental strength has been based upon the Northern Cheyenne's emphasis of leadership, centralization, and member involvement and upon the existence and functioning of effective checks and balances. As a result, Northern Cheyenne government has partially offset such potential reservation weaknesses as isolation, demands for sharing tribal income now, and sharp factionalism. Another consequence of this governmental strength has been the tribe's ability to keep alive in a meaningful way its traditional beliefs in homeland and harmony with all of life.

The strength of Northern Cheyenne government, in its design and results, becomes especially clear with the understanding that the tribe has faced political realities and made necessary adjustments. For example, the Northern Cheyenne government has listened to and responded to criticism without manipulation or intimidation; it has allowed strong leadership to develop and removed a politician from office when the traditional ideal of leadership was violated; it has resolved the most critical policy problems on their merits and without resort to personal attacks; it has achieved structural reform, rationalized on the basis of tribal need and not private advantage; it has entered into interbranch conflict, not for destructive ends but to preserve high ideals; and it has looked to the future and exercised fiscal prudence and restraint. The Northern Cheyenne government's strength and sophisticated politics have not been hostile to the tribe's values.

Notes

1. William Brandon, *Indians* (New York: The American Heritage Library, 1985), p. 329.

2. The discussion of the traditional values of the Northern Cheyenne Tribe is derived from Brent Ashabranner, *Morning Star, Black Sun: The Northern Cheyenne Indians and America's Energy Crisis* (New York: Dodd, Mead and Company, 1982).

3. Ibid., p. 30.

4. The discussion of the traditional organization of the Northern Cheyenne Tribe is derived from Katherine Morrett Weist, "The Northern Cheyennes: Diversity in a Loosely Structured Society" (unpublished Ph.D. dissertation, Dept. of Anthropology, University of California, Berkeley, 1970), pp. 30–41.

5. Karl N. Llewellyn and E. Adamson Hoebel, *The Cheyenne Way: Conflict and Case Law in Primitive Jurisprudence* (Norman: University of Oklahoma Press, 1941, 7th Printing), pp. 67–131.

6. Superintendents' Annual Narrative and Statistical Report, Tongue River, 1911, Frame 62.

7. Superintendents' Annual Narrative and Statistical Report, Tongue River, 1914, Frame 135.

8. Superintendents' Annual Narrative and Statistical Report, Tongue River, 1911, Frame 68.

9. Superintendents' Annual Narrative and Statistical Report, Tongue River, 1914, Frame 139.

10. Superintendents' Annual Narrative and Statistical Report, Tongue River, 1926, Frame 682.

11. U. S. Congress, House, Report with Respect to the House Resolution Authorizing the Committee on Interior and Insular Affairs to Conduct an Investigation of the Bureau of Indian Affairs, Pursuant to House Resolution 89, 83rd Cong., 2d sess., 1954, Serial 11747, p. 109.

12. Interview with Allen Rowland, President of the Northern Cheyenne Tribe, August 24, 1983.

13. Weist, p. 143.

14. See Ibid., pp. 141–169.

15. Tribal income figures come from budget documents provided by President Allen Rowland.

16. Weist, p. 35.

17. Ibid., p. 179.

18. Ibid., p. 140.

19. Ibid., p. 141.

20. Ibid.

21. Interview with Sylvester Knows His Gun, former Director of Natural Resources for the Northern Cheyenne Tribe, August 23, 1983.

22. Interview with Sharon Limberhand, Tribal Operations Officer of the Northern Cheyenne Agency, August 25, 1983.

23. *Plan of Operations of the Northern Cheyenne Reservation,* adopted on October 21, 1980, Art. I, sec. D and sec. E.

24. Interview with Llevando "Cowboy" Fisher, Northern Cheyenne Councilman and Chairman of the Executive Committee, August 25, 1983.

25. Interview with Ernest "Bud" Moran, Superintendent of the Northern Cheyenne Agency, August 25, 1983.

26. Interviews with Clara Spotted Elk, Northern Cheyenne tribal member and former aide to President Allen Rowland, January 28, 1986, and with Edwin Dahle, Northern Cheyenne tribal member and former Northern Cheyenne councilman, February 25, 1986.

27. Ibid.

28. Letter from Oliver Glenn Eaglefeather, member of the Northern Cheyenne Tribe, to the Assistant Secretary of the U.S. Department of Interior for Indian Affairs, January 7, 1983.

29. *Billings Gazette,* November 9, 1982.

30. Ibid.

31. Interview with Allen Rowland.

32. Ibid.

33. Interview with Bob Bailey, Northern Cheyenne Councilman and Vice President, August 24, 1983.

34. Ashabranner, p. 128.

35. Ashabranner, p. 67.

36. The discussion of the Northern Cheyenne Tribe's relationships with energy companies comes from Ashabranner, pp. 75–125.

37. Ibid., p. 95.

38. Ibid., p. 93.

39. Ibid., p. 124, quoting Joe Little Coyote.

6

The Fort Peck Reservation:
The Factor of Leadership

The struggle of Native Americans to regain the self-sufficiency they once possessed has been frustrating more often than fruitful. After United States soldiers and agents brought an end to the Indian way of life on the northern plains, the United States Congress asserted responsibility for its renewal or replacement, alternately adopting policies of assimilating Indian people into the white culture and preserving the reservation as an Indian homeland. Increasingly, though, reservation governments have taken control of Indian destiny. This has happened on the Fort Peck reservation, where strong political leadership has overcome deficiencies of governmental structure and obstacles of reservation life to bring about significant economic development. This chapter deals with the remarkable political economy of the Fort Peck reservation.

The Fort Peck reservation, whose boundaries were fixed by an 1888 Act of Congress, is located in the northeastern corner of Montana. Early in the 1800s the Assiniboine in separate bands came across the rolling prairies to the upper Missouri River valley. The Sioux arrived later in the century after evading the pursuit of the United States Cavalry. Today these two tribes are the inhabitants of the Fort Peck reservation. The reservation's land area is 2.1 million acres, covering parts of four Montana counties. The tribes have approximately 8,200 enrolled members, 4,400 of whom live on the reservation.

For generations, meaningful economic progress was a stranger to the Fort Peck reservation. This was not because of need. In the early 1970s, when major efforts to improve the reservation economy were beginning, about 49 percent of Indian residents were below the poverty level established by the federal government and the Indian rate of unemployment was 49 percent. One obstacle to economic development was that industry managers considering business relationships with Indian tribes were concerned about social conditions on the reservation.[1] Experience taught them that reservation politics could destroy continuity in tribal personnel and policies, making negotiations too expensive and investment too risky.

One cause of such political upheaval on the reservation is extreme factionalism. On the Fort Peck reservation, divisiveness stems primarily from the confederation of the Assiniboine and Sioux tribes. Their early history included frequent warfare, occasioned by the Sioux following the dwindling buffalo into Assiniboine country. Also, the tribes' political cultures were different.[2] The Assiniboine governed themselves through many groups, each subject to laws which were spotty in coverage and carried little authority. The Sioux also were divided into bands, but government within each was characterized by strict rule and rigorous enforcement. Additionally, tribal dispositions were quite opposite. The Assiniboine were restrained and politically conservative, and the Sioux were aggressive and exacting as a nation. Some tribal distinctions have been preserved today because of separate areas of residence at Fort Peck. The Sioux live in the eastern part of the reservation, and the Assiniboine reside across Toule Creek in the western portion.

Tribal identification is not the sole determinant of reservation factionalism. Political conflict also is based upon dissimilar heritage, memberships, and ideology.[3] For example, campaign appeals can invoke membership in a tribal band which has its roots in a past battle or leader's following. One Sioux band descends from widows and orphans of warriors who were killed by Custer's troops at the Little Big Horn. Today some Sioux Indians trace their family line to this episode and feel a strong bond with others who share this tie. Family relationships can have the same effect. Campaign strategy, voting in elections, and hiring practices often turn upon blood considerations.[4] Reservation factionalism also is caused by diverse views of natural resource development: the argument of "go slow" vying with the opposite position of "revenue now."[5]

The reputed work habits of reservation Indians also have been an obstacle to economic progress. In early negotiations with the Department of Defense to secure a minority business contract, the Fort Peck government had to overcome the belief of federal administrators that Indian workers lacked sufficient self-discipline to show up for work and meet production deadlines. To prevent the manufacturing projects from going elsewhere to black minority enterprises, it was necessary for the then Fort Peck chairman, Norman Hollow, to pledge his efforts to overcome this perceived weakness. The plant manager, hired from outside the reservation to run the manufacturing operation after the contract was received, established a personnel system which took into consideration the Fort Peck Indians' lack of work experience and supplied special incentives "to compensate for the Indians' poor work ethic."[6]

Another barrier to an improved economic condition on the Fort Peck reservation was a short-ranged attitude about getting ahead. This outlook had a number of manifestations, the most consequential being pressure for using revenue for per capita payments, manipulation of constitutionally provided procedures for personal gain, and a politics of illegal payoffs. What these practices had in common is rejection of a commonweal philosophy.

Approval of per capita payments rests with the tribes' governing body, the Executive Board. The constitution permits these disbursements to be a major draw on tribal income, authorizing the reservation government to allocate up to 70 percent of annual income for per capita payments.[7] The Christmas 1982 payment of $200 to each member of the two tribes cost the government in excess of $1.6 million. Two issues have been before the tribes: what share of the reservation's income should be diverted to per capita payments, and whether the revenue received from tribal industries should be shared by all through per capita payments. The constant dilemma is the proper balance to be struck between serving immediate needs and building up capital. Pressure for using all income to help the members directly is always strong.

An example of this pressure, which also illustrates manipulation of governmental processes, was a petition for a general council to adopt a requirement of annual per capita payments.[8] The petition also would have placed on the agenda an inquiry into official travel and land purchases. The backers of the petition, calling themselves proponents of "honest government," were opponents of Chairman Norman Hollow. The group's strategy included forgery of signatures, using signatures from an old petition form, and submitting the petition to the agency superintendent and not to the chairman as required by the constitution. Another example of manipulating political procedures was a petition for a general council which misrepresented the purpose of the meeting.[9] The real purpose—to set a new degree-of-blood requirement for sharing in a claim settlement—was different from the stated purpose. This willingness to falsify, misrepresent, and by-pass the constitution in order to gain advantage can harm the cause of economic development. Outsiders can thereby form the impression that legal understandings and processes will not be honored by the tribes.

Of the political attitudes on the Fort Peck reservation that are damaging to general economic betterment, the most harmful has been the belief on and off the reservation that payoffs are an ordinary part of political life. A leading political figure on the Fort Peck reservation has observed that, in the past, "Fort Peck Indians have believed that political support for an official was part of a deal."[10] A supporter could ask the official for favors, such as diverting equipment and materials from a government program to personal use. Rumor of these practices created an expectation among outside businessmen that they could get favorable terms by bribing a tribal official. The result was that the whole membership suffered while a few enjoyed their unethical gain.

These aspects of political life on the Fort Peck reservation were obstacles to economic development. Their common element was political fragmentation as opposed to unified purpose. Factionalism forced the tribal government to focus on narrow perspectives; per capita payments gave the many a little now but denied large benefits to the many in the future; and payoffs and political manipulation were inherently selfish tactics. The debilitating effects of fragmentation can be overcome by leadership, encouraged by a carefully rationalized governmental structure or provided by a person with exceptional political skills. While a leader with such attributes did emerge, the present constitution of the Fort Peck reservation is not designed to promote centralized power and strong leadership.

This fragmentation should not be surprising as the Fort Peck tribesmen long favored diffusing power through a general council and a dual court system. The voluntary participatory politics of the general council system worked against strong executive leadership and prevented one tribe from controlling the reservation. Two reservation Courts of Indian Offenses existed initially, also reflecting each tribe's refusal to submit to the other tribe's leaders. A Fort Peck superintendent reported, "We have two judges, one for the Assiniboines and one for the Yanktons."[11] The former held court at Wolf Point, and the latter held court at Poplar. The courts were combined after World War I, but group loyalty dictated reestablishing two courts in 1926, one for each tribe. Some tribal residents circumvented the courts' decisions, claiming the courts lacked jursidiction over the tribesmen after Congress passed the Indian Citizenship Act of 1924.[12]

This culture of diffused politics was again evident in 1927 when the assembled tribes abolished a short-lived business committee, favoring a return to the general council.[13] The superintendent claimed that the general council's "open" forum allowed opportunistic individuals to control the tribes' political destiny and discouraged potential leaders from working for the tribes. Political agitation also affected the courts, as tribal politicans interfered "with the action of the Indian court, contending that its actions are illegal." This discontent resulted in a damage suit being filed against the tribal court.[14] The tribes' preference for the open government of the general council continued until 1960.

The Assiniboine and Sioux tribes of the Fort Peck reservation did not choose to govern themselves under the terms of the Indian Reorganization Act. In 1934 they rejected the Act and its small council form of government by a vote of 578 to 276. This choice left in force the tribes' earlier constitution of 1927, which had as its central feature general council government. In 1960 the members of the tribes on their own initiative set aside the constitution of 1927 and adopted a new fundamental law which established a system of representative government and retained some elements of direct democracy.

Former tribal chairman Norman Hollow said that the tribes' motivation for adopting a new constitution was displeasure with general council politics and lack of economic progress.[15] General council government up to 1960 permitted the entire reservation electorate to debate and legislate for the tribes. Voting for officials also took place openly on the council floor, usually following a heated campaign. The politics of the general council meeting were characterized by ill feeling between factions, character attacks, and even bodily threats. Debate over purchase of Missouri River bottomland, for example, caused a physical confrontation between tribal members.

The turmoil of the general council prevented the tribes from learning from experience and laying a foundation for economic growth. General council government was a politics of starts, stops, and reversals. Different reservation factions would control different meetings. The majority of the moment would impeach officials, remove them from office, and overturn policies adopted at prior meetings. There was hope on the reservation that the representative features and secret ballot of the 1960 constitution would bring continuity and direction to Fort Peck government.

The 1960 constitution proceeded from the people of the Fort Peck reservation and not from agents of the federal government. Its provisions continued to emphasize the tribes' traditional concern for dispersed power and direct participation. It was a significant move away from general council government, but it was not a model of separated powers and a strong executive. The structural and electoral features of the constitution placed no premium on the kind of centralized leadership which could help the tribe achieve the progress it desired.

Under the 1960 constitution, the Tribal Executive Board is the governing body of the Fort Peck reservation. The Board has twelve members plus a chairman, vice-chairman, secretary-accountant, and sergeant-at-arms. All of these officials are elected at-large, except for the secretary-accountant who is appointed by the Executive Board. Candidates for the Board file for office on a district basis; for filing purposes there are two positions in each of the six districts. All of the elected officials have two-year terms of office, which run concurrently. There is no primary election.

The constitution retains the "General Council," but it no longer is the ordinary governing body. Instead, it is designed to operate as an institutionalized initiative and referendum. The Executive Board is subject to the power of the General Council, which can initiate ordinances and reject enactments of the Executive Board within ninety days of passage. The General Council does not meet regularly but is called to order by a petition of 10 percent of the reservation electorate. Since 1960, there has been only one General Council meeting, which was used to approve a land claim payment awarded by the federal government. There was only one agenda item, and adjournment followed upon questions and answers and the vote. The constitutionally provided referendum process could have been used, but it would have taken too much time.

The by-laws of the constitution do not provide for clear separation between the Executive Board and the chairman. The duties of the chairman include serving as presiding officer of the Executive Board, providing "general and active management of the affairs of the tribes,"[16] overseeing implementation of resolutions and ordinances, providing "general supervision of all other tribal officers and employees,"[17] reporting to the Executive Board concerning tribal operations, and voting on the Executive Board "in the case of a tie only."[18] These grants of executive authority to the chairman are compromised by the Executive Board's retention of significant fiscal and personnel powers. The governing body prepares and adopts the annual budget and administers the funds under the tribes' control. The Executive Board also controls the personnel system, deciding who is hired for each job opening.[19] The constitution, therefore, creates an expectation that the chairman will be in charge of running tribal operations, but it denies him the budgetary and personnel tools needed to carry out the task effectively.

A constitution could be the source of an executive's strength, even if clear divisions and strong grants of power were not provided. Such leverage can be achieved through differences in election calendar, constituencies, and terms of office. The idea is that the executive can build up political power because the position's constituency is larger than the constituencies of councilmen or because the position's term of office is longer or overlaps the governing body's tenure. These political benefits do not accrue to the chairman under the Fort Peck constitution.

The election schedule for reservation officials places the chairman in the position of first among equals rather than of undisputed leader of the tribes. The entire reservation electorate, consisting of enrolled members over eighteen years of age, elects through secret ballot all members of the Executive Board, except for the secretary-accountant. The chairman does not have the only at-large constituency. If the chairman were elected at-large and the other Executive Board members were chosen from districts, the chairman could claim the special privilege of defining the needs and goals of the whole reservation. Also, the chairman does not gain advantage over the Executive Board because of election timing or term of office. All officials serve two-year terms and are elected at the same time. If the chairman had a four-year term, he could be senior to the Executive Board in experience and better able to influence its decisions.

As a result of the Fort Peck governmental structure, the chairman and Executive Board have had to manage the reservation government as partners. Directors of tribal programs, for example, report to both the chairman and one of the six committees of the Executive Board. A different perspective comes from a Fort Peck reservation judge who said that the Executive Board "runs everything."[20] This judgment may be true with respect to the judicial branch, as the Executive Board appoints all of the judges and has tried to influence the judges' decisions.[21] This may be why the tribal court has never reviewed actions of the Executive Board. A long-time tribal chairman, on the other hand, worked with and led the Executive Board in other areas. By relying on political tactics and not just on constitutional grants of authority, he accumulated sufficient power to move the tribes toward the economic growth they desired.

The achievements of this chairman, Norman Hollow, were in spite of pressures for favoritism and the constitution's failure to underwrite a strong executive office. Most importantly, he understood the centrifugal nature of reservation politics and the obstacles to centralized government, and used opportunities to forge alliances with which he could lead the tribes. Serving as the reservation's executive officer from 1973 to 1985, Chairman Hollow constructed a base of power which was not formally defined but stemmed from his personal strengths, managerial style, and program successes.

As a perceptive politician, Norman Hollow realized that his accomplishments depended upon the backing of others. This support was not automatic but cultivated by him over time. To secure a following he formed a political ticket and, as its leader, worked for its election. He organized campaign rallies, potluck dinners, and occasions for speeches, and he purchased radio spots for himself and those on his ticket. The chairman thereby became head of a "political party."[22] The ticket's visibility helped to win elections, especially since as many as forty candidates normally seek Executive Board positions and turnout is close to 70 percent. The chairman's strong appeal was evident in his own political success. He has served on the Executive Board for three decades and was chairman for twelve years, an amazing feat considering that some reservation elections have removed most Executive Board members. Opposition groups elected some candidates, but the chairman's political strategy made him the "dominant force"[23] on the Executive Board.

The primary reason for Chairman Norman Hollow's political success, according to his successor, was that he became a "constant force"[24] on the reservation. He rarely took vacations or left the reservation, and he declined national Indian leadership positions. He spent long days at tribal headquarters and was available to tribal members at home. In maintaining a strong presence on the reservation, the chairman demonstrated that he was a "realist regarding his power and the politics that put him there."[25]

Norman Hollow's leadership extended to fiscal matters. For many tribes, the most certain means of expanding reservation employment opportunities has been to use "638 contracts" to assume many of the functions of the Bureau of Indian Affairs. Chairman Hollow called the promise of contracting more illusory than real because the federal government's financial support always seemed to decrease once a tribal government took over a program. On the Fort Peck reservation, contracting for the law and order function was followed by substantial cuts in the federal government's share of funding. The tribes then retroceded the contract to the Bureau of Indian Affairs and became selective about what other contracts they pursued. Chairman Hollow's position was that the Bureau of Indian Affairs owed a trust responsibility to the tribes and should be made to perform to the fullest extent.[26]

Norman Hollow's leadership also influenced industrial development. As chief reservation spokesman, he advocated the tribes' economic welfare in different settings. A key reason major industry came to Fort Peck was the chairman's persistence with the Montana congressional delegation. A reason for the industry's success was his insistence in the face of popular opposition that tribal government use profits for plant expansion instead of for per capita payments.[27] So significant was the chairman's role in industrializing the reservation that the plant manager believed the chairman's departure would precipitate the industry's downfall.[28]

The same kind of advocacy was evident in other business relationships. Chairman Hollow renegotiated contracts with oil companies and boosted rental fees from $1.00 per acre to $5.00 per acre and royalty rates from 17 percent to 25 percent. Knowing how the energy companies spoke of Indians—that a few dollars and scare tactics would be sufficient to obtain an agreement—he chose to use "hard-nosed tactics" and succeeded.[29]

Chairman Hollow's aggressiveness also won results with the Bureau of Indian Affairs. He acted on his belief that the tribes have the right to approve, disapprove, and transfer a superintendent. He insisted on these prerogatives regarding a superintendent who encouraged complaints about tribal government from members and outsiders and released press statements on such sensitive matters as law enforcement and per capita payments. The chairman's position was that the superintendent's role is to work with tribal officials and not to act as an "ombudsman."[30] Norman Hollow believed that reservation politics was capable of providing accountability of tribal officials to members. This assertiveness won the right for the chairman—and not the Bureau of Indian Affairs—to be the reservation's chief spokesman.

Norman Hollow's style of leadership also was effective with white residents of the reservation and with officials of the four counties the reservation encompasses. Such liaison is important because of the significant white presence on the reservation. Of the reservation's 2.9 million acres, 56 percent are non-Indian owned, the largest degree of white ownership on any of Montana's seven reservations. The chairman's relationship with whites enhanced the tribal government's ability to carry out air quality regulation, planning and zoning, hunting regulation, and solid waste disposal. White cooperation depended upon respect for the Fort Peck government, and Norman Hollow established a reputation for being both fair and a strong advocate of tribal authority.

Most importantly, Norman Hollow's executive leadership earned the Fort Peck government a reputation for integrity. The former chairman strictly adhered to a high ethical standard and thereby gave others a model to follow: he refused to convert public property to private use in exchange for political support, even though refusal meant strengthening an opposition faction; he rejected petitions based on fraud and misrepresentation; and he refused to extend the tribes' patronage practices to tribal industries. Similarly, the contracts he made for legal assistance were with out-of-state firms to preclude favoritism and conflict of interest.

Historically, the relationship with the surrounding white community held great potential for corruption on the reservation. White influence in the past had insinuated itself into reservation politics, and Norman Hollow tried to prevent such meddling. His knowledge of these tactics was firsthand, having been offered bribes by energy firms. Company representatives perceived that payoffs were an ordinary reservation business practice, but the chairman ignored this rationalization and threats of retribution. The companies persisted and formed a relationship with a tribal faction in opposition to Norman Hollow. This "pro-development"[31] group then advocated the energy companies' cause in campaigns and benefited from the companies' influence with radio stations. The chairman's behavior was in sharp contrast to such official venality.

Another characteristic of the Fort Peck government—its sense of institutional pride—can be attributed to Norman Hollow. Despite short terms of office, turnover of officials, and a weak executive position, the former chairman's constancy enabled the Assiniboine and Sioux tribes to "get a grip"[32] on the business of governing. Because of his leadership, the atmosphere of tribal headquarters was of purposeful work, deadlines to be met, and administrative accountability. The chairman's governmental service on the Fort Peck reservation has spanned three decades. The subsequent chairman believed that Norman Hollow was the "thread from the old days to the future,"[33] embodying the evolution from the wrangling of the general council to the responsibilities of a modern government. His longevity and presence gave definition to the tribes' mission and reassurance to tribal members.

Chairman Hollow's functioning as a symbol of reservation leadership was also evident in the fact that he was the only official who consistently rose above district politics. The Fort Peck constitution calls for district filing and at-large elections, although prior to 1968 members of the Executive Board were elected from districts. Even though the six districts are no longer used for elections, they still are "very dear to a tribal member's heart; one always belongs to a district regardless of later residence."[34] The Fort Peck government had used districts to distribute claim settlements, and a district organization—chairmen, monthly meetings, appearances of Executive Board members—had been the vehicle for deciding how money would be spent. This process brought "new life to the districts"[35] and resulted in closer ties between district residents and Executive Board members. The Executive Board's resulting tendency "to move cautiously and cover all bases"[36] was in contrast to the chairman's unifying force.

Norman Hollow's final political success before his leaving office, and possibly the tribe's most historic modern achievement, was in part due to the cohesiveness he provided to the Fort Peck government. In 1985 the tribal Executive Board and the Montana Legislature ratified a government-to-government compact that clarified the water rights of the Assiniboine and Sioux tribes on the Fort Peck reservation. Most outstanding issues were settled by the compact as to tribal, state, and federal water rights administration. Future disputes arising from the compact over water rights are to be referred to a special arbitration board made up of a tribal appointee, a state appointee, and a neutral party. The Fort Peck reservation was the first of Montana's seven Indian reservations to conclude an agreement with the Montana Reserved Water Rights Compact Commission, and the five-year process involving the Fort Peck tribes was fruitful in no small part because of Chairman Hollow's trustworthiness and resolve.

Today the Fort Peck reservation is probably best known for its industrial development, the most visible achievement of Chairman Hollow's leadership. The traditional economic base of the northeastern corner of Montana, however, has been agriculture. The inland continental climate of hot summers and the presence of the Missouri River on the reservation's southern border have permitted dryland wheat farming, irrigated hay production, and cattle ranching. Approximately 98 percent of the reservation's Indian population live within nine miles of the Missouri River valley, and many have tribal assignments of two and one-half acres. One hundred and forty-four tribal members are directly engaged in the farming and ranching business. The tribes and individual members receive significant income from leasing large portions of their land to white farmers and ranchers. In 1982, for example, farming and grazing leases brought in about $900,000. But because it is difficult both to start up an agricultural operation and earn an adequate return, Norman Hollow discouraged young tribal members from farming and ranching. Instead, his highest priority was creating job opportunities through industrial development. The success of this effort could be seen in the Fort Peck reservation's 1983 unemployment rate, the lowest of Montana's seven Indian reservations. That year the Bureau of Indian Affairs reported a 33 percent rate for Fort Peck and an average rate of 55 percent for the other six reservations.

An Indian reservation generally is not seen by American businesses as a good place for investment and location. The reasons have already been discussed—pressures for per capita payments rather than reinvestment, little work experience, political instability, a culture of patronage—and Chairman Hollow's offsetting role on the Fort Peck reservation has been detailed. Because of his influence, an outsider's view of Fort Peck government must take notice today of policy continuity, competent tribal members in managerial positions, and professional planning documents and project proposals. These accomplishments are notable, but not only because they are atypical of many reservation governments. More importantly, they represent an innovative attitude toward economic development which brought jobs to the Fort Peck reservation.

Probably the most effective innovation adopted by the Fort Peck tribes in their economic development effort has been enterprise boards. Each enterprise board has full control of a tribal business. The result is that tribal politics have not intruded in the operation of tribal enterprises, which has been a major reason for failure of reservation industries elsewhere. Tribal officials are not completely excluded from business operations, however, as many enterprise board members come from the Executive Board. But enterprise board meetings are conducted by outside managers hired to run the businesses, and Chairman Hollow insured that political favoritism was excluded from personnel decisions. The chairman's philosophy was: " 'Get key people in management, and caution the tribal council not to interfere with the decision-making power of management. . . . If we don't have the skilled people, trained business managers, we must go outside the reservation to find them.' "[37] The manager of the largest industry on the Fort Peck reservation believed that the "success of the tribe-enterprise relationship is dependent on this system."[38]

The first step in bringing employers to the reservation was construction in 1968 of a forty-acre industrial park. The site was jointly funded by the tribal and federal governments, demonstrating the tribes' willingness to invest their money to secure jobs. To attract manufacturing concerns, the tribes experimented with several types of ownership and operating relationships. They entered into joint venture arrangements with private businesses, hired an outside contractor to manage a corporation wholly owned by the tribes, and became the first tribal government in the Northwest to go into the oil business on its own. Most significantly, the Fort Peck tribes have had the confidence to forego reliance on their old bargaining partner, the Bureau of Indian Affairs, and to enter directly into business negotiations with outside manufacturing industries and energy companies.

The principal enterprise on the Fort Peck reservation is A and S Tribal Industries, one of Montana's largest employers. The manufacturing concern is totally owned by the Assiniboine and Sioux tribes. In 1984 its 125,000 square-feet facility was valued at $11 million; an annual payroll of $4.5 million supported 350 employees, 80 percent of whom were Native Americans; and annual sales approached $20 million. The major contracts have been with the U.S. Department of Defense for camouflage netting, medical supply chests, and insulated food containers. The company also had a manufacturing contract with Western Electric.

A and S Tribal Industries began operation in 1968 with a minority business contract to refurbish M-1 rifles for the federal government. Its successful completion of the project paved the way for bigger undertakings. To receive the first camouflage contract in 1975, Chairman Norman Hollow argued that deadlines had been met under the rifle contract and pledged that they would be met again. To make good this promise, he conducted a three-week orientation period for employees, explaining that it was up to them to overcome negative attitudes about Indian workers. Continued employee cooperation and productivity were aided by good reservations wages (average of $5.50 per hour in 1984), one-dollar meals, a bonus system for piecemeal jobs, and posting of wages to allow comparison. Employee reluctance to leave their districts and families and travel across the reservation to the plant was overcome by low-cost bus transportation, one-half hour meal breaks to shorten the workday, and pride in the meticulous work accomplished in the plants.

Chairman Hollow was instrumental in securing the initial contract and orienting workers, but the actual management of A and S was provided by the Brunswick Corporation. Under a 1975 agreement between the tribes and Brunswick, the corporation supplied management personnel and received actual costs plus 10 percent of net profit. The plant's manager, assistant manager, controller, design engineer, and quality control engineer were professionals from outside the reservation. All department heads were tribal members who in 1984 earned approximately $25,000 annually. The contribution of the Brunswick managers has been critical to the success of A and S. They have enlisted the corporation's political influence in Washington, D.C., to win additional contracts, initiated and supervised plant expansion, secured several 900-ton presses from the federal government's surplus inventory, and moved A and S into metal fabrication work. A and S Tribal Industries would be an impossibility without the Brunswick Corporation and the tribe's leadership, which was open to experiment and willing to commit tribal funds.

A and S Products Company is another manufacturing operation which is wholly owned by the tribes. It is a plastic injection moulding business begun in 1982. The plant originally employed six workers and manufactured valves for home sewer drains. Since that time it has hired additional employees and acquired contracts to make bumper guard plates for General Motors and plastic pen barrels for the Blackfeet Indian Writing Company in Browning, Montana. The $500,000 contract with the Blackfeet tribe was believed to be the nation's first joint venture involving two tribal governments.[39]

The Assiniboine and Sioux have had other business ventures besides A and S Industries and A and S Products. The capital to start A and S Products came from a joint venture involving the tribes' A and S Construction Company and a Minnesota company to work on the Northern Border pipeline which carries natural gas across the reservation. West Electronics is a wholly owned tribal enterprise which began as a joint venture in 1970 with Multiplex Communications of

New York. The tribal firm does light electronic manufacturing for the government and private industries. Contracts were first received on a non-competitive basis because of the company's minority status, but recent projects for the Department of Defense, RCA Global Communications, Western Electric, and IBM were awarded through bid competition. The twenty employees of West Electronics have manufactured such equipment as transmitters, receivers, and dollar bill changers. Another joint venture required an initial commitment by the tribal government of $1 million. In 1975 the tribally owned Fort Peck Manufacturing Company contracted with ESCO Corporation of Portland, Oregon, to machine, heat treat, and fit parts for ESCO's earth moving and excavation equipment. The tribes provided facilities in their industrial park and employees. ESCO supplied raw materials, machinery, and production managers. The benefit to the tribes has been a fixed return based on production and jobs for about forty tribal members.

Most of the money the tribes invested to get their businesses underway came from tribal oil and gas revenue. The reservation's greatest economic potential always has been oil, and the world energy crisis precipitated by the 1973 embargo was a boon to the tribes. Soon the return from exploration leases and actual production was "pumping millions into tribal coffers."[40] Over the years the tribes have committed to lease more than 90,000 acres of reservation land, and in 1983 fourteen oil fields were in production. The yearly revenue to the Assiniboine and Sioux tribes is significant. In fiscal year 1982, the tribes' income was $9.9 million; of this total oil and gas leases accounted for $358,969 and oil and gas royalties and bonuses brought in $6.4 million. The oil and gas income allowed the tribes to invest a substantial amount after the reservation budget was set at $4.4 million. Up to 1984, the Fort Peck Indian tribes conducted their oil business through leases with private energy companies. Then, utilizing a 1982 law providing for greater tribal control over resource development, the Fort Peck government decided to invest $500,000 for drilling its own oil well. The Winona well, now producing oil, could earn the tribes $4 million.

The Fort Peck reservation has natural riches in addition to gas and oil which could be the basis of future economic development. There are estimated deposits of one billion tons of lignite coal which can be extracted by strip mining. These reserves have the potential for conversion into synthetic fuels and fertilizer. The reservation also contains geothermal resources and large quantities of non-energy resources such as potash, bentonite, salt, and sand and gravel.

Tribal economic self-sufficiency has been the goal of every Native American leader. For generations, agriculture produced inadequate results, and hope was increasingly placed in reservation industries. Off-reservation investment, however, has been slow to materialize because of fears about reservation social and political conditions. On the Fort Peck reservation, this hesitation has been overcome by skillful leadership. A longtime chairman, relying not on constitutional grants of authority but on a power base of his own creation, guided the way to economic development. The reservation has no visible business failures because this chairman was a realist. The reservation's future is promising because, with his example, the tribes built up their confidence. In the words of Norman Hollow, "'We are proof that industrialization of Indian people is possible.'"[41] This reservation success story has many explanations, but competent political leadership clearly has been the critical factor.

Notes

1. "Fort Peck: A Study in Successful Indian Enterprise," *Site Selection Handbook,* XXVIII (February, 1983), p. 129.

2. Edwin Thompson Denig, *Five Indian Tribes of the Upper Missouri,* ed. John C. Ewers (Norman: University of Oklahoma Press, 1961), pp. 3–38 and 70–97. See also David Reed Miller, "Montana Assiniboine Identity: A Cultural Account of an American Indian Ethnicity" (Ph.D. diss., Indiana University, 1987).

3. Interview with Ken Ryan, Fort Peck tribal member and Administrative Manager of the Fort Peck Agency, September 7, 1983.

4. Interview with Jacke Miller, Fort Peck tribal member and Director of Environmental Protection of the Fort Peck Reservation, September 6, 1983.

5. Interview with Lonnie Red Dog, Fort Peck tribal member and Director of Planning of the Fort Peck Reservation, September 6, 1983.

6. Interview with S. D. Morris, General Manager of A & S Enterprises, September 6, 1983.

7. *Constitution—Bylaws of the Assiniboine and Sioux Tribes of the Fort Peck Indian Reservation, Montana,* Art. X, sec. 1.

8. Interview with Norman Hollow, Chairman of the Fort Peck Reservation, September 6, 1983.

9. Interview with Norman Hollow.

10. Source requested to remain anonymous.

11. Superintendents' Annual Narrative and Statistical Report, Fort Peck, 1910, Frame 921.

12. Superintendents' Annual Narrative and Statistical Report, Fort Peck, 1926, Frames 4–5.

13. Superintendents' Annual Narrative and Statistical Report, Fort Peck, 1927, Frame 55.

14. Superintendents' Annual Narrative and Statistical Report, Fort Peck, 1930, Frame 339.

15. Interview with Norman Hollow.

16. *Fort Peck Constitution and Bylaws,* Art. XI, sec. 6.

17. Ibid.

18. Ibid.

19. Interview with Jacke Miller.

20. Interview with Arlen Headdress, Fort Peck Associate Judge, September 6, 1983.

21. Ibid.

22. Interview with Jacke Miller.

23. Ibid.

24. Interview with Ken Ryan.

25. Ibid.

26. Interview with Norman Hollow.

27. Per capita payments flowing from the successes of reservation industries may be needed after a capital base has been built to guarantee that all income groups among the tribal membership are benefited. See David L. Vinje, "Cultural Values and Economic Development on Reservations," *American Indian Policy in the Twentieth Century,* ed. Vine Deloria, Jr. (Norman: University of Oklahoma Press, 1985), p. 170.

28. Interview with S. D. Morris.

29. Interview with Norman Hollow.

30. Ibid.

31. Ibid.

32. Interview with Ken Ryan.

33. Ibid.

34. Ibid.

35. Ibid.

36. Ibid.

37. *Western Business,* June 1984.

38. Interview with S. D. Morris.

39. *Western Business,* June, 1984.

40. *Site Selection Handbook,* p. 125.

41. Ibid., p. 124.

7

The Fort Belknap Reservation:
The Reality of Poverty

About thirty-five miles south of the Canadian border in north-central Montana lies the Fort Belknap reservation. The boundaries of the reservation—twenty-five miles from east to west and forty miles from north to south—surround rising and falling plains covered by buffalo grass and sagebrush. On the northern border is the Milk River which downstream joins the Missouri. In the southern extent of the reservation are the Little Rocky Mountains, rugged and forested and reaching to a height of 5,000 feet. In between is the prairie marked by an occasional stream, frequent gullies, and here and there a dominating butte. These are the 652,000 acres of the Fort Belknap Indian Community, the Assiniboine and Gros Ventre tribes. The land is naturally cattle country, although since the mid-1960s grazing land has been broken out for farming. Agriculture, however, has provided an adequate living only for a few. Once the tribal portion of the Little Rocky Mountains contained gold, but in 1895 the federal government arranged for loss of that land through cession of a twenty-eight square-mile section. As a result, the Indian residents have had limited alternatives for their livelihood. There have been agriculture and federal programs and always the stark reality of poverty.

Fort Belknap holds few surprises. The ordinary mode of existence—a struggle to make the land yield a living—is apparent to the visitor. The reservation is small, with only Rocky Boy's and Northern Cheyenne of Montana's seven reservations being smaller. The sparse Indian population of just over 2,000 persons is lowest of all Montana reservations except for the 1,900 on Rocky Boy's. The harsh climate, a tendency toward sub-zero winters and hot, dry and windy summers, can easily make farming and grazing losing propositions. The best use of the land is its original use—grazing, and many believe that the land should never have been tilled. Less than 2 percent of Indian-held acreage is in fee patent, and of these 10,100 acres very little is non-Indian owned. The reservation has had little appeal to whites as a place of permanent residency because of its isolation and lack of access to water and transportation.

The history of the Fort Belknap reservation is a story of special protection and repeated failure.[1] In 1873, Fort Belknap was made a sub-agency of Fort Peck to serve the needs of the Gros Ventre and Assiniboine. Both tribes had been severely diminished by smallpox and were easy prey for stronger tribes, especially the Sioux. The federal government's action was an attempt to protect two weak tribes from powerful neighbors. The agency was established in the north portion near the Milk River by statute in 1882, and members of both tribes were assigned plots of ten acres in the river valley. In January 1887, an agreement between a United States negotiating commission and the Indians of northern Montana set out the boundaries of the Fort Belknap reservation.

During the late nineteenth century and early twentieth century, irrigation became the most important project of the reservation agent because of the general belief that the tribes' welfare was linked to farming. Irrigation plans were premised on an important U.S. Supreme Court ruling of 1908, *Winters v. United States.*[2] That decision recognized significant water rights of the Fort Belknap tribes and came to be the "foundation of all Indian water law."[3] At issue were the conflicting claims of the tribes and off-reservation white farmers to the water of the Milk River, the northern boundary of the reservation. The Supreme Court agreed with the United States government's argument on behalf of the tribes that "lands would not have been reserved for the tribes unless water had also been reserved to make the reservation productive."[4] Reserved Indian water rights, or "*Winters* rights," therefore, are created by implication at the time a reservation is established. Subsequent cases have determined them to be equal to "that amount sufficient to irrigate all the practicably irrigable acreage of [a] reservation,"[5] when it was expected that Indians would develop agrarian economies.

By 1909 the Fort Belknap superintendent could optimistically write:

> As the system stands . . . it is capable of handling all of the irrigable lands upon the Milk River within the confines of the reservation, and for such it was constructed. We have our own dam and headgate, a main canal twenty-two miles long, with an approximate carrying capacity of 5,000 inches; we have a system of spreading laterals from the main canal that distributes the water over practically 24,000 acres of land.[6]

The next year, however, a report on the tribes' condition found that no progress had been made toward self-sufficiency. "Most of the Indians," the analysis found, "lived in poverty, misery and near starvation."[7]

The 1887 allotment policy of the federal government was another program aimed at achieving self-sufficient Indian agriculturalists on small land holdings. Its application on the Fort Belknap reservation was delayed as a result of federal promises in 1895 to defer allotment until it was requested by a majority of adult male members of the tribes. After the Fort Belknap reservation was allotted in 1921, most Indians decided to lease their land instead of using it for farming or grazing. Only a few allottees were knowledgeable enough and had sufficiently good land to make it the basis of a living. The result was that by 1925, almost all of the allotted land was leased to large white ranching interests. The income from the leasing permits, like the land itself, was not enough to support a family.

Some years later, special studies by the Department of the Interior and the U.S. Congress again pointed to the difficult job of eradicating poverty on the Fort Belknap reservation. The Preston-Engle Report of 1928 emphasized the "problems and failure of irrigation."[8] The next year a congressional committee held hearings on the reservation and presented its findings in the 1932 Liggett Report. The conclusions were that the "majority of Indians lived in a semidestitute state"[9] and that the irrigation system was serving fewer than one dozen residents. The congressional report was so critical of the reservation's farming potential that cattle raising came to be the new focus for bettering the Indians' economic situation. But the cattle industry also could know hardship, and in the early 1930s dry weather and the depression wiped out tribal livestock ventures.

In the years since enactment of the Indian Reorganization Act, the Assiniboine and Gros Ventre tribes have experimented with many approaches to economic development, but most have failed. Six leases with energy companies opened up 2,200 acres to oil exploration, but there is yet to be a producing well. The reservation has large bentonite, limestone, and low-grade coal deposits, but lack of demand precludes development. Nothing has resulted from attempts to secure Urban Development Action Grants from the federal government and to work through an economic development association in northern Montana. Attempts to relocate industry to the reservation have been equally futile, one opportunity being lost because the tribes did not have $10,000 for engineering assistance for rehabilitating a reservation building.

Today Fort Belknap is the poorest of Montana's seven Indian reservations, being "virtually undeveloped in every aspect."[10] In 1983, the median income for tribal members over sixteen years of age was $4,859, the lowest of all Montana reservations. The unemployment rate in September of that year exceeded 70 percent. Less than 20 percent of Fort Belknap Indians have completed high school. And in 1979, over 68 percent of the reservation inhabitants were below the federal poverty level. All of these statistics were the worst figures for Montana reservations. The reality is that members of the Fort Belknap Indian Community continue to be "heavily dependent upon federally subsidized programs"[11] and that federal assistance is the only certain route to self-sufficiency. The irony of this situation is not lost on one tribal official who observes, "we can be as self-determining as federal dollars allow us to be."[12]

Poverty is the dominant feature of life on the Fort Belknap reservation today. Its pervasiveness creates a commonality which has helped to obliterate differences between the Assiniboine and Gros Ventre tribes.[13] For decades, the tribes' relationship was characterized by tension stemming from different orientations. During the late 1800s, the Assiniboine were culturally conservative, shunning Christianity, intermarriage with whites, and white ideas and ways of doing things. The Gros Ventres, on the other hand, were open to contact with whites. As a result, the Gros Ventres were mostly Catholic, and many Gros Ventre women married white men. Their descendants, Gros Ventre mixed bloods, became involved in political conflict with Assiniboine residents in the early twentieth century. Reservation full-bloods, mainly Assiniboine, opposed allotment of land under the Dawes Act and secured delay of its implementation at Fort Belknap. Backing the agency superintendent and working for allotment were mixed blood families, mostly Gros Ventres, some of whom were prosperous farmers on irrigated lands. The Gros Ventres believed that the value of their tracts would be enhanced through allotment and tended to be insulted by the prospect of continued federal paternalism, while the Assiniboine held to notions of tribalism and wanted to preserve an unfenced reservation.

For years the two tribes lived separately at Fort Belknap, first in camps along the Milk River and then in different reservation communities. The western portion of the reservation, and especially Hays and St. Paul's, were Gros Ventre settlements, and Lodge Pole and the eastern section of the reservation were inhabited by Assiniboines. From the mid-1960s, most new housing was built near the agency in the "river district," and a large movement to the north of both Gros Ventres and Assiniboines has occurred. Population shifts and marriage between the tribes have progressively erased tribal differences. Much of the old tribal languages has been lost, and a "new tribe is developing—a Fort

Belknap tribe."[14] The Fort Belknap government keeps three membership rolls: a Gros Ventre roll, an Assiniboine roll, and a community roll. The young increasingly are being enrolled as "community" members.

Progressive assimilation has had an effect on reservation politics. It is rare today when an issue affects only one tribe or splits the tribes, an exception being distribution of settlement money from one tribe's land claims. The principal problem facing the Fort Belknap reservation is unemployment, and the common concern is for the tribal government to increase the number of jobs. In past years an "escape" from poverty on the reservation was to discuss mostly imaginary but "hoped-for settlements of claims against the government."[15] Today tribal officials dream of large infusions of federal money or the success of a plan for major economic development.

The government of Fort Belknap is not well designed for the task of moving its residents from poverty to prosperity. Fort Belknap is an Indian Reorganization Act reservation. The Assiniboine and Gros Ventre tribes in 1934 agreed to be governed under that federal enactment by a vote of 371 to 50. The IRA constitution was approved in 1935. There is nothing in the constitution to promote strong leadership, probably because the "legal detail"[16] of the document was supplied by the Bureau of Indian Affairs.

The Bureau's desire to run things on the Fort Belknap reservation and to discourage Indian political initiative has a long tradition. In 1904, the superintendent organized a tribal council of elected members representing four districts (Lodge Pole, Hays, Savoy, and the Agency). Although the superintendent's creation "smoothed [his] way politically and gave a semblance of popular support to his decisions," he disbanded the council because he found it to be "an element of disturbance."[17] In 1919, the reservation superintendent encouraged council intervention in the Court of Indian Offenses by making the combined Assiniboine and Gros Ventres business committees the court's jury.[18] Two years later the superintendent established another tribal council over which he presided. The council had twelve members, six Assiniboines and six Gros Ventres, elected from three districts (Lodge Pole, Hays, and Milk River) in proportion to tribal populations. The superintendent thought that the council would be a way of overcoming intertribal factionalism stemming from the allotment dispute. More importantly, as a new superintendent he wanted some method of gaining the "confidence of the people," and the council's proceedings would provide him with "Indian consent" for his managerial decisions.[19]

Another obstacle to cohesive self-governance at Fort Belknap, besides Bureau intrusiveness, was tribal loyalty. Three business committees, at the turn of the century, were composed of seven members who represented the River Assiniboines, the Mountain Assiniboines, and the Gros Ventres. Each tribe's representatives reflected a group loyalty,[20] and each, as previously mentioned, had a different political orientation: the Gros Ventres worked with the reservation administration while the two Assiniboine groups opposed federal officials.[21] This group allegiance also affected police operations, as members of one tribe often received better treatment than members of the other tribe.[22] A start at overcoming narrow loyalties occurred in 1929 when the tribes organized a twelve-member business committee. Even though the committee members were elected separately by the two tribes, "progressive" tribal members served as representatives and were "wide awake to those things which will be of most benefit" to the community.[23] A single tribal court accompanied the more unified business committee.[24] After the tribes accepted the Indian Reorganization Act, they maintained the reservation-wide council.

Department of the Interior lawyers drafting the Fort Belknap constitution of 1935 very likely read the reports of early twentieth century superintendents. The model of the IRA constitution appears to be more the ideas of federal Indian agents than the two tribes' traditional ideas of governance. Like the 1929 tribal council, the contemporary Fort Belknap Community Council has twelve members, of whom six must be Assiniboines and six must be Gros Ventres. These twelve positions are apportioned among Hays, Lodge Pole, and Milk River according to the population of the two tribes in each district. Council members serve four-year terms and are elected on a staggered basis. There is no district or reservation residency requirement, nor did the 1935 constitution provide for a primary election. The council from its membership chooses a president, vice-president, and secretary-treasurer, all of whom serve concurrent terms of only two years.

The Fort Belknap constitution, in a number of ways, is not truly a fundamental document—that is, reflective of the needs of residents. Some of its features are outdated and others are not descriptive of how the Fort Belknap government actually works. For example, there is little reason today for continuing the split in representation based on tribal identity.[25] The principal reason for the six-six division was that in 1935 the Gros Ventre tribe had a land claim pending and wanted to preclude the Assiniboines from using the Community Council to share in the settlement. Intermarriage has substantially eliminated tribal affiliation as an issue, but the custom of quota representation persists.

Districts also have ceased to have much political significance. The lack of residency requirements has allowed off-reservation tribal members to file for the council. Their absence from the reservation has not prevented them from being competitive candidates. District filing theoretically ties a councilman to local interests, but election realities have worked against such a relationship. The population shift to the north means that a close election is won only by carrying all three districts, and, as a result, councilmen do not speak for the districts in which they filed. The constitution also provides for the establishment of district councils, but limited experience with them was unsatisfactory and they are not now in existence.

The Fort Belknap constitution's provisions for the executive office do not accurately depict how that function is carried out. The president's stated duties are to preside over council meetings, appoint standing committees, "direct the work"[26] of the other offices, and "perform any and all duties devolving upon his office."[27] There exists by ordinance, however, an executive committee which exercises "shared leadership."[28] The executive committee is comprised of the president, the vice-president, and the secretary-treasurer, and has taken over such powers as setting the council's agenda, regulating salary levels, formulating the budget, and overseeing fiscal affairs. The president consults with the other two officers "as much as possible."[29] Even though final action rests with the whole council, the reality is that the executive committee "runs things."[30]

The position of president also has been diminished by the role of the administrative manager and the political strength of the vice-president. Department heads have reported to the manager, whose principal duties are to "oversee the operation of tribal programs, keep the government out of trouble with federal auditors, and keep the executive committee and council informed."[31] Tribal members and employees have gone more to the vice-president than the president with problems and complaints. In 1983 a Bureau of Indian Affairs official on the reservation said that the president "thinks he runs things, but he doesn't."[32] Asked what the president's main job is, the tribe's secretary-treasurer said that it is "hard to say."[33]

Another weakness of the Fort Belknap constitution is its silence about the Gros Ventre and Assiniboine treaty committees, which have a critical governmental function. The impetus for the treaty committees was a 1935 award by the U.S. Court of Claims to the Fort Belknap Gros Ventre tribe. The Gros Ventres argued that the court's judgment should benefit Gros Ventres alone and was proof that Fort Belknap belonged solely to them. The Gros Ventres backed away from this extreme position, which would have excluded the Assiniboines from the reservation, when the Interior Department included language in the Fort Belknap corporate charter providing for the treaty committees. The purpose of these bodies was to exercise separate and total control over implementation of each tribe's treaty affairs and claims settlements.

Only these money payments have sharply divided the Gros Ventre and Assiniboine tribes.[34]

The treaty committees' strength today has its roots in the early 1970s when both tribes received settlements for land claims. The treaty committees and not the tribal council had been spokesmen for the tribes and pushed for the claims. After the settlements were received from the federal government, the treaty committees decided how their respective tribal members would share in the money. Ordinarily, investment and expenditure decisions were reached after per capita payments were made.

Additional claims settlements have further strengthened the treaty committees. Even though they have no foundation in the tribal constitution, the treaty committees have come to overshadow the Community Council in important matters. For example, the Fort Belknap government has never authorized a per capita payment out of tribal revenue, but in recent years per capita payments of between $900 and $3,500 have flowed from actions of the two treaty committees. The committees meet regularly and operate "without clear rules."[35] Their continuing agenda is to decide how to use the 20 percent of the claims' settlements which the federal government requires to be invested and programmed. The treaty committees thereby control the only discretionary money on the reservation. Not only has this basic function of a governing body been denied to the council, but the council has "no control"[36] of the treaty committees.

Finally, the weakness of the Fort Belknap constitution is seen in its failure to establish directly the tribal court and provide for its independence. The court is established by ordinance, and the judges have realized that what the council creates it can abolish. The judges' sense of political vulnerability is increased by their appointment to office by the council. The court also is dependent on the council for financial support. While some of the court's funding comes from a contract with the Bureau of Indian Affairs, this share has progressively shrunk. Because of the declining budget, the council appointed for a long time only a chief judge of an authorized three-judge bench. The tribal council, therefore, has not provided for judicial independence, and over the years council members have pressured judges to dispose of a matter one way or another.[37]

The Fort Belknap court, however, has overcome its precarious status and is probably stronger than either the council or the president. Because of the chief judge's popularity, more than thirty years on the tribal bench, and "firm stand,"[38] the Fort Belknap court has experienced "less pressure than courts of other reservations."[39] The chief judge has gained the trust and backing of tribal members through his accessibility and flexibility. He makes himself available to tribal members day and night, and he has been willing to provide general legal advice and serve as a family counselor. He has listened to tribal members seeking redress for wrongs committed by the tribal government, and he has taken jurisdiction of election disputes and the composition of treaty committees. His approach has been more "common sense"[40] than application of traditional customs ("Who the hell knows what's tradition and custom anymore," he says[41]). The chief judge has gained for the court a degree of acceptance and influence usually absent on reservations. This accomplishment is all the more significant because the reservation's constitution almost totally ignores the court.

One reason the Fort Belknap community hangs onto ways of governing that have outlived their usefulness is the absence of political leadership on the reservation. Pervasive poverty and a resulting distrust of officials have kept tribal members from reforming their constitution to encourage the emergence of a leader. Tribal members also have been unwilling to nurture a leader under the present constitutional system. The absence of a strong leader has precluded vigorous debate, policy planning, and bold action on the reservation.

In the early 1980s, the president's office provided no leadership because of the position's design and the weakness of the incumbent. Because a president is chosen by and from the council every two years, and one-half of the council seats are up for election every two years, it is difficult for an incumbent to establish a power base. A president also may not possess the necessary political skills for turning the weak office into a position of strength. In 1983, for example, the president was politically insecure, not knowledgeable of policy matters, and viewed by his political peers more with amusement than respect. That president also was exceptionally passive, unable to identify the goals of his administration and waiting for the council to supply him with a job description.

The president's weaknesses are probably no greater than the weaknesses of the council. That body is not a source of leadership because six of its members face election every two years. The usual result is a split between a "new council" and an "old council" and no unity or continuity.[42] The observation of the tribal judge is that the council has been dominated by individuals who are uneducated and unprofessional, frequently seeking office because "they can't run a ranch or do other things."[43] Given its low level of competence, the council tends to concern itself with minor matters instead of long-range plans. Its approach to unemployment is to make each hiring decision a major issue—not wanting to say "no" to any of the forty to eighty applicants for an unskilled position.

Although filling jobs is one of the few ways the council can help an individual, council members have numerous opportunities for helping themselves. They receive $120 for each regular and special meeting, $75 for each committee meeting, and compensation for travel on the reservation. Only the three constitutional officers draw a full-time salary. The Council has one scheduled meeting a month, but special meetings are frequently called "by the president or by any four members of the council."[44] The council has four committees (credit, enrollment, land, and law and order) of six members each, which meet frequently. Each council member sits on two committees. According to a former tribal president, council and committee meetings have come to be devices for increasing pay and have put a severe strain on the tribal budget.[45]

Because of such practices, it is not surprising that the prevailing attitude on the reservation toward tribal government is not confidence in leadership but lack of trust. This political culture is the result of widespread want and politics being the principal avenue of material advancement. For years residents have seen how councilmen "corrupted democratic self-government" by favoritism—helping their constituents and increasing their own popularity by treating welfare and loan programs as per capita payments.[46] The treaty committees also have been highly suspect, especially in the past when they debated whether the blood quantum for per capita payments should be one-fourth or one-eighth.

The reaction of tribal members has been a desire to keep their leaders on a tight leash. This suspicion is obvious in continuing short terms of office, staggered elections, a large council, and a weak executive. High voter turnout and a large number of candidates also are indicators of members' concern. In 1981 there was a reservation turnout of 58 percent and an average of eight candidates for each position; in 1983 each opening attracted an average of seven candidates. The voters' watchfulness also is seen in their habit of cleaning house. Almost every election results in six new council members. Another example of the residents' suspicion of politics is their refusal to support a ticket of candidates. A former tribal president believes that the basic disposition of Fort Belknap voters has been to "vote to build in conflicting factions, that is, to vote out of a basic distrust of government and officials."[47]

The prospect of the Fort Belknap reservation moving beyond this politics of distrust is not good. The ordinary reform methods for achieving leadership in government have little popular support. The probability of a strong leader emerging from the present government and taking control of affairs is also slight. The Bureau of Indian Affairs seems to be more interested in obstructing tribal government than filling the leadership vacuum. And, the potential for economic development is no more promising than in the past.

An amendment to the Fort Belknap constitution could redesign the government so that an independently elected president might become a policy leader and tribal spokesman. The formal amendment process, however, has proven ineffective. A council resolution or a petition by one-third of the electorate can place a proposal on the ballot, but ratification of the amendment requires a turnout of 30 percent of qualified voters. This is extremely difficult to achieve because of the large number of off-reservation voters, who generally do not vote. As a result, would-be reformers have had to turn to other procedures.

In 1979 and again in 1981, the Fort Belknap Community Council attempted to use a "secretarial election" to reform tribal government. The proposed changes in both instances would have been lowering the voting age from twenty-one to eighteen and reducing the council from twelve members to seven, with three councilmen representing each tribe and the chairman being elected at-large. The process of a secretarial election calls for the tribal council to schedule the election to change the constitution and the Interior Department to supervise the voting. For each such election there is a separate registration, and a turnout of 30 percent of these registrants is necessary for change to occur. Because of administrative error and insufficient turnout, the ballots were not counted in either Fort Belknap secretarial election. In 1979, the proposition erroneously provided for four-year council terms instead of two-year terms. In 1981, the Bureau of Indian Affairs declared that a 30 percent turnout of the specially registered voters had not been achieved. Even an extraordinary process, therefore, failed to bring about reform on the reservation.

The next time the Fort Belknap council attempted to change the government it used an even more unusual approach—one arguably unconstitutional. In 1983, the council enacted an ordinance to require an at-large primary election. The problem the measure addressed was real, and the desirable addition of a primary election had been discussed for years. With one election to choose a councilman from seven or eight candidates, the winner normally had not received majority support. The 1983 ordinance provided for a preliminary election with the top three vote getters in each race advancing to the final election. The argument against the primary election has been on legal and not policy grounds. The Fort Belknap constitution authorizes only one election, and the council is not granted ordinance-making power to revise the election process. The council's resort to an ordinance for changing the constitutionally prescribed election system points to the difficulty of bringing about governmental reform on the Fort Belknap reservation.

A more basic obstacle to change at Fort Belknap has been the attitude of tribal members and the council. Although the ballots for the two secretarial elections were never counted, there is widespread belief on the reservation that voters were overwhelmingly against the substance of the reforms. One analysis is that the tribal membership would never support a reduction in council size, even though the budget cannot presently support twelve members, because a smaller council would lead to too much concentration of power and opportunity for "officials to better themselves."[48] Other interpretations of voter opposition turn on the proposed at-large council chairman and the potential voting majority of four this change could produce. Some suggest that Fort Belknap voters rejected a strong president because of their fear of "dictator"[49] tendencies, and others say that the seven-councilmen plan was opposed because it would have allowed either the Assiniboine or Gros Ventre tribe to dominate the council.[50]

The council has been as status-quo oriented as the reservation population. Its reputation is of a conservative body, unwilling to participate in political controversy. For example, the Fort Belknap constitution requires the council to submit to referendum upon the request of one hundred community members any "matter of great importance"[51] voted upon by the council. In the past enough signatures have been gathered, "but the council has never acted upon"[52] a petition. Instead, councilmen "have read the constitution as they want, ignoring the mandatory language."[53] The irony is that the council, amidst substantial poverty, seems to be opposed to anything that suggests change.

The council has also stood in the way of progress by denying the presidency to a leader who had been "chosen" by the electorate. An incumbent president, who had won his council seat with 80 percent voter support, was prevented from gaining a second two-year presidential term by a six-to-six council vote.[54] This president had taken office in 1976 at the age of twenty-nine. He was college educated and brought with him a well-defined philosophy of leadership and tribal government. Good leadership, he thought, meant long-range planning, consistent decision making, the ability to say "no," and a willingness to build support. His approach to government was modern tribalism. The reservation's hope, he believed, was in collective action by the tribes and not in individual ownership. Water policy, for example, should focus on tribal needs because only a few members could earn a living as entrepreneurial farmers or ranchers. As president he delegated duties to other officers and appointed strong program directors from among college acquaintances. A tribal education program, built from scratch by an Indian with a doctoral degree, had notable successes in adult education, curriculum development, and pupil aid.

Two years of progress, however, were apparently enough for the council. Opposition had mounted to the president's youth, educational background, and savior image. The basic problems were twofold. The president's vigor threatened the council's sense of being in control, and his questioning of individual ownership won the support of the young and old but alienated a middle generation, children of boarding schools and allotment. The rejection of this leadership core ("Most are still around, in and out of jobs") increased the likelihood that poverty at Fort Belknap would be abiding.

A source of change at Fort Belknap always could have been the Bureau of Indian Affairs if it had chosen to interpret its trusteeship function to include development of leadership on the reservation. Bureau officials, however, chose a different role. Tribal officials view the Bureau as an enemy instead of a helper. Their list of grievances is long. The secretary-treasurer alleges that the Bureau has withheld land ownership information, preventing tribal officials from advising members of their rights under the federal Land Consolidation Act.[55] An employee of the Fort Belknap natural resource department says that the Bureau refuses to give the tribal government mineral development information, forcing the tribe to duplicate the basic data gathering.[56] The president charges that the Bureau ignored its own procedures and the tribes' recommendation when a new superintendent was appointed.[57] The chief judge of the Fort Belknap court says that the Bureau used a pretense when it reassumed control of the law and order department and fired tribal police officers.[58]

There is agreement among tribal officials that a "communications barrier"[59] exists between the Bureau and tribal government. Their reasons are poorly trained Bureau employees, uncertainty as to the Bureau's function on the reservation, and competition with the tribal government for reservation primacy. The problem is intensified because a majority of the agency's employees are Fort Belknap tribal members who have used their position to reward friends and punish enemies.[60] One Bureau official agrees that the Bureau-tribal relationship has deteriorated badly. His conclusion is that the Bureau's purpose on the reservation has been "to hamper the tribes, not allowing them to go forward, to succeed."[61]

The future of the Fort Belknap reservation, as its past, is tied to land as well as to governmental leadership. But the adoption of fundamental land reform appears to be as unlikely as the emergence of a strong leader. Land at Fort Belknap, however, will continue to be central to reservation life. Agricultural leasing will be a significant source of tribal and individual income; land use will be the only realistic basis of economic development; and relationship to the land will continue to define the Indian experience.

The most dependable approach to economic development is a tribal farm, but this is hardly a plan for eradicating poverty. The reservation is 28 percent tribally owned and 58 percent allotted to tribal members. Of the reservation's 652,000 acres, 77 percent is used for grazing and 18 percent for crops. Both the tribal government and the Indian allottees lease most of their acreage to white operators, increasingly for farming because of the $16.00 per acre rate compared to $1.00 per acre for grazing. On the reservation there are about seventy Indian livestock operators and fifteen Indian farmers, most of whom have negligible Indian blood. The tribal farm would double the number of Indian cattlemen.

A tribal farm was begun in the 1930s on river bottom acreage. This "tribal original land" was left after allotment and reserved to the tribe.[62] Today its leasing income is the sole local support for tribal government. The tribe, through federal loans, has added to this acreage through purchases of allotments gone to fee status. On the original tribal farm, a tribal herd allowed members to enter the livestock business collectively. In the 1960s the council shut down this operation, but today the plan has support again. The grazing limit of the reservation is 18,000 head, and tribal officials want to remove the 9,000 cattle owned by non-Indians to make room for a new tribal herd.

Another economic development scheme related to agriculture has been discussed on the reservation. The tribes' water rights on the Milk River are substantial, and in the 1970s the council hired an engineering firm to study eight possible reservoir sites. The Fort Belknap government would fill a reservoir in times of high flow and irrigate tribal land or sell water to farmers in the area. Depending on the site, the project cost could be from $27 million to $70 million, and the irrigation potential would be from 9,500 acres to 25,000 acres. Funding would come from the United States government, but so far federal officials have shown no interest.

An accurate assessment of the Fort Belknap reservation comes with an understanding of the land and what it means to tribal members. Most of the land is poor, yet Fort Belknap Indians have a strong attachment to it. Over and over again, after relocation, adoption, or employment elsewhere, they have found their way back to the reservation. Some refuse to break the soil for farming, and most allottees prefer to sell their land only to other Indians or the tribal government. Not sharing in these sentiments are the reservation's "two-drop Indians,"[63] those relatively prosperous farmers of slight Indian blood who have abandoned Indian ways. The average Fort Belknap Indian, in contrast, perpetuates a sad irony—a deep love for a land that cannot pay. For this reason, Fort Belknap highlights the common experience of being a reservation Indian—a life of poverty because "only the reservation gives a feeling of belonging, only the reservation is home."[64]

Notes

1. The discussion of the early history of the Fort Belknap Reservation is taken from Edward E. Barry, *The Fort Belknap Indian Reservation: The First Hundred Years, 1855-1955* (Bozeman, Montana: Big Sky Books, 1974).

2. 207 U.S. 564.

3. William C. Canby, Jr., *American Indian Law* (St. Paul: West Publishing Company, 1981), p. 81.

4. Ibid.

5. Ibid., p. 244.

6. Barry, p. 130.

7. Ibid., p. 147.

8. Ibid., p. 194.

9. Ibid., p. 207.

10. Robert J. Swan, "Introduction" of a proposal for a grant to the Fort Belknap Reservation Department of Education (no date), p. 3.

11. Ibid.

12. Interview with Delmar "Pancho" Bigbee, Fort Belknap Natural Resources Department, September 8, 1983.

13. The discussion of tribal differences is taken from Barry and from David Rodnick, "The Fort Belknap Assiniboine of Montana" (unpublished Ph.D. dissertation, Dept. of Anthropology, University of Pennsylvania, 1938).

14. Interview with Jack Plumage, Administrative Manager of the Fort Belknap Agency and former Fort Belknap President, September 8, 1983.

15. Barry, p. 262.

16. Ibid., p. 233.

17. Ibid., p. 119.

18. Superintendents' Annual Narrative and Statistical Report, Fort Belknap, 1919, Frame 242.

19. Ibid., p. 182.

20. Superintendents' Annual Narrative and Statistical Report, Fort Belknap, 1911, Frame 48.

21. Superintendents' Annual Narrative and Statistical Report, Fort Belknap, 1914, Frame 101.

22. Superintendents' Annual Narrative and Statistical Report, Fort Belknap, 1918, Frame 180.

23. Superintendents' Annual Narrative and Statistical Report, Fort Belknap, 1928, Frame 898.

24. Superintendents' Annual Narrative and Statistical Report, Fort Belknap, 1930, Frame 945.

25. Interview with Jack Plumage.

26. *Constitution and Bylaws of the Fort Belknap Indian Community of the Fort Belknap Indian Reservation, Montana*, Art. I (Bylaws), sec. 1.

27. Ibid.

28. Interview with Henry "Prince" Brockie, President of the Fort Belknap Community Council, September 8, 1983.

29. Ibid.

30. Interview with George H. "Chub" Snell, Secretary-Treasurer of the Fort Belknap Community Council, September 7, 1983.

31. Interview with Jack Plumage.

32. Ibid.

33. Interview with George Snell.

34. Ibid.

35. Interview with Jack Plumage.

36. Ibid. The judgment that the treaty committees overshadow the Community Council is also found in Loretta Fowler, *Shared Symbols, Contested Meanings—Gros Ventre Culture and History, 1778–1984* (Ithaca: Cornell University Press, 1987), p. 121.

37. Interview with Cranston Hawley, Chief Judge of the Fort Belknap Tribal Court, September 8, 1983.

38. Ibid.

39. Ibid.

40. Ibid.

41. Ibid.

42. Interview with Jack Plumage.

43. Interview with Cranston Hawley.

44. *Constitution and Bylaws*, Art. IV (Bylaws), sec. 2.

45. Interview with Jack Plumage.

46. Barry, p. 262.

47. Interview with Jack Plumage.

48. Ibid.

49. Ibid.

50. Interview with Henry Brockie.

51. *Constitution and Bylaws*, Art. VI (Const.).

52. Interview with Jack Plumage.

53. Ibid.

54. The account of the tribal President elected in 1976 comes from the Plumage interview.

55. Interview with George Snell.

56. Interview with Delmar Bigbee.

57. Interview with Henry Brockie.

58. Interview with Cranston Hawley.

59. Interview with George Snell.

60. Interview with Delmar Bigbee.

61. Interview with Jack Plumage.

62. Interview with Delmar Bigbee.

63. Ibid.

64. Ibid.

8

The Rocky Boy's Reservation: A Struggle for Government

Of all Montana tribes, the Chippewa and Cree Indians of the Rocky Boy's reservation have made least progress in the return journey from forced dependency to the practice of self-government. There are a number of reasons for this lack of political development. The Chippewa and Cree did not share in the self-definition and pride which derive from a reservation being a traditional homeland. Rocky Boy's is a modern afterthought to the period of reservation making. It served as a collecting place for landless Indians who were viewed as nuisances to white communities and other tribes. These Indians, principally the Chippewa and Cree, looked to better times when they constituted themselves one people, "The Chippewa Cree Tribe."[1] Additionally, the Rocky Boy's reservation is chronically poor. Even though it has fewest residents of any reservation in Montana, it is overpopulated. Only a small percentage of tribal members can make a living by grazing cattle, the reservation's one dependable economic pursuit. Finally, the reservation's dearth of natural resource wealth and out-migration of human talent often make the public life of Rocky Boy's an approximation of government. It is the striving against these tremendous odds—a twentieth century attempt to create a tribe, a homeland, and a government in an impoverished setting—that characterizes the politics of Rocky Boy's reservation.

It was not until the last decades of the nineteenth century that the Chippewa and Cree came to Montana as permanent residents.[2] They were not native to the area, being refugees of major historical occurrences elsewhere. A band of Chippewas under the leadership of Rocky Boy (his name was Stone Child in his own language) was part of an Indian movement westward from Minnesota in the 1880s to escape confinement on reservations. During the same period, the Cree chief Little Bear led several bands of Indians into Montana from Western

133

Canada to avoid punishment after Louis Riel's unsuccessful 1885 rebellion against the Canadian government.[3] Some time after 1890, the two leaders combined their followers into a wandering group of landless Indians. They periodically moved their camp to the outskirts of different Montana cities and were heavily dependent on the charity of those communities. Their total number was under five hundred.

For twenty-five years, into the second decade of the twentieth century, the homeless Chippewa and Cree moved about the state and raised the anger more than the compassion of both Indians and whites. Proposals to locate the Chippewa and Cree on the Flathead, Blackfeet, and Fort Belknap reservations met strong resistance,[4] but slowly support grew to create a permanent settlement at the abandoned Fort Assiniboine south of Havre, Montana. This effort was motivated by dislike of the Indians' homeless and destitute state and not by the suitability of Fort Assiniboine for providing a living based on agriculture. Collected in one place, the Chippewa and Cree could more easily receive rations from the federal government and be kept from the sight and consciousness of disturbed Montanans.

On September 7, 1916, several months after Rocky Boy's death, the combined action of the United States Congress and President Woodrow Wilson created a reservation for the Montana Chippewa and Cree. Rocky Boy's reservation was originally 55,040 acres carved out of Fort Assiniboine. From an agricultural perspective, it was the "least desirable land"[5] on the military reserve. The same act of Congress gave the city of Havre creek bottomland for an 8,880 acre park. The variety and charm of the reservation terrain belie its inutility. The grass-covered plains in the north gradually turn into twisting ravines and brush-covered hills. Then, on the southern boundary, the Bear Paw Mountains with canyons, pine forests, and peaks of over 5,000 feet present a vivid contrast to the flat prairie and twisting gullies. A rural tranquility is created, especially in the reservation's middle section, by roads winding among the hills and home sites with corrals. But rainfall is sparse, the creeks have insufficient flow for much project irrigation, and two and one-half acres of range land are needed to support one cow.

It is somewhat symbolic that the reservation's location is not far from the site where the Nez Perce leader, Chief Joseph, bravely but futilely fought off pursuing soldiers in 1877. The Chippewa and Cree have been conducting an economic "last stand"[6] on the Rocky Boy's reservation, never rising above a state of complete federal dependency. The root cause of the Indians' abject poverty has been their population in relation to reservation size. In 1917, the Indian Office officially set the tribal enrollment at 425 on the reservation of approximately 55,000 acres. The absence of good farming land and the limited grazing opportunities because of large acreage requirements caused Rocky Boy's in 1924 to be "perhaps the poorest of any reservation in the United States."[7] In time land was added to the reservation, but the Department of the Interior continued to view Rocky Boy's as a refuge for landless Indians. By the late 1940s, the reservation had increased by 45,523 acres, but the tribes had been forced to accept 414 additional Indian residents. In 1946, there were 250 families (about 1,000 persons) at Rocky Boy's, and the "reservation could only support 20 percent of its population."[8] In 1949, the Bureau of Indian Affairs estimated that the resources of the reservation could "provide a reasonable standard of living for 30 families."[9] More recently, prospects for a good life on this reservation of 108,000 acres (the smallest in Montana) and a population grown to 1,900 have been no better.

Today the Rocky Boy's reservation is an isolated Indian community of profound deprivation.[10] Located in rural, northcentral Montana, the Rocky Boy's Indians are far removed from major employment centers. The harsh winter storms sweeping down from Canada further isolate them from jobs and urban amenities. In 1983, unemployment averaged 73 percent and "virtually all available jobs"[11] were tied to the federal government. In late 1983, there were 350 separate welfare cases being administered by the general assistance agency. The resulting federal dependency is no different than in the days of rations, and the effects are the same. In the matter of politics, it has been difficult to take the business of governing seriously when the realistic agenda of what reservation government can accomplish is so short. There has been little change from the mid 1930s. Then the government of the Chippewa and Cree

> . . . without control over the reservation's finances took on the character of a charade and, much like the student government of a public school, provided a forum for participation, but was recognized as not truly important in the real world.[12]

This bleak assessment of Rocky Boy's early IRA government could be applied just as well to attempts at early reservation government. The scarcity of governance caused one superintendent in 1917 to request a Business Committee to "help in the proper discharge of my official duties, provided that the personnel include the most reliable and intelligent" tribal members.[13] The superintendent also found it necessary to create and control the reservation Court of Indian Offenses. He appointed the tribal judge, made the complaints, and furnished the evidence while the tribal police arrested the offender.[14] The next year reservation residents organized a business council, but the superintendent claimed that "the conclusions of their councils have been a hindrance, . . . probably from the fact that they did not understand the exact line of their duties."[15]

Six years later the formerly active Business Committee lapsed into disuse. The superintendent expressed no remorse, calling it "a hindrance" to reservation operations.[16] Yet, the superintendent wanted a tribal organization to help him administer reservation affairs, provided that he could control the council members.[17] The tribe formed a second council composed of thirteen members, but, to the probable delight of the superintendent, the representatives were not popularly elected.[18] Several years later the tribal population accepted the Indian Reorganization Act and adopted a new constitution.

Blame for the shortcomings of the Rocky Boy's government cannot be attributed to the IRA tribal constitution. The "buckskin book," as tribal officials refer to their constitution, is in many ways a strong document which could serve as a model for other reservations. The governmental principles which are central to the constitution include separation of powers, accountability, continuity, fundamental rights, and popular participation. Although the Rocky Boy's constitution contains some serious weaknesses, as a paper document it is one of the strongest constitutions of the Montana reservations.

The constitution creates the expectation that the three branches of tribal government—council, chairman, and court—will be independent and separate from each other. The reservation electorate, which is comprised of tribal members of at least eighteen years of age, choose on an at-large basis the eight members of the governing body which is called the Business Committee. The entire electorate also votes for the tribal chairman, and candidates file specifically for that position. The Business Committee, therefore, does not select the chairman from among its members. This principle of separation is also maintained for the judiciary. A separate "Judicial Branch" article,[19] added to the constitution by amendment in 1972, mandates the establishment of a three-judge tribal court and an appellate tribunal. The trial judges are elected by the tribal members, not appointed by the council. The jurisdiction of the court extends to enforcing tribal ordinances and administering justice.

The election system, with some drawbacks, in theory provides for a considerable amount of accountability and continuity. The electorate chooses the chairman for a four-year term, and no other executive official is elected. Responsibility for leading the council and guiding the government arguably is thereby assigned, and the tribal members have the means of rewarding or punishing an incumbent chairman seeking another term. Four-year terms for members of the Business

Committee, as for the chairman, provide sufficient time for gaining experience and making informed and useful contributions. The provision of a primary election also enhances accountability as it guarantees that each elected official is chosen with majority support. Continuity of service on the council, and thus a constant reservoir of experience, is assured by the requirement of staggered elections. One weakness of the constitution is that this provision for bridging the service of officials is not extended to the court. All three tribal judges serve four-year, concurrent terms.

Another strong feature of the Rocky Boy's constitution is its recognition of the rights of tribal members. The importance of political involvement is reflected in many sections. A separate article, "Popular Participation in Government,"[20] requires the Business Committee to keep its regular monthly meetings open to the public. The council is also mandated to put its official enactments into writing and to post these ordinances and resolutions in public places. The constitution, in addition, provides for such vehicles of direct democracy as recall of elected officials, popular referendum on any proposed or enacted ordinance or resolution, and petitioned initiative of a constitutional amendment. Some drawbacks of these provisions are that the open meeting requirement does not apply to special meetings, the popular referendum requires a turnout of three-fourths of the registered voters (the turnout for the 1982 tribal election was 58 percent), and the signature requirement for an amendment initiative is two-thirds of the reservation electorate. The Rocky Boy's constitution protects individual rights in another important way besides providing for various modes of political participation. Article XI, "Rights of Members," lists all of the fundamental rights found in the federal Indian Civil Rights Act of 1968 and asserts that they cannot be abridged by the tribe's powers of self-government.

Despite possession of a relatively sound fundamental document, the government of the Rocky Boy's reservation lacks the constitution's high-minded tone and seriousness of purpose. There are several possible explanations for this incongruity. The simplest answer is that the government's weaknesses are due to the deficiences of the incumbent officials and not of the structure. Another explanation is the principal defect of the constitution itself, namely its failure to specify the chairman's duties and to distinguish these responsibilities from those of the Business Committee. Whatever the reason, the fact remains that the "buckskin book" of the Rocky Boy's reservation has not brought about the respect that was so much desired by the Chippewa and Cree. In 1934, tribal members accepted the terms of the Indian Reorganization Act almost unanimously, hoping that federal recognition of their constitution would dispel the common perception of them as Canadian exiles and impoverished drifters. The tragedy is, however, that the promise of the governmental plan in the IRA constitution has not been realized on the reservation.

The headquarters of the Rocky Boy's government are located in unassuming frame structures scattered about a hilly part of the middle reservation. Until 1988 the tribal offices were in a converted house, and council chambers were an ordinary meeting room in the basement. The superintendent and his staff are found in a military-looking barracks set on a hillside back down the reservation road. These government buildings were the most modest and least serviceable of the seven Montana reservations.

The Business Committee is the government of the reservation. There is general agreement that the success and failure of tribal operations stem from the Business Committee's strengths and weaknesses.[21] The governing task is especially formidable because the reservation's poverty accents the longstanding divisions within the tribe. Intense factionalism prevents the emergence of a true community spirit and promotes fragmentation on the tribal council.

The political tensions on the Rocky Boy's reservation have many sources. Some conflicts are old and some are more recent; some are reinforcing and some are off-setting. The oldest cause of factionalism is the rivalry between the Chippewa and Cree, grounded in the struggle between Rocky Boy and Little Bear for control of the confederated bands and influence with the federal government. Intermarriage, however, has substantially eliminated this intertribal source of contentiousness. Later, bitter feelings arose between original residents of Rocky Boy's and latecomers, landless Indians whom the federal government crowded onto the small reservation. For fifty years this divisiveness has persisted, and today its principal manifestation is bad feelings between those with land assignments and those without. There are other ties to the past which can be the basis of contemporary division among Rocky Boy's Indians. Political appeals are made to family and band membership and to district residency, even though election by districts has not been used since 1972. Today, however, the most significant lines of separation are based on recent developments. For example, older Indians tend to reject the ambitious and often reform-minded young, especially if the youths are educated, returning to the reservation after an absence, and seeking land assignments and the few positions which carry prestige, influence, and a salary.[22]

This factionalism has rendered the Business Committee, with its eight councilmen organized into two-person sub-committees, an ineffective governing body. The council has taken the tribal government, split it into eight parts, and handed over each piece to several individuals to control. The Business Committee's resulting mode of operation has been governance through blocs, nepotism, and political favoritism. The result has been frequent use of political power for selfish purposes and governmental drift.

One example of the council's weakness was its long inability to accomplish the important process of recodification. The reservation government was forced to use a 1958 code which was outdated and incomplete. It did not adequately address such topics as natural resource regulation, probate, juvenile delinquency, drug use, child welfare, and traffic control on reservation roads. Much of the 1958 code was compiled by way of reference to prior enactments, and those earlier measures were not readily acccessible.[23] For almost three decades after 1958 the council enacted only a handful of ordinances, ignoring such problems as improper hunting, fishing, and wood cutting practices. The result was that the Business Committee did not give officials and residents needed policy leadership. The legislative branch seemed more concerned with day-to-day administration than elementary lawmaking. Finally a persistent code revision committee, comprised of tribal officials and lay representatives, convinced the Business Committee to adopt a comprehensive tribal code in 1987.[24]

Because of the council's preoccupation with the detail of program operation, the tribal chairman does not function as a chief executive. Similar to the workings of a county commission or a weak mayor-council system, the council's eight committees—economic development, natural resources, health, housing, welfare, law and order, education, and tribal farm—exercise close supervision of tribal programs or actually control their operation.[25] The administrative reporting system is from program director to committee members and not to the chairman. When tribal members have a request of a tribal program, they seek the assistance of a member of the Business Committee and not the chairman. The appeals route of a complainant is from the program director to the Business Committee and then to the agency superintendent, bypassing altogether the chairman.

This system of fragmented administration has not served the Rocky Boy's reservation well. A repeated finding of federal auditors, according to an agency superintendent, is that tribal programs have "too many bosses."[26] Some results of this administrative splintering and ambiguity have been poor communication among officials, governmental delay and inactivity, and more seriously, appointment of incompetent managers. With administrative responsibilities spread among council members, council cliques have deferred to each other and patronage practices have become acceptable.[27] A Rocky Boy's tribal judge has charged that an even more disastrous result of fragmented control has been "neglect of duty" and "gross misconduct" by officials.[28] For example, "time and again"[29] there has been personal use of program funds, and "over and over again"[30] the reaction of the Business Committee has been to ignore the impropriety.

Political remedies for these problems do not appear to be at hand. Elections seem to "solve nothing" as the same individuals or caliber of officials are returned repeatedly to the council.[31] For example, a chairman was retained for eight years, according to a Rocky Boy's judge, because the reservation electorate preferred a candidate "too dumb to steal" over an opponent with a reputation for being "dishonest."[32] The constitution's removal provision also has been of no utility because the council has lacked the courage to act. The judgment of one tribal official on the effectiveness and prospects of the Rocky Boy's system of government is, "it's just not working . . . I have given up."[33]

Given the strong judiciary article in the Rocky Boy's constitution, the tribal court conceivably could have been and still could be a source of redress and correction. The judges, however, have never exercised judicial review over the legislative and executive branches (they have, however, accepted cases dealing with the Election Board). The reason for the court's timidity has not been a philosophy of judicial restraint. Instead it has been a kind of judicial abdication evident in some judges' sacrifice of independence, disregard of the law, arbitrary administration of court affairs, and collusion with the tribal police. The court has not taken seriously its obligations under the tribal constitution.

An associate judge's analysis of the tribal court is that much of the court's weakness can be attributed to a past chief judge.[34] According to Geneva Stump, this chief judge provided little guidance to the court's staff and stayed away from the court to avoid answering the questions of parties and the public. He regularly delayed criminal cases without good reason, eventually disposing of most with a guilty plea.[35] The chief judge also was unwilling to assert jurisdiction over civil matters, partially because of his own inadequacies. Feeling uncomfortable with procedural technicalities, he avoided embarrassment by discouraging litigation. Jealousy also prevented him from assigning cases to another judge more able than he or more concerned about procedural guidelines.

The greatest failing of the court, however, has been its lack of judicial mentality, not its administration of business. Simply put, the Rocky Boy's judiciary has not always behaved like a court of law. Several judges have not known tribal law well, and this deficiency and the absence of formal rules because of delayed code revision caused the court to use illegal procedures or to dismiss cases. Political pressure on the court has been especially intense after dismissal of charges because there was no law to apply, for example, in drug-use cases. One tribal judge acknowledged that the council has placed "pressure" on judges "concerning the disposition of cases"[36] and that the chief judge did not come to the defense of the court's independence. Rather, the chief judge, himself, told the other judges "what to do" about settlement of matters before them.[37]

Most seriously, the Rocky Boy's judiciary has earned a reputation of acting in an unauthorized and irregular manner. A 1975 study of tribal government found that the Rocky Boy's police are viewed by tribal members as agents of raw power rather than enforcers of the law.[38] Their abuses have included inhumane arrest procedures and indifference toward the law and order code. The court has supported police misconduct by allowing the police to prosecute individuals "throughout the complete trial."[39] The extent of police influence on the reservation can be seen in the court's working with the police to silence members' criticism of tribal government. A tribal judge has alleged that the court has "often" upheld police enforcement of a "creating a disturbance" resolution against persons protesting how they were treated by program officials.[40] The result of such official arbitrariness is loss of governmental legitimacy. Tribal members "fear the court" and feel that they are "beaten down and have no place to go."[41]

The tribe has not ignored or failed to address these serious difficulties. From 1982 to 1987, with assistance from the judicial services division of the Bureau of Indian Affairs area office, a tribal committee worked on code revision and better rules of procedure for the tribal court. Judges, police, game wardens, and council members participated in the reform effort. The Business Committee adopted the reforms in 1987.[42]

A possible avenue of redress for Rocky Boy's Indians, besides the political branches of tribal government, is the Bureau of Indian Affairs. Any superintendent must determine the degree the agency should enter into the affairs of a tribe. At Rocky Boy's, the Bureau has not become an ombudsman or an alternative to tribal government. As a result, there has been little competition between the tribal and agency units. Generally, tribal members have had mixed feelings about the Bureau, being fearful of self-government because they harbor no illusions about the resources or competence of their own officials. On the other hand, the Bureau has willingly contracted programs to the tribe and thereby given tribal officials something to do.

Contracting with the Bureau for federal programs is the tribe's best opportunity to act governmental. An historian of the Rocky Boy's reservation observed that the Bureau of Indian Affairs, because of its centrality to the economy of the reservation, had become the "new buffalo" in the Indian Reorganization Act era.[43] The situation has not changed. Because of the isolation and poverty of the reservation, operation of federal programs essentially defines the Rocky Boy's government. The tribe had sixteen contracts in 1984 worth $2.1 million. Included were all of the Bureau's program responsibilities except for vocational education and management of forest and grazing land. These were law enforcement, courts, lease compliance, housing improvement, and social services. So extensive were these responsibilities that the tribe's grantsman, an outside professional hired to work with the council's economic development committee, devoted most of his time to the reporting requirements of the contract process.

Unlike some other reservation governments, Rocky Boy's officials believe that they have no choice but to contract to run federal Indian programs. Failure to seek these responsibilities would be "an admission of incompetence."[44] But the tribe's takeover of Bureau programs has not resulted in progress toward self-government. The Bureau has reserved for itself funding discretion and thereby maintained the traditional Bureau-tribal relationship. There is little difference from the situation decades ago when the superintendent refused to recognize the chiefs' authority over their followers and functioned as mediator between Washington and the tribe. Rocky Boy's officials today believe that the discrepancy between promise and performance that characterized federal action under the 1934 Indian Reorganization Act continues to typify implementation of the 1975 Self-Determination Act, the authority for contracting. The position of the Chippewa-Cree tribe has been that the federal government has nullified its own self-government policy:

> Tribal programs are not being funded at the level necessary to adequately run these programs, nor are they being funded at the same level of funding they would be were the Bureau running these programs. Repeated requests for additional funding have been denied. This situation is clearly inconsistent with the concept of self-determination. . . .[45]

The reality of the contracting situation is that both the tribe's ability and the Bureau's actions point to the same conclusion about the potential of self-governance at Rocky Boy's. Some tribal officials say optimistically that they are ready for "BIA extinction and total tribal absorption."[46] Bureau employees dutifully say that they look forward to the day when "there will be no need for a BIA agency office because the tribe will be competent to handle its own affairs."[47] The tribe, though, is fearful of its own limitations, and the Bureau consistently interprets its role as one of providing protection. The result is that the tribe is really the ward of the federal government, despite the pleasant sound of self-rule rhetoric.

Ultimately, the basis of true self-governance must be the people, and the Rocky Boy's constitution clearly calls for a political democracy. It creates an expectation that tribal members will speak out and be heard through such vehicles as fair elections, open meetings, referendum and recall, and amendment initiatives. The political culture of the reservation, however, is not in tune with that dogma. Few members have sustained interest in policy issues; the reform agenda of politics has been limited; and the willingness of governmental officials to tackle major problems has been nearly non-existent. Government on the Rocky Boy's reservation is not likely to improve, therefore, until a public consciousness grows among the people.

The politics of the Rocky Boy's reservation, that is, the characteristics which define the relationship between tribal members and their governmental officials, is both personal and material. On the impoverished reservation, almost all income and goods pass through the tribal government. The ordinary concern of each member is "How much am I getting," and "How well are others doing." This constant assessment by the individual of governmental distribution and comparative shares is enhanced by the reservation's small size and population. As the Rocky Boy's natural resource officer observed, on the reservation "everyone knows everybody and nothing can be hidden."[48] The result of this poverty and proximity is that the ruling passions on the reservation are jealousy, distrust, and cynicism. The jealousy of others' gain, expressed in an old clan joke: "You made it, you're at the top," is said to "run the reservation."[49] The distrust of tribal officials stems from repeated incidents of favoritism and misuse of tribal funds. The political cynicism is a logical conclusion from the fact that things go on the same despite promises, elections, and new faces.

The shining democratic provisions of their "buckskin book" are not central, therefore, to the political experience of the Rocky Boy's people. In general, tribal members have not known the law and have not expected that legal procedures will be followed. The governmental process for tribal members, according to a tribal judge, has been having decisions "shoved down their throats."[50] The contrast between principle and practice is striking. A discussion of several areas of tribal affairs— enrollment regulation, land use, and economic development—will help to illustrate the shortsighted and ineffectual nature of Rocky Boy's politics.

No area of tribal politics has generated as many promises, disappointments, and suspicions as economic development. The history of projects to create jobs is a story of repeated failure. In the early years of the reservation there were unsuccessful attempts to make the Chippewa and Cree self-sufficient farmers on small pieces of land, establish a saw mill to process the scrub pine of the Bear Paw Mountains, and mine precious metals which were thought capable of producing handsome royalties. These were not undertakings of tribal government but plans of the Indian Service. In later years the tribe itself set out to build a local economy, using a wide variety of approaches. A few were successful, though not one notably so, and most achieved nothing at all.

The economic programs which failed have included a greenhouse, hay project, bird farm, livestock project, and vo-tech construction project. The greenhouse was to raise seedlings for lodgepole pine and ornamental trees and shrubs. It ran out of funding when just 75 percent complete. The goal of the tribal bird farm was to raise game birds and make them available for hunting. The livestock and hay projects were tribally run commercial ventures to sell agricultural products. The vo-tech project called for construction craft trainees to build and sell different kinds of structures. It was to have been 100 percent tribally financed, but tribal money was insufficient. The recurring reasons for failure of these projects were the tribe's lack of seed money, the burdensome matching requirements of federal economic development programs (sometimes as high as three-to-one), the hiring of poorly qualified tribal applicants for administrative positions, and intrusive Business Committee oversight. The latter factors were the most significant.[51] The Business Committee did not want to surrender influence over operation of the programs, and its members retained a right to intervene at will by selecting reservation residents as managers. The repeated result of these decisions was incompetent personnel.

Some success has been or may be achieved through a number of other projects. The Baldy Mountain recreation area, a ski run and lodge, failed under Economic Development Administration funding but has been given new life by the Office of Minority Business Enterprises. Poor management and inadequate snow have hurt the project, but its lack of competition in northcentral Montana provides hope for the future. The post and pole plant also failed because of incompetent tribal management, but the Bureau of Indian Affairs has tried to rehabilitate the operation.[52] Talk of a contract for power line poles indicates that the project may have a chance for success. Most economic potential on the reservation rests with the Dry Forks Farm. This tribal operation began with federal revenue sharing money and now has $1 million in assets. Its purpose has been to produce and sell agricultural products, but recently there has been discussion about turning it into a community farm. One sure source of income for the tribe has been a $20,000 annual lease for an antenna on Centennial Mountain, the highest peak of the Bear Paws. Other possibilities are mineral mining (so far there have been only exploration leases), oil and gas production (there are no producing wells and recently there has not been a good market for even exploration), and timber harvesting (this market also is poor and the tribe is still angry over past clear cutting which was unauthorized). A 1975 assessment of the Rocky Boy's economy[53] concluded that any success with business development could be attributed principally to the hiring of outside managers,[54] Business Committee restraint, and Bureau of Indian Affairs supervision.

The tribe's attitude toward economic development and the prospects for any major project can be surmised from the fate of a recent proposal for a meat packing plant on the reservation. The Montana Livestock Cooperative in 1981 approached ten Montana communities, including the Rocky Boy's reservation, with a plan for a slaughterhouse. The reservation was selected as the site because of its location, tax advantages, high unemployment, and good likelihood of grant support from the Department of Housing and Urban Development. The total project investment was estimated at $20 million; 165 jobs were designated for Indian preference, with an average beginning salary of $10,000 a year. The tribe's responsibility was to construct a $4 million building which was to be funded by a $400,000 federal grant and debt obligations. The plan ran into trouble when the Montana Livestock Cooperative had difficulty securing an outside corporation to manage the plant, and tribal members learned of the tribe's possible financial obligation. The tribal population was generally "not enthusiastic"[55] about the project, submitting a 200-signature petition opposing the plant. The major concerns of members were that tribal land would be used to secure the debt and that the reservation would be lost in the event of default.

In 1982, negotiations fell apart. The tribe's distrust was too great to permit it to incur substantial financial risk. Too many times in the past business failure had been followed by the question, "What happened to the funds?" The tribe also had come to suspect the promises of corporations, especially because of dealings with energy and timber companies. This distrust of both insiders and outsiders, plus the fear that the reservation itself could be lost because of yet another failure, doomed the plan for the meat packing plant. The tribe, fearful of going outside for assistance, chose not to endanger its land, the only economic certainty it possessed.

This attachment of the Chippewa and Cree to their land also explains the tensions created by land use regulations on the reservation and puts into perspective other failings of the Business Committee. The Rocky Boy's reservation never was allotted and today is totally owned by the tribe. Assignments of land to individuals, however, long had been the plan of the Bureau of Indian Affairs for Indian self-sufficiency. Two hundred and five assignments of tribal land have been made; of this number, most assignments are in the 160-acre range, but some are more than 160 acres and some are 80 acres. Assignees have the right to pass on their land selections to one heir and to arrange an exchange of assignments.

Assignment holders on the Rocky Boy's reservation are viewed as a privileged class. Most assignments are longstanding, and today there is a waiting list of applicants for assignments. The inclusion on the reservation of landless Indians several times in the past created a division of "haves" and "have not" regarding land, and return of Indians to the reservation and a high birth rate have accentuated this problem. There are no land assignments for those coming of age today; and if tribal holdings were to be distributed equally among the membership, each member would receive only thirty-five acres of land.

To some degree the Business Committee has been faced with a "damned if I do, damned if I don't" situation. Since 1916 the critical problem of the reservation has been "too many people on too little land."[56] The council's choices seemed equally bad—insufficient land for everyone or enough land for some and nothing for the rest—and policy failure seemed inevitable. The tribal constitution, however, does give the Business Committee authority to see that some fairness is observed in the matter of assignments. The council can keep selections within the 160-acre range, make certain that the land is actually being used, and require that members be given preference in the leasing of assignments.

In each of these oversight responsibilities, the Business Committee has been delinquent.[57] It has, for example, failed to take up the matter of non-resident members holding but not using assignments. It has not reduced assignments which exceeded 160 acres in size. And it has not punished assignment holders who have been influenced by white money to lease land to outsiders rather than to tribal members. The land pressures at Rocky Boy's continue to grow as young Indians return to the reservation, feeling "uptight on the outside."[58] The response of the Business Committee to these land problems, which are at the core of reservation life, is inaction. Instead, it strikes a note of unreality by entertaining the idea of using a 1939 congressional enactment to annex 82,000 acres to the reservation. The critical fact that 99 percent of this land is white owned—raising serious jurisdictional and political problems—has not deterred the council.

In some ways the most heated area of politics on the reservation has to do with tribal enrollment, even though the poverty of the reservation leaves so little to contest. Per capita payments from the tribal farm, for example, were irregular in the 1960s and 1970s and always within the constitutional limitation of twenty dollars. In recent years these bonuses for members have been non-existent. The centrality of the membership question can be seen in the fact that it was the sole issue considered by a constitutional revision committee meeting monthly in 1983.

The value placed on tribal membership is evident in the illegality which surrounds administration of the constitution's membership language. Article II has three provisions which are especially important: membership can be lost if a person is "away from the reservation for a period of ten years"; adoption by election is open to any Indian of at least half-blood who is not a member of any other tribe; and membership is granted to all children of members of the tribe who are reservation residents at the time of the child's birth. The most serious abuse of these regulations has been "inconsistent"[59] administration of the ten-year absence provision. The Business Committee has dropped persons from membership without grounds and kept individuals on the roll when they did not satisfy the ten-year requirement. Most importantly, the council has not taken up the problem of assignment holders who have been absent from the reservation for more than ten years. The Business Committee also has not required adherence to the adoption procedure for taking Indians into the tribe. During the 1970s, many persons were drawn to the Rocky Boy's reservation by talk of claims settlements and oil and gas production. A former tribal judge remembers how a "lot of illegal enrollees" later appeared "mysteriously" on the membership roll with the expectation of sharing in large per capita payments.[60] Finally, there has been arbitrary rejection of membership applications by treating the hospital in the nearby city of Havre as off-reservation and the parents as non-residents at the time of birth.[61]

These practices of the Business Committee concerning tribal membership point to key determinants of Rocky Boy's politics: economic isolation and hope for material well-being. A high value is placed on tribal membership, despite the tribe's poverty, because there is so little economic opportunity for a reservation Indian on the northern Montana prairie. The Chippewa and Cree hope that one day the tribe will strike oil or find gold, and then per capita shares will make membership a road to prosperity. The resulting membership politics is characterized by favoritism and an arbitrary use of power, feeding off an elementary desire for a better life.

In a sense, the Chippewa and Cree who wandered throughout Montana seeking identity and security are still adrift. Facing the Rocky Boy's reservation has been adversity different from that of other reservations. The Chippewa and Cree have struggled to create a new political community in a place that is economically inhospitable and without traditional ties. The short distance the Chippewa and Cree have come is seen in the irregularity of their government and in the cynicism and desperateness of their politics. But, despite the approximations of tribal bureaucrats and the outpost behavior of tribal police, the activities of Rocky Boy's officials are more than a parody of government. They represent sincere and genuine steps in the tremendously difficult journey from political decimation to self-determination.

Notes

1. *Constitution and Bylaws of the Chippewa Cree Indians of the Rocky Boy's Reservation, Montana,* Preamble.

2. The discussion of the early history of the Rocky Boy's Reservation is taken from Thomas R. Wessel, "A History of the Rocky Boy's Indian Reservation" (No publisher or date of publication given) (photocopy).

3. For an account of Louis Riel and the Meti Indians' rebellion, in which Big Bear and the Crees joined, see Verne Dusenberry, "The Rocky Boy Indians," *Montana Magazine of History* (Winter, 1954), pp. 1–15, and Joseph Kinsey Howard, *Strange Empire: A Narrative of the Northwest* (New York: William Morrow and Co., 1952), p. 546.

4. Thomas R. Wessel, *Historical Report on the Blackfeet Reservation in Northern Montana* (U.S. Indian Claims Commission, Docket No. 279-D, 1975), pp. 133–134.

5. Wessel, "A History of the Rocky Boy's Indian Reservation," p. 71.

6. Ibid., p. i.

7. Ibid., p. 108.

8. Ibid., p. 187.

9. Ibid., p. 203.

10. Thomas Wiest (Grantsman for the Rocky Boy's Reservation), "Project Narrative" (Photocopy, 1983), p. 2.

11. Ibid.

12. Wessel, "A History of the Rocky Boy's Indian Reservation," p. 179.

13. Superintendents' Annual Narrative and Statistical Report, Rocky Boy's, 1918, Frame 27.

14. Superintendents' Annual Narrative and Statistical Report, Rocky Boy's, 1928, Frame 526.

15. Superintendents' Annual Narrative and Statistical Report, Rocky Boy's, 1920, Frames 55–56.

16. Superintendents' Annual Narrative and Statistical Report, Rocky Boy's, 1926, Frame 471.

17. Superintendents' Annual Narrative and Statistical Reports, Rocky Boy's, 1928, Frame 536.

18. Superintendents' Annual Narrative and Statistical Reports, Rocky Boy's, 1930, Frame 676.

19. *Constitution and Bylaws of the Chippewa Cree Indians of the Rocky Boy's Reservation, Montana,* Art. XII. The judiciary article was added to the Rocky Boy's Constitution by amendment, the ratifying election being held on April 22, 1972.

20. Ibid., Art. VII.

21. Interviews with John J.V. Pereau, Superintendent of the Rocky Boy's Agency, September 9, 1983, and with Geneva Stump, Associate Judge of the Rocky Boy's Tribal Court, September 9, 1983.

22. Jim Morsette, the Rocky Boy's tribal prosecutor, upon his return to the reservation felt that the door was closed to him. For a long time he was unsuccessful in his attempt to get a land assignment, the Business Committee telling him that there was no land available. He had become a force for tribal government reform, and believed that the council was using land assignments politically. Finally, when he threatened a law suit, the Business Committee "found" a 400-acre bull pasture and converted it to five, eighty-acre assignments, one of which went to Jim Morsette. Morsette interview, September 26, 1986.

23. In effect, the 1958 code was a reprint of a 1935 code, and the reservation's official statutory law until 1987 was what remained of the first code as amended by ordinances.

24. The post-1958 attempts at recodification on the Rocky Boy's reservation have included two comprehensive drafts, 1975 and 1982. Neither was ever implemented. The 1978 U.S. Supreme Court decision, *Oliphant v. Suquamish Indian Tribe,* made the 1975 draft out of date. The 1982 code, written by an Indian attorney, was adopted by the Business Committee but disapproved by the Bureau of Indian Affairs because of inconsistencies with the Indian Civil Rights Act. At that time the Bureau asked the University of Montana Indian Law Clinic to give drafting assistance to the Rocky Boy's council. The Clinic worked for the next five years with a tribal code revision committee.

25. Interview with Bruce Measure, Manager of the Rocky Boy's Tribal Forest Enterprise, 1979–1981, on November 6, 1986. Measure said that councilmen "kept their hands in everything" he did, and that these contacts were "meddlesome and contradictory."

26. Interview with John J.V. Pereau. A similar observation by Bruce Measure, ibid., was that it was impossible for tribal program managers to get agreement on goals and means from members of the Business Committee. As a result, it was "very difficult for a program to push ahead."

27. Interview with Bruce Measure. Measure said that managers of tribal operations generally were "hand picked" by members of the Business Committee and that the "family and political connections" between council members and managers were "obvious."

28. Interview with Geneva Stump, Associate Judge of the Rocky Boy's Tribal Court, September 9, 1983.

29. Alan Parker, *Indian Tribes as Governments* (New York: John Hay Whitney Foundation, 1975), p. 86.

30. Interview with Geneva Stump.

31. Ibid.

32. Ibid.

33. Ibid.

34. Ibid. The description of the Rocky Boy's tribal court is largely dependent on this source.

35. Bruce Measure, a former manager of the tribe's forest enterprise, said that he was assaulted by a tribal member in the tribal headquarters building and the chief judge refused to impose a sentence. The chief judge told him, "You can leave the reservation, but I have to live here."

36. Interview with Geneva Stump.

37. Ibid. The chief judge, David Mitchell, chose to run as associate judge in 1984 and was elected. The retirement of the other associate judge in 1985 left on the court Mitchell and the new chief judge, both possessing minimal training for their positions.

38. Parker, p. 186. Bruce Measure, in an interview, provided a different perspective on police behavior. From 1979 to 1981, he found tribal police to be passive and unwilling to make arrests. As a result, "members could get away with anything," and Rocky Boy's became a "lawless reservation."

39. Parker, p. 1986.

40. Interview with Geneva Stump.

41. Ibid.

42. Ever since the Fall of 1983, the University of Montana Indian Law Clinic has held meetings on the Rocky Boy's reservation with tribal government officials concerning code reform. The staff of the Indian Law Clinic developed a new code after receiving the suggestions of tribal leaders. Public hearings on the draft elicited many technical criticisms and calls for more time for review. Elections in 1984 and 1986 prompted the Business Committee to take no action until new council members were seated. The Business Committee, in general, took the position that caution was best, based upon its reading of the political winds, not adopting the code until 1987.

43. Wessel, "A History of the Rocky Boy's Indian Reservation," p. 205.

44. Interview with Gary Eagleman, member of the Rocky Boy's Business Committee, September 9, 1983.

45. Statement of John Windy Boy, Rocky Boy's Chairman, to the Billings, Montana, Area Officer of the Bureau of Indian Affairs, September 8, 1983.

46. Interview with Daryl Wright, Natural Resource Officer of the Rocky Boy's Reservation, September 9, 1983.

47. Parker, p. 160.

48. Interview with Daryl Wright. Also present and concurring in his statements were Gary Eagleman, member of the Rocky Boy's Business Committee; Peter St. Marks, member of the Rocky Boy's Business Committee; and Earl Arkinson, Rocky Boy's Police Chief.

49. Ibid.

50. Interview with Geneva Stump.

51. Interview with Bruce Measure. Although tribal applicants frequently were not qualified for managerial and technical positions, Measure emphasized

that this observation must be made with some qualification. Generally those getting jobs were "heads over others" in education and experience. The problem was that "people with a little competence stood out and got too much responsibility handed to them."

52. Bruce Measure, manager of the Rocky Boy's forest products operation from 1979 to 1981, said that another cause of failure, in addition to poor management, was the job skills and work ethic of tribal employees. Measure said that forest products manufacturing, like the ski lift, was "too mechanical oriented and not well suited to the reservation culture." The Indians' skills and cultural disposition, Measure observed, were very adaptable to the forest end of the timber industry: "It was like a hunting camp in the woods." But "Indians in the mill became nervous with machinery, fixed work schedules, and the monotony of the work."

53. Parker, p. 90.

54. An outside manager's success might be attributed to being an outsider as well as to training and experience. Bruce Measure observed that a managerial position would bring a tribal member "too much responsibility or money for anyone to handle." Relatives, friends, and acquaintances would immediately seek money, favors, and jobs. The person in authority would escape this dunning by denying power ("I'm not responsible for that") or passing the buck ("See this other person"). Measure called the effect of these intense social pressures an "institutionalized incompetence." Tribal managers "ran away from responsibility rather than give away the business."

55. Interview with Thomas Wiest, Grantsman for the Rocky Boy's Reservation, September 9, 1983.

56. Wessel, "A History of the Rocky Boy's Indian Reservation," p. 193.

57. Parker, pp. 181–184.

58. Interview with Daryl Wright.

59. Parker, p. 180.

60. Interview with Geneva Stump.

61. Parker, p. 180. Enrollment issues continue to be highly political on the Rocky Boy's reservation. In 1983 the federal government announced a $46 million judgment in the Pembina-Chippewa claims case, an award to which all Chippewa-Cree felt entitled. The Business Committee, however, had disenrolled 150 members in 1958 because of their absence from the reservation for ten years or more. The constitutional revision committee meeting in 1983 proposed the remedy of amending the ten-year provision out of the constitution before receipt of the cash settlement in 1987. According to Kathleen Fleury, Bureau of Indian Affairs attorney in the Billings Area (October 6, 1986, interview), the amendment proposal was made politically unnecessary by Business Committee action. A council resolution allowed many people to return to the tribal roll by creating education, health, and employment exceptions to the constitutional residency requirement.

9

The Flathead Reservation: From Enclave to Self-Government

The Flathead Indians have been involved for several centuries in a process of political evolution. Change precipitated by outside forces has been a constant in their lives, from the time they governed themselves on the plateaus of the Continental Divide to the last quarter of the twentieth century when they have struggled against the pressures of external governments and corporations. Native American life generally, of course, has been a story of attempted recovery from savage assaults of various kinds, and in this respect the Indians of the Flathead reservation are typical. What is distinguishing in their lives is an openness to change—a native disposition to borrow and adapt—marked by progressive admixture and assimilation. As a result, the contemporary politics of the Flathead reservation are based upon values and expressed in words which are the common currency of any progressive American government. Fighting few rear guard actions against traditionalists from within, Flathead government has made significant progress toward achieving political sophistication and administrative competence.

The Flathead reservation, established in 1855 by the Hellgate Treaty, contains some of the most beautiful land in the Pacific Northwest. The reservation's majestic mountains, charming valleys, and picturesque lakes, however, were not the homeland of its Indian inhabitants. Not only were these Indians native to other locales of the Mountain West, but they also had various tribal affiliations. What have been obstacles to the political development of other reservations—a setting which was not a homeland and the bringing together of different Indian cultures—however, did not stand in the way of Flathead success. Early in the reservation's history, it was said that "[n]o Indian agency in the United States has a better record than the Flathead"[1] in terms of material progress. Today the same statement could just as well be made and found true.

Brought together in a confederation by the treaty of 1855 were the Salish people and the Kootenai people.[2] This division, though, was only the beginning of tribal distinctions on the Flathead reservation. The Salish group, who also came to be known as the Flathead, was made up of four tribes: Flathead, Pend Oreille, Kalispel (or Lower Pend Oreille), and Spokane. The Kootenai people consisted of three tribes: The Lower Kootenai, the Upper Kootenai, and the Kutona. All of these tribes were Plateau Indians, occupying different portions of a vast territory stretching from the McKenzie Basin drainage south to the California-Oregon border, and from the Cascades in the West to the buffalo ranges on the east slopes of the Rocky Mountains. The Lower Kootenai lived near Kootenai Lake in British Columbia, while the Upper Kootenai dwelled along the Kootenai River north to the headwaters of the Columbia. The Kutona occupied land east of the Rockies in Alberta and Montana (including the territory of the contemporary Blackfeet reservation). The Pend Oreilles had claims to Washington and Idaho lands, while the Spokane inhabited the Coeur d'Alene area. The Salish Indians claimed the high plains of eastern Montana until Blackfeet warriors and smallpox drove them in the late eighteenth century across the Rocky Mountains and into the Bitterroot Valley of western Montana. This was the home of the Salish when the Hellgate treaty council, with a good deal of arbitrariness, created a loose political union of separate Indian peoples and began demarcation of a new homeland for these several tribes.

There are significant similarities among the different Salish-speaking tribes, and important differences exist between the Salish and Kootenai peoples. The word "Salish" means the "people who speak Salish,"[3] and this language and other cultural characteristics were common to the Salish group. Kootenai Indians, however, had their own separate language. The Salish Indians, especially the Flathead, were open to other cultures, both Indian and white, and intermarried frequently. In contrast to the Salish traits of friendliness and hospitality, the Kootenai were known for their social reserve and caution and preserved a more undiluted blood line. The Salish perceived the Kootenai as an inferior people. They were hesitant to enter marriage with Kootenai Indians, and at the time of the Hellgate council they expressed "disgust"[4] at political association with the Kootenai which was commanded by the treaty.

For several reasons the culture and outlook of the Salish Indians came to be of greater political consequence on the Flathead reservation than the ways of the Kootenai. The Salish were numerically greater than the Kootenai, accounting for 75 percent of the population at the reservation's outset. Also, the Salish adapted well to change, primarily because they were a socially open people and genuinely interested in understanding the differences and advantages of other cultures. One history of the Flatheads relates that in early times they

> . . . adopted social forms as well as manufacturing techniques and weapons from peoples they encountered. . . . Other borrowings seem relatively recent. A pure Flathead tradition, if one existed, was progressively diluted by cultural borrowings, intermarriages, and adoptions, so that the Flatheads as a society combined features of the original Plateau and adopted Plains cultures.[5]

Such cultural flexibility became attractive to the federal agents appointed to manage the affairs of the new reservation. In 1855 the U.S. Government preferred the Salish to the Kootenai for leadership positions, naming Victor, a Flathead, the head chief of the reservation. In later years, Indian agents found performance of their duties to be an easier task when dealing with the Salish than with the Kootenai. This difference was explained in terms of blood quantum. Fullbloods, which generally included the Kootenai band, were described as "non-progressive and backward."[6] On the other hand, a Flathead of unmixed ancestry was quite uncommon.

The Salish Indians' adaptability came to play a significant role in the early development of the Flathead reservation. Such openness was important because reservation life was long characterized by nagging differences and disturbing intrusions from the external world. For most of the nineteenth century, for example, the various tribes on the reservation tended to maintain separate areas of residence. The Salish Indians remained until 1891 in their ancestral home, the Bitterroot Valley, for several decades resisting orders to move to the Jocko Valley reservation preferred by the federal government. The Pend Oreilles camped near the Jesuit fathers' St. Ignatius Mission, occupying a southern valley of the reservation eighty miles distant from the Salish. In the northern reaches of the reservation lived the Kootenai clustered in their Dayton Creek village on the west shore of Flathead Lake. As one historian described the situation, these "three disjoined peoples" rendered the "Flathead nation . . . merely a phrase."[7]

The federal government in the late nineteenth century did additional damage to the possibility of Indian nationhood when special commissions, reacting to white pressures for more land, displaced northwestern tribes and moved outside Indians to the Flathead reservation. In 1886 the Northwest Indian Commission added to the Flathead population several Kalispel bands and some Spokane Indians who had been uprooted from their Washington and Idaho lands. Six years later the federal Indian Office moved Kootenai Indians from the Bonners Ferry area in northern Idaho to the Flathead reservation. These Kootenai, made refugees by federal Indian policy, chose to settle at the Dayton Creek encampment. This forced intermingling, without the addition of new land to the reservation, further eroded a spirit of community and rendered the Flathead Indians' flexibility an especially practical virtue.

Preclusion of a cohesive identity on the reservation can be attributed as much to the authorized admission of whites as to tribal differences and the mixing of displaced Indians. The setting of the Flathead reservation was not only beautiful; it was also highly desirable for planting crops, raising livestock, hunting game, and fishing. As good land for general settlement became progressively more scarce in the nineteenth century, pressure on Congress grew to open the reservation to white settlers. The Montana legislature in 1895 resolved that Congress take such action, and Congress sent a commission to negotiate with the Flathead Indians in 1897. Despite several attempts, the commission was unsuccessful in gaining tribal consent to a cession of a portion of the reservation. Then, bolstered by a 1903 decision of the United States Supreme Court upholding broad Congressional authority over Indian lands, newly-elected Montana Congressman Joseph M. Dixon secured the enactment of the Flathead Allotment Act in 1904.[8] Without providing for Indian consent, the Act authorized the survey and allotment of the reservation and the sale and disposal of all surplus lands after allotment. Proceeds from land sales were to be paid to the United States to be expended for the benefit of the Flathead Indians. The Act and its amendments also led to the designation on the reservation of approximately 61,000 acres as Montana school lands, 18,500 acres for the National Bison Range, and smaller acreages for tribal usage, the Indian agency, townsites, power and reservoir sites, and missionary churches and schools.

After tribal enrollment lists were completed, 2,390 Indians received either 80-acre allotments of agricultural land or 160-acre allotments of grazing land. These allotments secured for the Indians only 245,000 acres, or about one fifth of the 1,245,000 acres within the reservation. Next, a presidentially appointed commission classified and appraised the remaining lands as a preliminary step to their availability to homesteaders. A 1909 proclamation by President William H. Taft formally opened the nonmineral, unreserved agricultural and grazing lands to settlement by non-Indians and prescribed procedures for the filing of applications for homestead entries.

The actual opening of the Flathead reservation occurred May 2, 1910, and in the following years more than 4,500 homestead patents were issued for some 404,000 acres. Indian-held lands also moved into non-Indian ownership, initially as a result of Congressional action in 1910 authorizing the sale of up to 60 acres of the 80-acre farm allotments if the land was irrigable, and later through sales and foreclosures after Indians received fee patents for their allotments. By 1960, members of the confederated tribes owned only one of every seven farms on the reservation. In 1983 less than 4 percent of the reservation's 1.24 million acres belonged to individual Indians (in addition, the tribes through an aggressive land purchase program held ownership to 46 percent of the acreage). In 1984 the Indian population on the reservation was a little over 19 percent, the lowest of all Montana reservations. Once again, changing circumstances placed a high premium on the Flathead Indians' disposition to adjust to an alien culture.

The Flathead tribes' openness to the political values of other cultures has been a constant phenomenon, and no outside influence has been more significant than the counsel and subtle coercion of white advisors ushered in by the era of the 1934 Indian Reorganization Act. But this was not the beginning of the Flathead Indians' shedding of their traditional ways of governance. The Flathead tribes, along with other Plateau Indian groups such as the Kootenai and Nez Perce, had in common a form of social organization whose roots were found on the Plains. This type of political structure included such features as a council of headmen, a system of leadership including a head chief and lesser chiefs, and a pronounced ethic of individual autonomy. While this basic framework was borrowed from hunting tribes of the Plains, whose primary political need was flexibility and adaptation, the Flatheads did develop several of their own practices, such as the disuse of bands, the emergence of the tribe as the prinicipal political unit, and the election of chiefs. For the most part, however, the Flathead system of governing was borrowed, and as far back as the 1920s an observer in the field reported: "The ancient social organization changed so long ago that very little authentic information about it can be secured."[9] This trend has continued into modern time. The confederated tribes of the Flathead reservation were the first of all American Indian groups to adopt, under the Indian Reorganization Act, a tribal constitution which in reality far more represented white views than Indian values. And in 1979 when the culture committee of the Flathead tribes published *A Brief History of the Flathead Tribes,*[10] the account was largely derivative of the work of prior white historians.

The government of the Flathead reservation has gone through several phases, and overall the changes have taken the tribes from political isolation to active involvement. In the years between establishment of the reservation and the Indian Reorganization Act, the Indian agent controlled to what extent tribal leaders participated in decisions of consequence. Prior to 1909, general councils elected individuals to represent the tribes on specific matters. In that year, the general council chose nine members from the reservation's districts to serve on a business committee. These committee members were young, reliable, and progressive mixed-bloods who sought to improve reservation conditions. Former leaders and young malcontents, who were generally full-bloods, opposed the new leaders and undermined the business committee whenever possible, and they also favored abolishing the Office of Indian Affairs on the Flathead reservation. Discussions concerning the reservation's abundant natural resources and enrollment questions provided ample opportunities for confrontation between the two groups. Both groups favored using the reservation's natural resources, but they differed on who should enjoy the proceeds of such use.[11]

By 1929 the business committee had gained enough strength to subdue its rivals and to carry out its social and fiscal responsibilities. Committee members, for example, opposed the appropriation of tribal funds for industrial purposes, preferring to use congressional money for that objective and tribal funds for other reservation purposes.[12] These early, astute reservation leaders provided considerable political stability. The tribes took another step toward self-rule when they approved in 1935 the Indian Reorganization Act.

The Flathead tribesmen continued their quest for greater self-government in 1944 when their leaders requested full tribal control of tribal resources. Such tribal opposition to the decisions of the Office of Indian Affairs resulted in federal authorities depicting tribal leaders as incapable of governing. The tribal council, however, confident of its own abilities, requested the removal of the Office of Indian Affairs from the reservation for "a trial basis for a period of 5 years, using tribal funds for said administration . . . subject to review and audit by the Congress."[13] Though not approved, the tribes' advocating the removal of federal supervision in favor of self-rule made the Flathead reservation a candidate for the eventual complete withdrawal of federal regulation.[14] Though never the subject of termination legislation, the Confederated Salish and Kootenai tribes agreed to a system of concurrent reservation jurisdiction with the State of Montana under the provisions of Public Law 280.

Despite early self-rule gains, the government that was established under the Indian Reorganization Act presided over the residual politics of a protectorate. Roughly for forty years, from 1934 to 1974, the agency superintendent was the dominant force on the reservation and even routine enactments by the tribal council were subject to the Secretary of Interior's review. It was not until the mid 1970s that the

government of the Flathead reservation began to take on the appearance
of an organization of serious purpose and strong will. The following
discussion will trace the development of the Flathead government from
the early IRA years, a system of limited scope and responsibility, to
the reforms and bold ventures of modern times. Evident in these two
stages, just as in the pre-reservation period, is the use of nontraditional
concepts of political structure and process.

Reservation politics for the first four decades under the IRA constitution were the concerns of an Indian enclave. The form of government was suited to routine domestic tasks. The political value most
emphasized was representation as opposed to leadership, professional
administration, or responsiveness. The tribal council, true to the design
of the IRA, was the principal branch of government, and it functioned
as a forum for hearing and discussing complaints about reservation life
and not for making and implementing policy. The atmosphere of the
council was informal, and there was immediacy in the relationship
between councilmen and tribal members. The ten councilmen came
from election districts which reflected old settlement patterns. Jocko
Valley and Mission had two members each and Ronan, Pablo, Polson,
Dixon, Elmo-Dayton and Hot Springs-Camas Prairie each had one
councilman. Councilmen were required to have district residency of
one year and to make regular reports to their districts concerning
actions taken by the council.

As council members were tied to their districts, so the tribal chairman operated within the orbit of the council. The constitution contained
no expectation that the chairman would be an independent political
force. For example, the councilmen, who had four-year staggered terms,
chose from among their membership the chairman who had an indef-
inite term of office. The constitutionally prescribed duties of the chairman were presiding at council meetings and other functions "detailed"
by the council.[15] No parallel between the chairman and a mayor, a
governor, or even a chairman of a board of county commissioners was
contemplated. The tribal chairman was simply a presiding officer, like
a president of a city council, and not an executive official in charge of
running a government. Other minor offices were vice chairman, secretary, treasurer, and sergeant-at-arms.

For many years the operation of the Flathead tribal government
under its IRA constitution was similar to the experience on other
reservations. Council business was infrequent and of little importance,
and meetings were scheduled for only four times a year. The superintendent of the Bureau of Indian Affairs exercised the dominant political
power on the reservation. He gave the Bureau's trusteeship role a
paternalistic interpretation when passing upon tribal resolutions, man-

aging the tribes' natural resources, and running the federal programs on the reservation. The chairman's position remained structurally weak and staffed by weak politicians, and members—especially older Indians—opposed the council's hiring of experts to whom would be given discretionary powers. This concern and watchfulness about the doings of government, grounded in the Indian traditions of individual autonomy and consensus politics, also extended to the council. Councilmen were frequently the target of harsh criticisms—for example, that they shut themselves off from the tribal community and failed to communicate adequately their agenda and decisions.

Flathead politics, therefore, was characterized by dissatisfaction. In general, it had two basic themes.[16] First, it was grounded in the understanding that the reservation was an Indian homeland, despite the massive white presence within its boundaries. The second theme was that each member had rights that stemmed from this homeland status, the least not being a share in the reservation's resources and income. Reservation politics, based on these premises, could easily shift from a questioning of what the council was doing to a distrust of the intentions and capabilities of the tribal government. Frequently heard were such complaints as favoritism in hiring, closed-door meetings, and council meddling in business enterprises. The central issue of reservation politics was per capita payments: What was the tribal council doing to turn the reservation's resources into income-making property, and was the council passing on a large enough portion of this revenue to tribal members.

Several examples of reservation politics will illustrate its tendency to have an enclave or inward perspective. Disputes over developing natural resources have frequently followed tribal or generational lines. The young and old or Salish have favored development while a conservation philosophy was more apt to be found among the Kootenai or middle-aged.[17] The reasoning of the middle-aged group has been that caution and balance is best, while the young and old have feared that blood-dilution and death would prevent them from sharing in the wealth of the reservation.

The issues of blood quantum and membership eligibility are other examples of enclave politics. Given the significant white presence on the reservation and the Flathead Indians' openness to intermarriage, membership criteria long have been the subject of heated dispute. On both sides of the question has been not a little self interest: small slices of the pie for many or large shares for a few. In 1960 fear of de facto reservation termination through interracial marriages was sufficient to cause a major change in the membership requirement. Assimilation was impeded somewhat when the council threw out a one-sixteenth

Salish-Kootenai blood requirement and adopted in its place a rule of one-fourth.

The elements of enclave politics have also been evident in recurrent popular movements on the reservation to distribute among the membership the resources of the Flathead government. In 1972 there was a push to authorize "optional withdrawal" from tribal membership whereby a member would be "entitled to receive his share of all tribal assets."[18] Failure of this "prodigal son" strategy led to a subsequent proposal to reduce the tribal council's size from ten to five. The primary rationale for this plan was to cut the cost of government and use the money saved for payments to members instead of for councilmen's paychecks. In 1984 during negotiations with the Montana Power Company about the utility's annual rental payment to the tribes for the Kerr Dam site on the reservation, a small group of members stirred up support for a proposal in opposition to the position of the tribes' bargaining team. This approach called for an up-front $5,000 cash payment to each tribal member, rather than large annual payments to the tribes. The common threads of these popular movements were distrust of reservation government and the hope of more tribal money for the members.

With Flathead politics characterized by fragmentation, suspicion, and self-seeking, it is not difficult to understand how the agency superintendent remained the dominant force on the reservation. He could speak for a broader interest when councilmen were advocates of narrow district interests and tribal members felt free to speak out only at district meetings.[19] The superintendent could be a source of cohesion when there was tension between the tribes—for example, when the Kootenai felt ignored by the tribal government and wanted to divide the reservation and take their share of the assets. And, the superintendent could urge caution when the tribal membership defined politics in terms of direct payments. With no rival for political prominence, the Bureau of Indian Affairs on the Flathead reservation became a bureaucracy primarily dedicated to self-perpetuation and comfortable procedures. Even the tribes' chairman and executive secretary were accustomed to argue that the Bureau was needed and on the reservation to stay.[20]

No change in Flathead reservation politics better symbolizes its emergence from an enclave mentality than the developing conviction among outspoken council members that the Bureau of Indian Affairs had become too dominant. This belief is based upon the routine performance of the Bureau, such as its forest road closure program. Relying on an expression of approval by the tribal council in the early 1970s, the Bureau for years has closed the tribes' forest roads whenever it wants and for its own reasons.[21] The Bureau has disregarded Indian usages of the forests, ignored council protestations, avoided answering to the tribes, and justified its action by adherence to its own procedural requirements. The tribal government, as a result, has come to view the Bureau as a smug bureaucracy operating without comment, access, or accountability. A common judgment is that the Bureau makes no contribution at all to the welfare of the tribes. A derogatory appellation for the Bureau is "leather balls,"[22] a collection of insensitive bureaucrats committed only to their governmental careers.

The desire to reduce sharply the superintendent's role on the reservation comes after tribal leaders have tried less drastic measures to solve their problems with the Bureau. The confederated tribes in good faith have entered into contracts with the Bureau under the 1975 Self Determination Act, but they have soured on this process. The normal pattern of events has been tribal assumption of responsibility for a function previously performed by the Bureau, severe cutbacks in federal funding of the service and proportional increase in the tribes' financial contribution, and increased interference by the Bureau in terms of performance standards. The tribes have responded to this experience with political realism. "Why should we," they ask, "pay the bill and let the Bureau call the shots?"[23] As a result, the Flathead tribal government has become very cautious about "contracting." The contemporary approach is to maintain the present contracts—as retrocession would undercut arguments of sovereignty and fuel the Bureau's claims of tribal incompetence—and to hold the Bureau accountable for its responsibilities with respect to non-contracted functions.

Besides experimenting with assumption of governmental services, the Flathead tribal government attempted to develop a more fruitful working relationship with the Bureau of Indian Affairs by changing its Area Office affiliation from Billings, Montana, to Portland, Oregon, in 1982. The reasons for this move were twofold. The Bureau's Portland staff would be able to give tribal officials better advice concerning the management of natural resources and the new Portland connection might provide opportunities to by-pass the local superintendent.[24] The move backfired and the Flathead tribes since have sought realignment with the Billings office. The Portland office, tribal officials discovered, operated with extreme paternalism, "fifty years" behind the Billings philosophy regarding self-government.[25] This mentality—possibly a result of the fact that Portland is responsible for forty-two tribes and Billings for seven Montana reservations—was transmitted to the Flathead superintendent, and the tribes' new situation seemed worse than before. Tribal officials view the logical next step as complete independence from the Bureau of Indian Affairs.

This challenge to the agency system was only part of the assertiveness that characterized 1974–1984 on the Flathead reservation. The hallmark of these ten years was quiet confidence and not noisy displays of self-determination rhetoric. Its manifestations were organizational reform, successful negotiations, increasing regulation of non-members, and strong leadership. The significance of the progress made can be measured by reaction as well as results. Non-Indians on the reservation formed groups to resist through political and legal means the tribes' increasing exercise of jurisdictional authority. On the Flathead reservation, therefore, the last decade of a half-century under the Indian Reorganization Act marked the transition from subjugation to meaningful steps toward self-governance.

Indian self-government on the Flathead reservation is not an insignificant undertaking. The land area is in excess of 1.2 million acres, the fourth largest of Montana's seven reservations. This territory includes parts of four counties. The reservation's population is approximately 20,000, and only 19 percent are Indians. The tribes' official enrollment is 6,150, of whom about 3,800 members live on the reservation. The substantial white presence can be appreciated in terms of land holdings as well as population. Fifty percent of the acreage within the reservation boundaries is held by non-Indians, the second highest land ownership by whites among Montana reservations.

In recent times the Flathead tribal government, with general service and regulatory responsibilities for members and a liaison role regarding the state and many local governments, has grown to be large and costly. In 1984 there were thirty-eight departments, seven semi-autonomous enterprises, and 589 employees. The tribes' own operating budget was $4.8 million and, in addition, there were $31 million worth of federal projects on the reservation. Beginning in the 1970s, concern grew among tribal officials about the adequacy of their political system for handling its expanding responsibilities. A series of subsequent changes points to an openness to practical reforms, awareness of the demands of self-government, and erosion of the enclave mentality perpetuated by decades of Bureau paternalism.

The first set of reforms affected the tribal council, the reservation's governing body. Historically the council had been a forum where headmen had discussed tribal problems and searched for solutions. It was a body that respected interest representation, fullness of access and participation, and conscious accommodation. During the fifty years of the Indian Reorganization Act era, the activities of the council involving special influence and favor began to conflict with its new tasks of governance. Changes in the election system and the council's internal organization then were adopted to create a government which was both more open and more rational. The success of these reforms lies partially in the fact that they represent a balance between the tribes' past practices and values and present challenges and needs.

Election reform was achieved in two stages, changing from district to at-large representation in 1977 and adding a primary election in 1981. Behind both changes was a desire to make tribal government less dominated by minority interests and more responsive to the collective concerns of the tribal community. It was argued, for example, that councilmen should truly represent the entire membership because their decisions affect everyone. The election plan now calls for district residency but at-large primary and general elections. The expectation is that a councilman's inevitable district perspective will be tempered by a sensitivity to the reservation-wide implications of policy issues.[26]

Of the two election reforms, the efficacy of the primary is the least apparent in terms of broadening representation. This change, though, was the result of strong feelings and a petition movement to amend the constitution, while at-large election was the result of a referendum sought by the tribal council as a means to forestall challenges of council elections on equal protection grounds. The leaders of the drive for primary elections argued that voters were splitting their support among many candidates, and winners received the backing of relatively few members. The result of this scheme was manipulative campaigning, minority based councilmen, little voter control, and little changeover.[27] On the other hand, the result of the primary has been what the reformers intended.[28] The two-election system has brought to reservation politics new candidates and councilmen and responsive policies. Elections have been made a vehicle of accountability rather than a tool of favoritism. The election reforms thus indicate that tribal members respect classic as well as native political values.

Another far-reaching reform that reveals the public philosophy of the Flathead tribes was elimination of the council's committee system in 1983. The impetus for this change was new membership on the council brought about by the newly implemented primary election.[29] The supporting arguments once again called attention to a lack of representation and accountability, although advocates in their public case stressed potential cost savings. The problem with the committee system was that a minority of council members were effectively making policy in a given area.[30] For example, the land committee of three councilmen was comprised of persons with vested interests. Rancher-councilmen would become expert on land issues and make recommendations to a deferential council. Discussion on the whole council would not include varied and opposing views. A land use decision would turn upon grazing needs and ignore recreational and cultural considerations.

And often, when only a quorum of seven was present, an ad hoc coalition of four councilmen would "ram through a new policy."[31]

The reform was to abolish the council's committees. The committees, intended to be thorough and objective, became selective, narrow, costly, and time-consuming. They often gave birth to bad ideas, and innovative thinking was being stifled. Without the committees, the entire council has felt the responsibility of becoming informed. Policy discussion has become more sensitive to complexities and details, and council members now rely on the tribe's departmental staff for advice rather than on committee members.[32] This reform, along with the requirement for at-large and primary elections, reflects the confederated tribes' opposition to narrowly concentrating power in reservation government. The ideal governmental form from the perspective of tribal members appears to be a system which allows the entire membership to select its policy makers, who in turn develop the expertise to be able to respond to the collective needs of the reservation.

These structural changes have reflected considerable agonizing by councilmen about their proper role. Present on the council are both an old mentality and a new outlook, with reformers gaining the upper hand. Both the old and new are evident during proceedings in the council chambers, a large room decorated with wildlife trophies and the banner of the Flathead nation. During its twice-a-week meetings (no longer the quarterly sessions), the council at times still finds itself immersed in the detail of program implementation: receiving a report about an illegal structure diverting a stream, giving instructions about timber bidding, or learning about recent developments in a housing project. The atmosphere can be light and informal, with bantering between the council and the audience displacing debate among council members. At its serious moments, however, the discussion turns to the desirability of separating council work from routine administrative matters. At these moments the council defers to the action of the credit committee, considers a new Indian preference hiring policy, or approves implementation of portions of an executive reorganization plan. The council, therefore, is increasingly serious minded and public spirited and less given to a vigilance for narrow interests. More pointedly, the council is feeling its way through a role transition, learning what it means to be a policy making body rather than an administrative power.

Besides changes in the election system, there has been another structural reform which has moved the Flathead tribal council and government toward the political maturity necessary for self-governance. This is the executive reorganization project.[33] One of the critical weaknesses of the council has been its lack of distance from the problems it is being asked to solve. Its informal mode of proceeding has tended to immerse council members in the "heat of the moment."[34] A layer of bureaucracy, a formal executive officer, or even time have not been present to serve as barriers to the people's passion. The traditional justification for such a system has been participation—that is, government can then be reflective of the people. The growing criticism is that such immediacy magnifies problems and suffocates policy making. The council's recent response has been to initiate the demanding and politically difficult task of reorganizing the tribes' administrative machinery, thereby realigning the bureaucracy's relationship with the council.

Prior to the reorganization study, the administrative system on the Flathead reservation lacked discipline and order. The council or the agency superintendent might have been in charge, but the chairman was not. The heads of more than thirty departments and programs reported directly to the council. The tribal chairman lacked the formal authority of a chief executive officer, and incumbents of this office were traditionally weak and did not use their power of building the council's agenda or their strategic position at the center of operations to enhance their influence.[35] As a result, the chairman's potential leadership role was often co-opted by the superintendent. In 1969 the council created another rival when it established by ordinance the position of executive secretary. Over time, because of the incumbent's force of personality and the chairman's deference, the executive secretary evolved into a position of quasi executive. There were obstacles, however, to the executive secretary's full realization of the prominence and power of a chief executive—such as frequent tensions between this office and the chairman, the executive secretary's lack of constitutional authorization, and popular resistance to concentration of power in an untraditional position.

In the fall of 1984, the tribal council approved a seventy-five page executive reorganization plan which had been prepared by the tribes' management analyst. The report was controversial, as is the case with any administrative restructuring, because of the threat it presented to employees' jobs, authority, status, and accustomed way of doing things. The plan called for consolidation of the more than thirty departments into eight units. A new chain of command was created, with a full-time tribal chairman at the top and a redefined executive secretary under the chairman. The eight department heads would report to the executive secretary, who now was formally termed the chief administrative official with full responsibility for overseeing program operations. But the executive secretary was to report to the chairman, who formally became the tribes' chief executive officer and was vested with the council's delegated power. The chairman reported directly to the council and assumed the role of *primus inter pares*. Rather than supervising the workings of the tribal government, the chairman was given the responsibility of unifying and speaking for the council. For this office, the skills of an expert politician would be more in demand than the training of an administrator.[36] To these two positions, somewhat analogous to a head of state and prime minister, the executive reorganization plan added a minister of finance, the executive treasurer. Equal in status to the executive secretary, the executive treasurer became the tribes' chief fiscal affairs officer and also reported to the chairman.

The political values that underpinned this major governmental reform effort did not reflect traditional Indian social organization—informality and consensus decision making. Instead, the tribes' rationale sounded as if it were borrowed from some state's little Hoover Commission. The plan was justified in terms of "obvious overlapping and duplication"[37] resulting from rapid and unplanned growth of federally funded programs. The principal motivation of the council was achievement of "accountability"[38] in the administrative system. No other word was repeated so often, regardless of which positions were being discussed: chairman, executive secretary, executive treasurer, or department heads. The advertisement for the new position of executive secretary carried out this theme common to so many contemporary government reforms. It contained such phrases as "cost effective management control functions," "efficient and effective results," "goals and objectives," "program management systems," and "assigns responsibility clearly."[39]

What was evident in executive reorganization was the existence of a new kind of cultural assimilation. As the tribes emerged from their sheltered status as a special type of federal enclave, they began to interact increasingly with governments and corporations. The tribes discovered that they could deal successfully in these relationships only if they adopted organizational values and processes that outsiders respected and that they themselves discovered were necessary. The tribes at the same time came to recognize that reliance on the rhetoric of Indian sovereignty would produce no lasting results. Overcoming the similar pitfall of simply mouthing the platitudes of the governmental efficiency movement, the tribes selectively took on new attitudes and forms. These, in turn, have generated on the Flathead reservation an assurance and competence which have marked the tribes' recent participation in their new high-stake games.

The movement of the Flathead reservation from enclave to interaction has been impressive even though it is not yet complete. Examples of political sophistication are matched by persisting evidence of adherence to old ways. At Christmas time in 1984, for example, the tribal council authorized a $200 per capita payment instead of the scheduled

$100 distribution, even though the reservation was experiencing a significant income shortfall from timber sales and facing unanticipated budget modifications totalling $500,000. Earlier in 1984, the council removed a councilman with thirty-four years of service because he allegedly used his official position to collect wrongfully $5,000 in expense money. And the executive reorganization plan has been implemented on a piecemeal basis, partially because of the entrenched resistance of current employees. The important conclusion, however, is that there does exist a pattern of positive and continuing change: the council was divided on the per capita issue; it did impeach the official charged with improprieties; and it has put into place 70 percent of the reorganization plan. More than any other reservation government in Montana, the Flathead tribes are prepared for contemporary challenges. A discussion of some of their recent activities and successes will illustrate the Flathead government's comparative strength.

The building and grounds of the tribal complex and community college at Pablo, Montana, are a symbol of the Flathead tribes' new self-confidence. Their structures are modern, highly functional, and handsome in appearance. The surrounding property is tastefully landscaped and well cared-for. Together they speak of discipline and pride in education and self-governance. These qualities are also present in routine tribal operations. The tribes, for example, have saved a considerable amount of income and have held this reserve constant. In 1984 the interest on tribal investments amounted to $1.5 million. But most importantly, discipline and pride are seen in the tribes' selection and prosecution of major undertakings. For example, the Flathead tribal government has put together an aggressive and extensive natural resource effort, begun regulation of non-members as part of an attempt to preserve the beauty and quality of Flathead Lake, and negotiated with the Montana Power Company to get better terms for having Kerr Dam on the reservation. These activities, which will be discussed below, chart the Flathead reservation's emergence as a government of consequence.

Natural resources on the Flathead reservation are both a cultural heritage and a door to self-determination. There are 2.5 billion board feet of timber, 34,000 acres of trust grazing land, the Flathead River with good hydroelectric generating sites, Flathead Lake with excellent recreation potential, and an abundance of fish and wildlife. These natural assets have been a major source of revenue. Forest income has been as high as $4 million a year, and for years the tribes received $2.6 million annually from the Montana Power company for the Kerr Dam site.

Since 1981 the tribes' work in natural resource management has outpaced the Bureau of Indian Affairs in terms of expertise and ambition. The tribal Department of Natural Resources, established in 1981, is involved with forest management, minerals, water resources, hydro-power development, realty, and air quality. Its staff includes geologists, hydrologists, and biologists and represents the first collection of administrative professionals in the tribal government. Because of this specialization, the council has referred many matters to the department which were outside of the boundaries of natural resources. The goal of the department is to assume all of the Bureau's natural resource functions.[40] The tribes presently prevail in the areas of hydroelectric development and recreation management, and they are seeking to take over responsibility for environmental quality regulation, mineral development, and wildlife management.

No instance of the Flathead tribes' natural resource management better illustrates responsible entry into intergovernmental relations than their creation of a wilderness area on the west side of the Mission Mountains. In so acting in 1981, the Confederated Salish and Kootenai tribal government became the first Indian jurisdiction and one of a very limited number of governments besides the United States to set aside its rare and wild country. The cooperative dimension of this action is significant because the tribes' 89,500 acres of wilderness on the western slopes of the Mission Mountains matches the federal government's 73,877 acres of wilderness on the eastern side. The two tracts of primitive land meet at the top of the Mission range and create in reality a single wilderness area. Moreover, the Flathead tribes and the federal government have worked out a joint plan of management.

In the judgment of most outsiders, the true importance of the tribes' action is that it assured maximum protection and preservation of some of the most beautiful terrain in North America. The view is well described by two Montana naturalist writers:

> The bold peaks of the Mission Mountains crown a wilderness range unique in the West both in majesty and management. Soaring more than a mile above the farms and villages of the Mission Valley, the austere western front of the Missions forms one of the most striking mountain valleys in the Rockies.
>
> A dozen peaks over 9,000 feet rise from the southern end of the Missions, dominated by the great snowy head of 9,820-foot McDonald Peak. The tall central crest of the range catches the prevailing westerly winds, wringing down more than 100 inches of annual moisture, most of it snow. Alpine snowfields linger year-round, feeding a half dozen named glaciers and melting into icy streams and springs that purl through a remarkable 350 lakes, ponds, and pools.[41]

Tribal members live with and appreciate the beauty of their reservation daily, and conservation values are important to them. The land they contributed to the Mission Mountains Wilderness, however, means something more than scenery or recreation. It is tied intimately to their lives, present and past. They remember these mountains as the site of their ancestors' berrying parties, hunting expeditions, and vision quests. And today the mountains play a part in their plans for economic and political independence. As a result, the tribal management plan differs from federal policy in that it permits timber cutting on the lower flanks of the mountains and the taking of game by tribal members.

The Flathead tribes' confidence in the natural resource policy area went considerably beyond intergovernmental cooperation when the tribal council set out to include a vote for non-members in its regulation of the Flathead Lake shoreline. By terms of the 1855 Hellgate Treaty, the Flathead reservation includes the southern half of Flathead Lake, a snow and glacier-fed body of water twenty-six miles long and five miles wide. The tribal constitution authorizes the council to

> . . . regulate the uses and disposition of tribal property, to protect and preserve the tribal property, wildlife and natural resources of the Confederated Tribes, . . . [and] to protect the health, security, and general welfare of the Confederated Tribes.[42]

Acting on the assumption that ownership of the bed and banks of the south half of the lake rested with the United States and the tribes, the council in 1977 enacted a "Shoreline Protection Ordinance" for control of docks and other structures on the lake or extending over the lake bed. The stated aim of the tribes was "maintaining and improving the environmental quality of the shoreline."[43] The Secretary of the Interior subsequently approved Tribal Ordinance 64A, noting that he "fully endorse[d] the motivation behind the creation of the Ordinance."[44]

Soon after the ordinance received Department of the Interior approval, the council set into motion its regulatory program affecting the entire length of lakeshore within the reservation regardless of the ownership of adjacent lands. A challenge to the tribes' regulatory authority arose when the ordinance was enforced against owners of a marina near the resort community of Polson, who had built docks, a breakwater, and a storage shed extending from the lake onto the banks beyond the highwater mark. In federal district court the marina owners, joined by the City of Polson and the State of Montana who also were owners of frontage on the southern half of Flathead Lake, argued that the "Tribes have no power to regulate how a non-member exercises his or her riparian rights."[45] The tribes' position was that regulation of the marina, owned and operated by non-Indians, was necessary for protection of water quality and tribal fishing rights. A federal district court judge ruled in 1980 that the Flathead tribal government had no authority to regulate the marina, the city, and the state. Determined to push on, the tribes with the counsel of a Washington, D.C., law firm carried the case to the Ninth Circuit Court of Appeals.

The tribes' persistence in the Flathead Lake case cast them in an explorer's role. Both gains and losses were possible when they sought confirmation of their regulatory authority over both Indians and non-Indians. One potential drawback was intensifying bad feeling between Indians and whites on the reservation. In reaction to the tribes' assertiveness, 1,500 non-Indians formed Montanans Opposing Discrimination (MOD) to lobby the United States Congress to limit tribal governing power. MOD, and its successor organization, All Citizens Equal, rallied around the arguments that Indians of small blood quantum were enjoying unreasonable privileges and that non-Indians were being regulated by a government in which they had no voice. In addition to these groups, the Flathead Defense Fund was created to pay the legal fees of non-Indians who were sued by the tribes. On the benefit side, the Flathead tribes could obtain a decision that would resolve confusion in the law and secure for all tribal governments the authority to act more as governments and less as docile protectorates.

The decision of the Ninth Circuit Court of Appeals had that result. Before the court were two arguments: that the shoreline ordinance was inconsistent with the tribes' dependent status and with overriding federal interests, and that the tribes had inherent power to regulate non-Indians within the reservation to protect "the political integrity, the economic security, or the health or welfare"[46] of the reservation. The judges, well aware of the opposition in these arguments, ruled for the tribes. In its opinion the court observed:

> The conduct that the Tribes seek to regulate in the instant case—generally speaking, the use of the bed and banks of the south half of Flathead Lake—has the potential for significantly affecting the economy, welfare, and health of the Tribes. Such conduct, if unregulated, could increase water pollution, damage the ecology of the lake, interfere with treaty fishing rights, or otherwise harm the lake, which is one of the most important tribal resources.[47]

Following the decision, the United States Supreme Court denied a petition for review, even though Justice William Rehnquist pointed out that the "issues present important questions having ramifications throughout the many Western States."[48] As a result, the rule of the

Flathead Lake case—recognition of enhanced tribal power over non-Indians—is the law throughout the seven western states in the Ninth Circuit.

After the Supreme Court's 1982 action upholding tribal jurisdiction, the Shoreline Protection Board of the Flathead reservation proceeded with its regulatory program. It set an annual mooring fee for buoys and proposed fees for shore stations, docks, breakwaters, and other permanent facilities built on the lake bottom. Comments were received on the proposed regulations, and some modifications were made. This mode of proceeding by the tribes is significant because it demonstrates an intent to be open and fair. Having won their case in court and having experienced the hostility their aggressiveness had generated, the tribes resorted to political measures to disarm their opponents. In addition to hearings, the tribes held out an olive branch to their opponents by implementing the provision of the Shoreline Protection Ordinance which called for three non-Indians as voting members on the seven-person Shoreline Protection Board. Such participation is not nominal because the board chairman, the seventh member, does not vote. It is especially noteworthy because it represents such a rare occasion—admission of whites by an Indian tribe into its governing processes. This also speaks loudly about the Flathead tribes' self-confidence and political sophistication.

There is another example which points to the Flathead tribes' emergence as an autonomous and active government. This was its case before the Federal Energy Regulatory Commission (FERC) and negotiations with the Montana Power Company to acquire the license for Kerr Dam. While wilderness creation and shoreline protection represent intergovernmental cooperation and regulation of non-Indians (certainly major accomplishments for a tribal government), the Kerr Dam episode stands for something more. Here the Flathead tribes took on directly the most graphic symbol of established political power in Montana. The Montana Power Company and Anaconda Mining for years were known together as "the company" because of their integrated economic interests and astounding political power. Though those days of captive government are now gone, the Montana Power Company remains a formidable opponent for any organization. In the compromise settlement regarding Kerr Dam, the Flathead tribes clearly got the better deal.

Kerr Dam is the oldest federally licensed hydroelectric facility in the United States and only one of nine dams built for hydropower on Indian reservations. It spans the Flathead River, southwest of Polson, Montana, and has a generating capacity of 180 megawatts, which represents 31 percent of Montana Power's hydroelectric output and 11.5

percent of the utility's total electric product. The Flathead tribes' calculations placed Montana Power's annual profit for operating Kerr Dam at $12 million to $14 million. Montana Power's fifty-year operating license was due to expire in 1985, and in 1981, when the tribes petitioned the federal government for the license authority, the utility was making an annual payment to the tribes of $2.6 million.

The contest before the Federal Energy Regulatory Commission for a fifty-year license for the Kerr Dam pulled many sideliners into the fray. The Montana Power Company especially was active in recruiting allies with the argument that tribal operation would mean higher electricity rates. Consequently, irrigators, industry representatives, business groups, and home owners testified against the tribes' petition at FERC hearings. The controversy also came to be framed in terms of the tribes' competency and good will. The federal hearing examiner, whose charge was to weigh the testimony and recommend a decision, found that the tribes had failed to prove that they had a purchaser for the dam's electricity and asked the two parties to negotiate a settlement. The tribes rejected the utility's first two offers: an annual payment of $5 million or continuation of the current payment of $2.6 million a year plus a onetime, up-front payment of $5,000 to each tribal member. Despite Indian protestations that 75 percent of the tribal membership preferred the cash-now option, the council resisted popular pressure and held out for something better.

The eventual settlement, unanimously approved by the council in late 1984, provided for Montana Power operation of the dam and an annual payment of $9 million to the tribes for thirty years. This rental fee would be adjusted for inflation using the consumer price index. In 2015, the tribes will assume operating authority for the dam, paying the utility for its net investment in the facility. To ease the transition, Montana Power will supply training to tribal members and use its transmission network to conduct the tribally produced electricity. After twenty years of tribal operation, the dam will again be subject to relicensing. Achieving the agreement was a major success for the Flathead tribes, but implementing the takeover in thirty years will be an even greater challenge. Responsible use of the $9 million annuity and preparation for the day of assumption will try the discipline and vision of the tribal government.

A councilman on the Flathead reservation said that two themes have traditionally run through the tribes' politics: the reservation as a homeland and rights of members. For many years emphasis was placed on the rights theme. It was defined in terms of a member receiving a fair share, and the reservation was viewed primarily as a material resource to gratify this demand. The values of this political culture were suspicion of the motives of officials and an extraordinary degree of participation by members in tribal politics ("nowhere else in the United States is participation more intense than on this reservation").[49] The symbol of this era of reservation life is the federal ration or the tribal per capita payment.

The public life of the Flathead reservation is moving beyond proprietary politics. The same two central themes persist, but they are given a different interpretation and emphasis. Increasingly, today, the reservation is being viewed as a vulnerable trust which must be carefully conserved. In many ways, members' rights are seen as subordinate to tribal interests and members are increasingly asked to exercise prudence and restraint. The political values of the emerging period are accountability and efficiency, as well as participation. The symbol is a strong government, which is both professional and representative.

The Flathead tribes have been able to approach their goal of self-determination for many reasons. There has been a high demand for their natural resources, namely timber and water. The membership has been willing to use the ideas and approaches of outsiders, and such political acculturation has made adaptation to change easier and more successful. But most importantly, tribal leaders have been able to manage the reservation's evolution, preserving the past and accommodating it to the unrelenting internal and external pressures of the present by bringing realism and balance to the interpretation of the tribes' basic principles. To do this without cynicism or contrivance is a masterful feat, and yet the future of the reservation depends upon it.

Notes

1. John Fahey, *The Flathead Indians* (Norman: University of Oklahoma Press, 1974), p. 263, quoting Agent Peter Ronan, *The Missoulian,* August 23, 1893.

2. The discussion of the early history of the Salish and Kootenai Indians is taken from Ibid. and James A. Teit and Frank Boas, *The Flathead Group* (an extract from *The Salish Tribes of the Western Plateaus,* 45th B.A.E. Annual Report, 1927–1928; Seattle: Facsimile Reproduction of the Shorey Book Store, 1975).

3. Fahey, p. 6.

4. Ibid., p. 94.

5. Ibid., p. 7.

6. Ibid., p. 279.

7. Ibid., p. 108.

8. The Court's opinion is *Lone Wolf v. Hitchcock,* 187 U.S. 553 (1903). Dixon's role in introducing the Flathead Act is treated in Jules A. Karlin,

Joseph M. Dixon of Montana, Vol. I: *Senator and Bull Moose Manager, 1867–1917* (Missoula: University of Montana, 1974), pp. 56–59. For a detailed account of the allotment and opening of the Flathead reservation, see *Confederated Salish and Kootenai Tribes v. United States* 437 F.2d 458 (1971). This decision of the United States Court of Claims awarded the Confederated Salish and Kootenai Tribes $6,066,668.78, based on the fair market value of the lands lost under the 1904 Act, calculated at $7,410,000.00, less the $1,343,331.22 that the tribes had received for the lands.

9. Teit and Boas, p. 374.

10. Flathead Culture Committee, *A Brief History of the Flathead Tribes* (2d ed.; St. Ignatius, Montana: Confederated Salish and Kootenai Tribes, 1979).

11. Superintendents' Annual Narrative and Statistical Report, Flathead, 1911, Frame 747; 1917, Frame 819; 1919, Frame 864; 1922, Frames 1035–1036.

12. Superintendents' Annual Narrative and Statistical Report, Flathead, 1929, Frame 220.

13. U.S. Congress, House Select Committee for Indian Affairs, *Hearings before a Subcommittee of the Committee of Indian Affairs, Pursuant to H. Res. 166,* 87th Congress, 2nd Session, 1944, pp. 461–462.

14. S. Lyman Tyler, *A History of Indian Policy* (Washington, D.C.: Government Printing Office, 1973), p. 163.

15. *Constitution and Bylaws of the Confederated Salish and Kootenai Tribes of the Flathead Reservation,* Article I (Bylaws), sec. 1.

16. Interview with S. Kevin Howlett, member of the Tribal Council of the Flathead Reservation, December 12, 1984.

17. Interview with James Paro, Director of the Flathead Reservation's Department of Natural Resources, July 5, 1983.

18. *The Missoulian,* March 23, 1984.

19. Interview with James H. Steele, member of the Tribal Council of the Flathead Reservation, July 5, 1983.

20. Ibid.

21. Interview with S. Kevin Howlett.

22. Ibid.

23. Ibid.

24. Interview with James Paro.

25. Interview with James H. Steele.

26. Interview with S. Kevin Howlett.

27. Interview with James H. Steele.

28. Ibid.

29. Ibid.

30. Interview with S. Kevin Howlett.

31. Interview with James H. Steele.

32. Ibid.

33. Greg Dumontier (Management Analyst for the Flathead Reservation), "Reorganization Plan" (Photocopy, August 31, 1984).

34. Interview with James Paro.

35. Interview with Joe McDonald, former member of the Tribal Council of the Flathead Reservation, July 5, 1983.

36. Interview with S. Kevin Howlett.

37. Ibid.

38. Ibid.

39. *The Missoulian,* October 21, 1984.

40. Interview with James Paro.

41. Steve Woodruff and Don Schwennesen, *Montana Wilderness: Discovering the Heritage* (Kansas City: The Lowell Press, 1984), p. 83.

42. *Constitution and Bylaws of the Confederated Salish and Kootenai Tribes of the Flathead Reservation,* Art. VI, sec. 1.

43. Flathead Tribal Ordinance, p. 64A.

44. *Confederated Salish and Kootenai Tribe of the Flathead Reservation, Montana v. James M. Namen, City of Polson, Montana, and State of Montana,* 665 F.2d 951, 964 (1982).

45. Ibid., p. 953.

46. *Montana v. United States,* 450 U.S. 544, 566 (1981).

47. *Confederated Salish and Kootenai,* p. 964.

48. *James M. Namen, et al. v. Confederated Salish and Kootenai Tribes of the Flathead Reservation, Montana et al.,* 459 U.S. 977, 981 (1982).

49. Interview with S. Kevin Howlett.

10

Reflections on Tribal Government

Each of the foregoing chapters focused on one reservation and what is special about its politics. It is also apparent from these sketches that the seven Montana reservations have much in common. They are like brothers and sisters in a family, each with particular cares and pursuits but bonded by a commonality both superficial and profound. Without disregarding the unique, this final chapter will explore the political attitudes and practices which Montana reservations share. Against this background of Indian political culture, the discussion will turn to reform considerations. Given the aim of this chapter, a point stressed preliminarily requires reemphasis: tribal government is the sovereign prerogative of the tribes. This essay thus cautiously presents the observations of interested outsiders.

The contemporary Indian view of politics on the Montana reservations has its roots in the northern plains of several centuries ago. The American Indian Policy Review Commission concluded that "each tribe has retained, in varying degrees, traditional, cultural, and religious societal practices which influence the manner and form in which the tribal government is operated."[1] Some of these past practices comprised a political economy which was based upon growing seasons and the movement of wild game. For some plains tribes, small bands were the best way to respond to the ever-present condition of economic and military vulnerability. Other tribes used a governing system that was more centralized, but even in these instances a premium was placed on broad participation and consensus decision making. Seemingly inconsistent political values could coexist, both between tribes and within a tribe. For example, individual autonomy could be prized at the same time that group loyalty or cultural conformity was expected. Loyalty to a band or tribe did not inevitably translate into subservience to a tribal government, and the importance of personal relationships and expedient actions was recognized in even the most centralized tribes. There appears to be, therefore, one constant in political attitudes among the plains Indians: an inclination to remain somewhat aloof from formal government and to hold oneself separate and ready. Thus the old Sioux saying, "On each individual rests the survival of the group."

Some of this outlook persists today on the reservations and can have a pronounced effect on the principal modern source of livelihood, the tribal government. Vestiges of the days of buffalo, berrying, and vast unrestricted homelands can be found in council decisions, campaign rhetoric, and attitudes about government and officials. While it is often observed that reservations are governed under alien forms imposed by whites, in fact there frequently exists an unwritten constitution of traditional Indian political values. This set of political attitudes and practices is consistently neither good nor bad in terms of reservation welfare. They are, though, often unrecognized as distinctively (but not uniquely) Indian, and in prior writings they have not been suggested as a basis for reform or a possible obstacle to progress.

A central value of a tribe's political culture is personal autonomy, in the sense of preserving some meaningful separateness from the various groups with which the individual identifies. Its roots are far different from a laissez faire rationalization or the born-again philosophy of urban escapees. It is a cultural inheritance that developed of necessity and was continuously nurtured by experience and myth. Reservation Indians, as a result, do not readily submit themselves to government, whether tribal or white. The values of representative institutions can seem infirm beside the traditions of self-direction, direct involvement, and personal obligation. Viewed positively, this shared attitude permits any tribal member to address the council and be listened to with attention and respect. But if strongly held, the value of individual autonomy can call into question the very legitimacy of tribal government.

Related—possibly by contradiction, in some cases—to individual autonomy is a loyalty to the familiar and near. Of the first order is an emotional and symbolic attachment to the reservation as a homeland. More important for internal politics is identification with a district, local settlement, or group, which is often more intense and meaningful than identification with the tribe or tribal government. Associations based on family, clan, or historical events also can be politically more significant than reservation-wide movements or issues. These local relationships and small groups create the opportunity for involvement, and the resulting expectation on the reservation has been that politics should be highly personal and participatory. But this traditional outlook can also be the basis of disparaging the benefits of more formal government.

Another ingredient of the political culture of Montana's Indian reservations is a view of government that is grounded in proprietary—as distinguished from public—considerations. This attitude is obviously not limited to Native American society, but in this context it is especially understandable given the poverty, overpopulation, and limited economic opportunity of the typical reservation and the mandates of fundamental tribal documents. For example, the Blackfeet constitution characteristically authorizes the tribal council to "manage all economic affairs and enterprises of the Blackfeet Reservation . . . in accordance with terms of a charter to be issued to the Blackfeet Tribe by the Secretary of the Interior."[2] The Blackfeet Corporate Charter permits the tribal council to

> . . . issue to each of its members a nontransferable certificate of membership evidencing the equal share of each member in the assets of the Tribe and [to] distribute per capita, among the recognized members of the Tribe, the net income of corporate activities including the proceeds of leases of tribal assets. . . .[3]

The reservation setting and legal provisions such as these can raise legitimate expectation among tribal members that politics is a means of bettering one's personal material situation, as well as being a vehicle for improving the tribe's general welfare. This belief, when coupled with other commonly held values, can lead to political dysfunction. The stage is set by tribal members' inherent suspicion of formal government. The pervasiveness of per capita and patronage politics and an understandable jealousy—that tribal officials and employees are getting rich and you are not—then can cause political competition to become intense and mean. Challengers to incumbents frequently play to this distrust and attack existing programs as corrupt and selfish. The result can be short political careers, flip-flop in policies, and little continuity in tribal government.

There is another common feature of reservation politics that is closely tied to individual autonomy, local identification, and political involvement for personal gain. This is the belief that reservation government should be relatively informal, that is, structured loosely and operated with vaguely defined procedures. The underlying disposition—deference to the individual and aversion to concentrated power and overly strong leaders—stems from the power and role of traditional chiefs. The influence of these leaders was due to finely developed political skills and not grants of authority. Such leadership values as strong character, humility, and articulateness are clearly still prized. In contemporary reservation politics, however, informal government can be maintained for additional reasons and with mixed results. Informal government, that is, vague and dispersed grants of power and poorly defined procedures, allows for personal political participation with immediate and predictable results. Political factions can thereby gain favors, such as jobs, and serve up retribution more easily. On the other hand, formal government, a system of fixed responsibilities and clear procedures, is not as susceptible to individual manipulation.

Because of the informality of tribal government, its functioning is often characterized by poor communication among the parties involved in reservation politics. This at first seems ironic given the persisting vigor of such features of traditional Indian society as proximity and personal involvement. A principal cause of the communications problem is that the tribe's part-time governing body must all too often carry out its substantial responsibilities without adequate information and counsel. Like other part-time legislatures—city councils, county commissions, and some state legislatures—tribal councilmen normally do not have adequate staff to rely upon, and the Bureau of Indian Affairs has not had the willingness or ability to provide the necessary assistance. A tribal council is also similar to other legislative bodies in that it lacks the time and training to make itself expert concerning the many complex issues on its agenda. This deficiency can result in defensive and evasive actions by the council, especially when members, events, and outside interests apply pressure for council decisions. For example, councilmen can resort to closed meetings and refuse to explain council deliberations. Because of these realities of council politics, it is not surprising that tribal members become ill-informed and confused about tribal matters. Having no reliable source of political information, they depend instead on rumor and gossip, which only tend to fuel their suspicions about official waste and fraud. Poor political communication, therefore, can be a problem for both officials and members, and lack of information can diminish the effectiveness and acceptance of tribal government.

Finally reservation political culture is influenced by an extremely conservative outlook which cherishes the past and is tied to age and bloodline. Elderly and full-blood Indians, especially, tend to emphasize treaty rights, the longstanding role of the federal government and its obligation to the tribes, and even the tribe's modern constitution. While younger and more progressive Indians (usually mixed bloods) work to hasten the end of colonial rule, more traditional elements on the reservation fear the termination of Bureau protection and federal benefits and want to avoid constitutional revision and the risks of Indian self-government. Reservations are similar to third world nations which face tremendous tasks of economic and political development. The fact that there is no Indian consensus, that reform-minded leaders must constantly do battle with those who are more strongly wedded to the past, makes the agenda of tribal governments as demanding as the challenges facing emerging countries.

The just-discussed themes of politics on Montana's Indian reservations are also found in differing degrees on reservations throughout the country. This phenomenon becomes clearer when two essential characteristics of reservation politics are used as shorthand for the values of Indian political culture. The two composite features are a politics of scarcity and a politics of interference. These dimensions can be used to summarize and demonstrate the practical dynamics of the constituent values. An underlying basis of this political commonality is undoubtedly some similarity in the reservations' political traditions and economic and demographic features. But past common experience with the United States government and more recent relations with local political forces also account for some of the shared traits and political threads tying one reservation's political heritage to others.

A politics of scarcity stems understandably from the high unemployment, high illiteracy, and poor health that characterize the nation's reservations. Economic scarcity, coupled with pronounced loyalty on reservations to the social group, influences the political behavior of tribal leaders. Their principal task is to overcome scarcity, and they accordingly seek outside dollars to improve the reservation's economic opportunities and social conditions. Even though getting outside help is critical for the reservation, a negative effect is inevitable: compliance with outside regulations and acceptance of other forms of interference.

Reservation politics continues to tolerate outside interference and increased reservation dependency because outside funds are absolutely crucial to both the tribal community and to the reservation political machine. The economic need is more obvious but no more critical than the political need. The mark of a tribal leader's success and longevity in office is an ability to bring outside funds into the reservation without lining one's pocket. Hence, a tribal leader demonstrates public concern and improves community welfare for the short term by minimizing scarcity.

A good example of the politics of scarcity is the Quechan Reservation in California, where politicians are judged on how well they "get something for the people." The primary objective of Quechan tribal members is funding for reservation projects, jobs, and per capita payments. Quechan leaders, therefore, must secure federally financed community development programs because scarcity is minimized only by getting something for the reservation. Then a leader "must make a series of strategic choices about how best to allocate his and the tribe's resources to gain desired ends."[4]

Overcoming scarcity has tremendous ramifications for participation in reservation politics. If voter turn-out tends to be high, a tribal political leader must expand his probably fragile political base or be willing to accept the alternative of certain ouster. Successful Quechan politicians, consequently, make emergency loans to tribal members to hold old supporters and attract new supporters. A successful tribal chairman knows that getting something for the people means more than providing for the social welfare.[5]

The politics of scarcity gives understanding to the politics of interference and explains a reservation's tolerance for intrusion in its politics. Two kinds of political interference exist on reservations, one culturally based and from within and the other governmentally associated and from the outside. Two values of Indian political culture are especially pertinent to the former, individualism and group loyalty. For example, the loyalty of tribal members is to social groups sharing the same territory, language, and world view, and not to the reservation-wide tribal government composed of many social groups and even different tribes. This political fragmentation is especially true of, but not limited to, multi-tribal reservations where distinct social divisions have perpetuated group loyalties.

The value of personal autonomy or individualism also influences quietly though profoundly the politics of interference. A traditional disposition toward self-autonomy among plains Indians was reinforced by subsequent United States Indian policies emphasizing wage work, land allotment, military service, relocation, and formal education. These were programs that stressed and strengthened individualism. Evolving personal autonomy encouraged tribal members to challenge tribal governmental authority and obstruct, either overtly or covertly, the reservation's political process.

These dichotomous social values, individualism and group loyalty, maintain the reservation's politics of internal interference. Corollaries are a fluid tribal administration, constantly changing political factions, and a constant vigil on those who are in power. Individualism and group loyalty, coupled with an innate cultural conservatism, mean that there is lacking on the reservations a sufficient political and administrative basis for changing the political system. The politics of interference produces little loyalty to a reservationwide government.

The 1974 Pine Ridge election for tribal chairman illustrates the dynamics of the politics of interference. The politically significant social and cultural groupings were young versus old, full blood versus mixed blood, educated versus uneducated, and off-reservation and urban versus reservation and rural. American Indian Movement leader Russell Means, an urban tribal member, opposed incumbent chairman Richard Wilson, a reservation resident, for control of the reservation government. This notorious tribal political campaign pitted candidates from different cultural and social backgrounds. The stakes and the polarities caused both candidates to overstep the established proprieties of tribal elections.[6]

Outside interests, as well as internal factions, contribute to the politics of interference on Indian reservations. The reservation political process can be obstructed by Congress, federal agencies, local governments, and business corporations. This outside interference contributes to the tribal political culture of suspicion and hostility toward government.[7]

The initial outside wedge into tribal politics was Congress' trust relationship with federally recognized tribes. Intrusion into the reservation political process began with treaties and continued with periodic legislation. It varied from authorizing the establishment of a tribal government to placing limitations on tribal actions. In 1892 Congress approved the Osage tribal constitution which established the community's political forum.[8] In 1906 Congress enacted legislation forbidding the governments of the Five Civilized tribes to pass specific laws and requiring the United States President to approve all tribal actions.[9]

Executive departments of the federal government also have frequently invaded tribal politics. The Secretary of the Interior, because of authorizations in federal statutes and secretarial approval clauses in most contemporary tribal constitutions, can either approve or disapprove tribal actions. The reservation superintendent also has jurisdiction to review specific tribal decisions. Congress' policy of Indian self-determination thrusts other federal agencies into reservation politics. The requirements of Public Law 93-638 contracts have made tribal officials low level administrators for many federal assistance programs, ironically under the guise of a law enacted to enhance tribal self rule.

Examples of the politics of interference based on outside pressures are unfortunately not hard to find. The circumstances, though, can vary significantly and the results are not uniform. In 1976 the Navajo tribe negotiated a coal lease with El Paso Natural Gas-Consolidated Coal Company, setting the company's rate at 8 percent of the coal price. Acting in a trust capacity, Secretary of the Interior Cecil Andrus refused to approve the lease until the negotiated rate increased to 12.5 percent.[10] On the other hand, the Northern Cheyenne demanded federal intervention to prevent coal mining on their reservation. These differences in circumstances illustrate that federal intervention in the reservation political process can be either solicited or opposed, beneficial or damaging.

Tribal governments continue to depend upon Congress and comply with agencies' intrusive regulations out of necessity. The reality is that federal funding is essential to implement the policy of Indian self-determination, not to mention the alleviation of tribal poverty. Tribal populations have been forced to accept grudgingly this interference, creating a culture that tolerates outside influence in their internal affairs. The politics of scarcity and the politics of interference make clear that a counter culture is necessary to promote the change that is needed in different aspects of tribal government. The addressing of reservation political reform requires more than a constitutional amendment or a council ordinance; it first requires building a tribal reform tradition. In the absence of a culture open to reform, tribal politics will continue to be based on scarcity and interference.

Any suggestions for reforming tribal government, therefore, must be tied to an analysis of Indian political culture. The central values of this tradition can serve both as a foundation for growth and as an indication of needed change. Overall, the following would seem to be helpful changes for tribal governments: movement toward separation of powers, redefinition of the role of the Bureau of Indian Affairs, and acceptance by tribal members of their constitution as fundamental law. For years, such reform discussion was dismissed as a plot to impose "Anglo" values on Indians. Recently, however, Indian leaders are distinguishing between which of their traditional values should be the basis of reform and which should be the object of reform. For example, Joe McKay, a Blackfeet lawyer and councilman, has said:

> Revision of constitutions and charters must center on a tribe's own needs and cultural values. Goals should be arrived at through participation, not by using model constitutions or the documents of other tribes. To be really respected, though, tribes must begin to act like governments— to follow their constitutions. Now this pressure is coming from the outside. Soon, the pressure will come from within. It is growing now.[11]

Many reservation problems stem from a lack of separation of powers. This situation should not be surprising given traditional tribal forms, the expedience and intrusiveness of Indian agents, and the prescriptions of the Indian Reorganization Act. Montana reservations have provided numerous examples of usurped powers. A Northern Cheyenne president fired a judge because of a decision opposing energy development. On the Rocky Boy's reservation, councilmen have told a judge "how to try a person" despite the constitution's provision of an independently elected judiciary.[12] The singular influence of the Crow General Council means that there is no forum for a complaint against the tribal government: "You must swallow your grievance."[13] And on the Blackfeet reservation, the expectation that the "council handles everything" resulted in council meddling and the bankruptcy of a business enterprise.[14] Tribal councils in Montana, despite their part-time status, have assumed an almost swaggering supremacy. This phenomenom is by no means limited to Montana reservations. A broader survey observed that tribal "council members wield extraordinary power: They control the biennial elections, they distribute jobs and housing," and they control the 638 contracts.[15] Such substantial power at times can be corrupting. In 1981 Rosebud petitioners claimed that the tribal council was buying votes at Ideal, South Dakota. The tribal judge ordered a temporary halt to the election, but the council suspended the judge and appointed another judge who overturned the election stay. The election was held, with the long-term result that the council had thoroughly politicized the court.[16] Reservations would be better served by accountable policy makers, professional administrators, and an independent judiciary.

Certainly the unique conditions, traditions, and present strengths of each tribal government must be recognized when examining the proper relationship between the branches of government. Some across-the-board observations, though, will probably stand up. For most tribal governments, accountability is an absent virtue. The blurring of lines separating the Bureau from the tribe, the membership from officials, and the council from all other government functions makes it difficult to assign credit or blame for actions. On many reservations, sharper delineation of duties would be an improvement. The council should be the policymaking arm of tribal government, a good-sized representative body close to the membership and with clear limits on the extent of its authority. The chairman should be a chief executive who is an effective leader and has strong administrative assistance. The chairman's principal source of power should be an at-large political base, and the critical check should be responsibility to the tribal electorate. The tribal court, the most studied but often the least developed branch of tribal government, should become a dependable forum for resolving members' grievances and reviewing the actions of tribal officials, in addition to exercising the criminal and civil jurisdiction delineated by federal and tribal law. The independence necessary for these functions would come mainly from constitutional status, elected judges, adequate resources, and specialized training.

Separation of powers will become especially important if progress is made on the second suggested reform, redefinition of the role of the

Bureau of Indian Affairs. The hypothesis, very simply and not at all novel, is that the Bureau must withdraw from tribal political affairs for self-government to become a reality. For over fifty years and despite federal policies of self-determination, the Bureau—principally in the form of the superintendent, an outsider and career administrator—has been present on reservations in a patriarchal and protective capacity. The intent of the 1934 Indian Reorganization Act could well have been to make the tribal council the policy formulator and the superintendent the combined judiciary and executive with a veto, because this has often been the reality. The 1975 plan for tribes to contract to provide services previously administered by the Bureau also has had self-government shortcomings because the Bureau did not remain at arms-length and was unwilling to trust or help tribal governments in their assumption of greater authority.[17] The Bureau has been dedicated to preserving its own system of regulatory control and its own economic security.

The tribal-Bureau relationship has been an affair of love and hate. For some tribal members the Bureau has been a Santa Claus, maintaining the predictable and reassuring role of provider.[18] These tribesmen fear the loss of federal intervention. Tribal leaders, too, have benefited from the Bureau's presence. Federal assistance makes it easier for tribal politicians to live up to their constituents' expectations, while their own failures can be blamed on the federal government. The ambivalent nature of federal intrusion explains the federal investigation of the 1974 Pine Ridge tribal elections, even though the tribal constitution requires that a tribal committee handle all election disputes.[19] Tribal leaders have frequently found it convenient to have the Bureau as "the bureaucracy of last resort."[20]

The political convenience the Bureau provides the tribes cannot hide the fact that the Bureau's self-interest and insensitivity have been despised. Tribal populations regularly view the Bureau in several negative ways. The Bureau has been a scapegoat for failure, a step-father refusing to let the tribes exercise their own authority, or an unfeeling case worker dispensing welfare.[21] All of these perspectives emphasize the tribes' dependency on the federal government. But Indian self-government can be achieved only if tribal leaders and communities learn and grow through the experience of full risk assumption, independent action, and complete accountability. Such a set of conditions requires at a minimum Bureau withdrawal from the arena of tribal governments. Then tribal governments will come to accept the "complete equation of their proposed conduct"—rights and responsibilities.[22]

The self-government lessons learned from Bureau withdrawal would be more painfully acquired on some reservations than on others. This is because there are two tiers of Indian communities, those with governmental sophistication and economic promise and those that are politically weak and chronically poor. The Presidential Commission on Indian Reservation Economies recognized such a diversity among Indian tribes in its recommendation for reorganizing federal systems with trust responsibilities.[23] The many factors of reservation progress can be grouped into four categories: good leadership, which includes stability, strong character, and political realism; effective structure, which consists of enhanced separation of branches, professional and managerial expertise, and formal procedures; adequate revenue, which depends upon marketable natural resources, imaginative economic development, proximity to jobs, and fiscal restraint; and reservation unity, which is tied to shared values, pride in identity, and considerable homogeneity—whether based upon common roots or practical experience.

Viewed according to these four factors of progress, the Montana reservations have a considerable range. Flathead, Fort Peck, Northern Cheyenne, and the Blackfeet are grouped toward the top, and Crow, Fort Belknap, and Rocky Boy's have the greatest distance to travel. The phase-out of the Bureau would necessarily vary in pace from reservation to reservation, just as the Bureau's contemporary role and influence have been anything but uniform. On the Blackfeet, for example, the Bureau has been intrusive; paternalistic on the Crow; a check on the Northern Cheyenne; obstructionistic on Fort Belknap; either a back-up or meddlesome on Rocky Boy's; wisely and prudently used on Fort Peck; and useless on the Flathead. In each instance, however, Bureau withdrawal would not mean the end of United States trust responsibility or the loss of trust status for tribal lands and resources. This formal federal obligation also should be met by generous block grants to tribal governments.[24] The tribes, in turn, would assume total political responsibility for their accomplishments and failures.

Thirdly, the strength of reservation governments would be enhanced by broad acceptance of the concept of fundamental law, as well as by increased separation of powers and redefinition of the Bureau's role. Up to now, the tribes have not viewed their constitutions as documents to legitimate and guide political actions. Instead, tribal governments have ignored their constitutions when the provisions were inconvenient. On the Northern Cheyenne reservation, for example, both a tribal president and an agency superintendent have found it necessary to remind the council repeatedly of the constitution's authorizations and limitations. The council finally passed a resolution "to follow the constitution from here on out."[25] Such an action would not have taken place if the concept of fundamental law had been meaningful to the tribe.

The fact that tribal governments have often ignored their constitutions does not mean that fundamental law has no place on Indian reservations. There have been good reasons for rejecting a constitution's authority. Both tribal members and officials have tended to view their constitutions as hastily adopted foreign documents imposed upon them by the federal government. This attitude is reinforced by the Bureau's long practice of functioning as a reviewing body, interpreting a constitution and telling a tribe whether or not a certain action can be taken, or determining if the tribe's amendment can be added to its constitution. As a result, a tribe comes to see its constitution as the federal government's document, not its own. The Bureau's paternalism has trivialized the tribal constitutions, and, consequently, the council and officials do not hesitate to act without authority or in direct contradiction to constitutional requirements. This does not mean, though, that reservation politics would not be better off if the constitution embodied an expectation for fair and limited government.

The necessary reform is for the tribes to make their constitutions their own. The political values contained in a constitution would then be fundamental because they would have come from the tribe itself. There are several possible vehicles of constitutional change, the two principal modes being total revision and step-by-step reform.[26] Many reasons exist for arguing in favor of the piecemeal approach. Wholesale constitutional reform has little chance for success if the stories of recent failures on the Flathead, Blackfeet, and Crow reservations are given credence. There appears to be no dependable strategy for overcoming tribal members' deep conservatism and distrust when faced with a proposal for wholesale change. A better approach is a continuing constitutional commission, comprised of members and officials, which studies the reservation's constitution and periodically recommends amendments. The merits of such a process is that it is tribally run, permits broad-based participation, and promotes gradual and orderly change. Even major revision—such as changing the size of the council or strengthening the power of the chairman—could become acceptable if grounded in open deliberation and compromise.

This process of incremental revision could create a truly fundamental law. A series of amendments, initiated and ratified by the tribal membership, could in time "repatriate" a tribal government's constitution. The substance of these proposals would vary from reservation to reservation, but they undoubtedly would be a reflection of both traditional values and contemporary needs. A growing sentiment among tribal officials is that concern for preserving native traditions does not have to stand in the way of strengthening government. For example, advisory community councils, the initiative and referendum, and an open meeting requirement could be adopted to accommodate a tribe's participatory culture. A code of public ethics in the constitution could articulate a tribe's expectations for its officers and renew the high regard in which tribal leaders traditionally were held. Separation of enterprise management from community politics could announce that the tribe's resources are meant for the general welfare and not for the benefit of a favored few. Clear election procedures spelled out in a constitution could build up trust in tribal politics and dispel the impression that government is the captive of factions. Through careful and sustained attention to constitutional reform, tribal members could formally reclaim their own governments—enshrining the values of the past and building a strong foundation for the future.

Notes

1. American Indian Policy Review Commission, *Report on Tribal Government* (Washington, D.C.: U.S. Government Printing Office, 1976), p. 28.

2. *Constitution and Bylaws of the Blackfeet Tribe of the Blackfeet Indian Reservation, Montana,* 1935, Art. VI, sec. 1 (e).

3. *Corporate Charter of the Blackfeet Tribe of the Blackfeet Indian Reservation,* p. 5.

4. Robert L. Bee, *The Politics of American Indian Policy* (Cambridge, Mass.: Schenkman Publishing Company, 1982), p. 3.

5. Ibid.

6. U.S. Commission on Civil Rights, *Report of Investigation: Oglala Sioux Tribe, General Election, 1974* (Washington, D.C.: The Commission, October, 1974), pp. 1–28.

7. Russell Lawrence Barsh and James Youngblood, *The Road: Indian Tribes and Political Liberty* (Berkeley: University of California Press, 1980), pp. 230–240.

8. U.S. Commissioner of Indian Affairs, *Annual Report, 1892* (Washington, D.C.: U.S. Government Printing Office, 1892), p. 26.

9. 434 U.S. Statutes at Large 148.

10. Philip Reno, *Navajo Resources and Economic Development* (Albuquerque: University of New Mexico Press, 1981), pp. 110–112, 120–121.

11. Joe McKay, "Achieving Constitutional Revision," Presentation at the Forum on Tribal Constitutional and Code Revision and the Implications for Tribal Courts, University of Montana School of Law, Missoula, August 3, 1984.

12. Duncan Standing Rock, member of the Rocky Boy's Reservation Business Committee, remarks at Ibid., August 2, 1984.

13. Jim Vogel, Tribal Court Adviser on the Crow Reservation, remarks at Ibid., August 2, 1984.

14. Jackie Parsons, Chief Judge of the Blackfeet Tribal Court, remarks at Ibid., August 2, 1984.

15. *Washington Post,* September 11, 1984, p. 15.

16. Ibid.

17. Interview with Ted Meredith, Department of Interior Field Solicitor, Billings, Montana, August 22, 1983.

18. U.S. Congress, House, *Investigation of Bureau of Indian Affairs.* Report No. 2680 (Washington, D.C.: 83rd Congress, 2nd sess., 1954), p. 78.

19. U.S. Commission on Civil Rights, pp. 1–28.

20. American Indian Policy Review Commission, p. 355.

21. U.S. Congress, *Investigation of Bureau of Indian Affairs,* p. 78.

22. Fred L. Ragsdale, Jr., "The Deception of Geography," in *American Indian Policy in the Twentieth Century,* ed. Vine Deloria, Jr. (Norman: University of Oklahoma Press, 1985), p. 80.

23. Presidential Commission on Indian Reservation Economies, *Report and Recommendations to the President of the United States* (Washington, D.C.: The Commission, 1984), p. 31.

24. The Presidential Commission on Indian Reservation Economies at ibid. reported that a "reorganization of government systems which focuses on trust responsibility from the perspective of protection, rather than management, which provides a population-resource formula for block-grants to tribes, and which acknowledges their rights to manage their own affairs, would provide the right kind of support."

25. Clara Spotted Elk, Member of the Northern Cheyenne Constitution Committee, remarks at University of Montana forum, August 3, 1984.

26. Joe McKay, "Achieving Constitutional Revision."

Bibliography

American Indian Policy Review Commission. *Final Report.* 2 vols. Washington, D.C.: U.S. Government Printing Office, 1977.

American Indian Policy Review Commission (Task Force Two: Tribal Government). *Report on Tribal Government.* Washington, D.C.: U.S. Government Printing Office, 1976.

Arizona Affiliated Tribes. *Self-Determination: A Program of Accomplishment.* Arizona: Indian Community Action Project, 1971.

Ashabranner, Brent K. *Morning Star, Black Sun: The Northern Cheyenne Indians and America's Energy Crisis.* New York: Dodd, Mead, 1982.

Barsh, Russel Lawrence, and Henderson, James Youngblood. *The Road: Indian Tribes and Political Liberty.* Berkeley: University of California Press, 1980.

Bee, Robert L. *The Politics of American Indian Policy.* Cambridge, Mass.: Schenkman Publishing Company, 1982.

Brakel, Samuel J. *American Indian Tribal Courts: The Costs of Separate Justice.* Chicago: American Bar Foundation, 1978.

Bryan, Jr., William L. *Montana's Indians: Yesterday and Today.* Helena, Montana: Montana Magazine, Inc., 1985.

Bunch, Steven L. *Treaties and Statutes Pertaining to Montana Indian Reservations.* Helena, Montana: Montana Legal Services Association, 1985.

Cadwalader, Sandra L., and Deloria, Jr., Vine (eds.). *The Aggressions of Civilization: Federal Indian Policy Since the 1880s.* Philadelphia: Temple University Press, 1984.

Canby, William C. *American Indian Law in a Nutshell.* St. Paul, Minn.: West Publishing Co., 1988.

Cohen, Felix S. *Felix S. Cohen's Handbook of Federal Indian Law.* Albuquerque: University of New Mexico, 1971.

_____. *Handbook of Federal Indian Law.* Charlottesville, Virginia: Michie Bobbs-Merrill, 1982.

Deloria, Jr., Vine (ed.). *American Indian Policy in the Twentieth Century.* Norman: University of Oklahoma Press, 1985.

Deloria, Jr., Vine, and Lytle, Clifford M. *American Indians, American Justice.* Austin: University of Texas Press, 1983.

_____. *The Nations Within.* New York: Pantheon Books, 1984.

Ebbott, Elizabeth. *Indians in Minnesota.* Judith Rosenblatt (ed.). Minneapolis: University of Minnesota Press, 4th ed., 1985.

Ewers, John C. *The Blackfeet: Raiders on the Northwestern Plains.* University of Oklahoma Press, 1958.

Fahey, John. *The Flathead Indians.* Norman: University of Oklahoma Press, 1974.

Fowler, Loretta. *Shared Symbols, Contested Meanings—Gros Ventre Culture and History, 1778–1984.* Ithaca: Cornell University Press, 1987.

Getches, David H., and Wilkinson, Charles F. *Cases and Materials on Federal Indian Law.* St. Paul, Minnesota: West Publishing Co., 1986.

Haas, Theodore H. *Ten Years of Tribal Government Under IRA.* Washington, D.C.: United States Indian Service, 1947.

Hagan, William T. *Indian Police and Judges: Experiments in Acculturation and Control.* Lincoln: University of Nebraska Press, 1980.

Institute of the American West. *Indian Self-Rule: Fifty Years Under the Indian Reorganization Act.* Sun Valley, Idaho: Institute of the American West, 1983.

Johnson, Ralph W., and Lupton, Susan (eds.). *Indian Tribal Codes: A Microfiche Collection of Indian Tribal Law Codes.* Seattle: University of Washington School of Law, 1981.

Knight, Yvonne T. *Tribal Regulation Manual.* Boulder, Colorado: Native American Rights Fund, 1982.

Llewellyn, Karl N., and Hoebel, E. Adamson. *The Cheyenne Way: Conflict and Case Law in Primitive Jurisprudence.* Norman: University of Oklahoma Press, 1941.

Lopach, James J., Brown, Margery H., and Jackson, Kathleen (eds.). *Tribal Constitutions: Their Past and Their Future.* Missoula, Montana: University of Montana Bureau of Government Research, 1978.

McBeath, Gerald A., and Morehouse, Thomas A. *The Dynamics of Alaska Native Self-Government.* Washington, D.C.: University Press of America, Inc., 1980.

McNickle, D'arcy. *Native American Tribalism: Indian Survivals and Renewals.* London: Oxford University Press, 1973.

Miller, David Reed. "Montana Assiniboine Identity: A Cultural Account of an American Indian Ethnicity" (Ph.D. diss., Indiana University, 1987).

Olney, Orville N., and Getches, David H. (eds.). *Indian Courts and the Future.* (National American Indian Court Judges Association) Washington, D.C.: U.S. Government Printing Office, 1978.

Olson, James Stuart, and Wilson, Raymond. *Native Americans in the Twentieth Century.* Provo, Utah: Brigham Young University Press, 1984.

Ortiz, Roxanne Dunbar. *Indians of the Americas: Human Rights and Self-Determination.* New York: Praeger Publishers, 1984.

Parker, Alan (ed.). *Indian Tribes as Governments: An Analysis of the Governing Institutions of Selected Indian Tribes.* (American Indian Lawyer Training Program) New York: John Hay Whitney Foundation, 1975.

Philp, Kenneth R. *John Collier's Crusade for Indian Reform.* Tucson, Arizona: University of Arizona Press, 1977.

Presidential Commission on Indian Reservation Economies. "Report and Recommendations to the President of the United States." Washington, D. C.: The Commission, 1984.

Prucha, Francis P. *The Great Father: The U.S. Government and the American Indian.* Lincoln: University of Nebraska Press, 1984.

Reno, Philip. *Navajo Resources and Economic Development.* Albuquerque: University of New Mexico Press, 1981.

Schusky, Ernest L. (ed.). *Political Organization of Native North Americans.* Washington, D.C.: University Press of America, Inc., 1980.

Stanley, Sam (ed.). *American Indian Economic Development.* The Hague, Paris: Mouton Publishers, 1978.

Taylor, Graham D. *The New Deal and American Indian Tribalism: The Administration of the Indian Reorganization Act, 1934–1945.* Lincoln: University of Nebraska Press, 1980.

Taylor, Theodore W. *American Indian Policy.* Mount Airy, Maryland: Lomond Publications, 1983.

Tooker, Elizabeth (ed.). *The Development of Political Organization in Native North America.* Washington, D.C.: American Ethnological Society, 1983.

Tyler, S. Lyman. *A History of Indian Policy.* Washington, D.C.: U.S. Government Printing Office, 1973.

U.S. Congress, House. *Investigation of Bureau of Indian Affairs.* House Report No. 2680. 83rd Congress, 2nd sess., 1954, Serial 11747, p. 78.